RELIGION AFTER METAPHYSICS

How should we understand reli̦   ...ould it hold, in an age in which metaphysics has ѵѵ̣ие into disrepute? The metaphysical assumptions which supported traditional theologies are no longer widely accepted, but it is not clear how this "end of metaphysics" should be understood, or what implications it ought to have for our understanding of religion. At the same time there is renewed interest in the sacred and the divine in disciplines as varied as philosophy, psychology, literature, history, anthropology, and cultural studies. In this volume, leading philosophers in the United States and Europe address the decline of metaphysics and the space which this decline has opened for non-theological understandings of religion. The contributors are Richard Rorty, Charles Taylor, Jean-Luc Marion, Gianni Vattimo, Hubert L. Dreyfus, Robert Pippin, John D. Caputo, Adriaan Peperzak, Leora Batnitzky, and Mark A. Wrathall.

MARK A. WRATHALL is Associate Professor at the Department of Philosophy, Brigham Young University, Utah. He has published articles in a number of journals and has contributed to books in the Cambridge Companions to Philosophy series. He is co-editor of *Appropriating Heidegger* (2000), *Heidegger, Authenticity, and Modernity* (2000), and *Heidegger, Coping, and Cognitive Science* (2000).

RELIGION AFTER METAPHYSICS

EDITED BY

MARK A. WRATHALL

CAMBRIDGE
UNIVERSITY PRESS

PUBLISHED BY THE PRESS SYNDICATE OF THE UNIVERSITY OF CAMBRIDGE
The Pitt Building, Trumpington Street, Cambridge, United Kingdom

CAMBRIDGE UNIVERSITY PRESS
The Edinburgh Building, Cambridge, CB2 2RU, UK
40 West 20th Street, New York, NY 10011–4211, USA
477 Williamstown Road, Port Melbourne, VIC 3207, Australia
Ruiz de Alarcón 13, 28014 Madrid, Spain
Dock House, The Waterfront, Cape Town 8001, South Africa

http://www.cambridge.org

First published 2003

Printed in the United Kingdom at the University Press, Cambridge

Typeface Adobe Garamond 11/12.5 pt   *System* LATEX 2$_\varepsilon$ [TB]

A catalogue record for this book is available from the British Library

Library of Congress Cataloguing in Publication data
Religion after metaphysics / edited by Mark A. Wrathall.
p.   cm.
Includes bibliographical references and index.
ISBN 0 521 82498 2   ISBN 0 521 53196 9 (paperback)
1. Religion – Philosophy.   2. Metaphysics.   I. Wrathall, Mark A.
BL51.R3455   2003
210 – dc21   2002041693

ISBN 0 521 82498 2 hardback
ISBN 0 521 53196 9 paperback

Contents

v

Contributors

LEORA BATNITZKY, Princeton University

JOHN D. CAPUTO, Villanova University

HUBERT L. DREYFUS, University of California – Berkeley

JEAN-LUC MARION, Université de Paris I – Sorbonne

ADRIAAN PEPERZAK, Loyola University Chicago

ROBERT PIPPIN, University of Chicago

RICHARD RORTY, Stanford University

CHARLES TAYLOR, McGill University

GIANNI VATTIMO, University of Turin

MARK A. WRATHALL, Brigham Young University

Preface

I would like to thank Julie Lund, Andy West, Katie Treharne, James Olsen, and James Faulconer for their invaluable help in the preparation of the typescript of this book. Many people and entities at Brigham Young University contributed time and resources in support of the conference out of which this volume has grown. I am indebted in particular to Alan Wilkins, Van Gessel, Ron Woods, Dennis Rasmussen, Andrew Skinner, and Katie Treharne for their contributions to the conference. It was Bert Dreyfus who provided the inspiration for this project, and I am grateful to him for the many conversations and correspondences we have had on the subject.

CHAPTER I

Introduction: metaphysics and onto-theology

Mark A. Wrathall

I

Since Plato, philosophers in the West have proposed various conceptions of a supreme being that was the ground of the existence and intelligibility of all that is. In the works of St. Augustine (and perhaps before), this metaphysical god became identified with the Judeo-Christian creator God. In modernity, however, the philosopher's foundationalist conception of God has become increasingly implausible. The decline of the metaphysical God was perhaps first noted when Pascal declared that the God of the philosophers was not the God of Abraham, Isaac, and Jacob. In any event, by the time that Nietzsche announced "the death of God," it was clear that something important had changed in the form of life prevailing in the West.

Whether Nietzsche's actual diagnosis of the change is right, most contemporary thinkers agree with him that the metaphysical understanding of God is no longer believable. But several of the most distinguished thinkers of the nineteenth and twentieth centuries – for example, Søren Kierkegaard, Fyodor Dostoevsky, Martin Heidegger, and Nietzsche himself – held that the loss of belief in a metaphysical god that is the ground of all existence and intelligibility, and even the loss of belief in a creator God who produced the heaven and the earth, is not itself a disaster. These thinkers argue that the absence of a foundational God opens up access to richer and more relevant ways for us to understand creation and for us to encounter the divine and the sacred. Thus, the death of the philosopher's God may have provided us with new and more authentic possibilities for understanding religion that were blocked by traditional metaphysical theology (or onto-theology).

A note is in order about the title of this volume, and the idea of metaphysics and "onto-theology." This volume grew out of a conference entitled "Religion after Onto-Theology," which was held at Sundance, Utah in July, 2001. The term "onto-theology," as it figured in that title, was popularized by Heidegger as a catch-phrase for the failings of the metaphysical tradition in philosophy. A central problem of that conference, and consequently of this book, is understanding the consequences of the demise of the metaphysical tradition for thinking about religion.

In the twentieth century, philosophers in both the analytic and continental traditions became concerned to free philosophical inquiry from the dominance of "metaphysics." The oddity of these parallel calls for the "overcoming of metaphysics" lies in the fact that the analytic and the continental camps saw one other as the main culprit in the continuation of metaphysical modes of inquiry. For the analytic, the error of the metaphysical tradition consisted in its striving for an "alleged knowledge of the essence of things which transcends the realm of empirically founded, inductive science."[1] For Heidegger (and the continental philosophers influenced by him), on the other hand, the analytical "elimination" of metaphysics through logical analysis and deference to the empirical sciences could, in fact, only lead to a deeper entanglement in metaphysics. This is because the dominance of logical, scientific, and mathematical modes of thought is, according to Heidegger, the result of the prevailing metaphysical understanding of being, an "alleged knowledge of the essence of things" – one in which beings are best represented in logical and mathematical terms – which fails to ask about the foundation of this understanding of being. Indeed, Heidegger believed that a central trait of metaphysical thought is a preoccupation with beings and a failure to ask properly about their being: "As metaphysics, it is by its very essence excluded from the experience of Being; for it always represents beings (ὄν) only with an eye to that aspect of them that has already manifested itself as being (ᾗ ὄν). But metaphysics never pays attention to what has concealed itself in this very ὄν insofar as it became unconcealed."[2]

According to Heidegger, all metaphysical philosophy was essentially oblivious to being, because all metaphysics took the form of "onto-theology." This means that metaphysics tried to understand the being of everything that is through a simultaneous determination of its essence or most universal trait (the "onto" in "onto-theology"), and a determination of the ground or source of the totality of beings in some highest or divine entity (the "theo" in "onto-theology"). This amounts, according to Heidegger, to a profound confusion, for it tries to understand the transcendental ground of all beings as a transcendent being.[3] In "The Onto-Theo-Logical Constitution of Metaphysics,"[4] Heidegger argues that the onto-theological structure of metaphysical inquiry has had deleterious effects on both philosophy and theology: it has prevented philosophy from thinking about being as something that is not itself a being, and it has misconstrued the nature of God, thereby obstructing our relationship with the divine.

It is worth observing that the contributors to this volume are anything but unanimous in their assessment of the details of Heidegger's critique of onto-theology, and one can find them disagreeing on issues such as: is it indeed the case that all philosophy is "always" metaphysical / onto-theological?,[5] or, what precisely is the failing of onto-theological metaphysics?, or even, is onto-theology something that we should want to overcome?

What does unite the essays in this volume is an interest in the state of religion in an age in which metaphysics has come into disrepute. And whatever their opinion of Heidegger's critique of onto-theology, the contributors all tend to think about metaphysics along the lines projected by Heidegger, rather than along the lines of the analytic opposition to metaphysics. That is to say, the concern is not primarily with metaphysics as a speculative, non-empirical mode of inquiry, but with metaphysics as an obliviousness to the understanding of being that governs an age. In the Heideggerian tradition, the project of overcoming metaphysics cannot be accomplished through logical or conceptual analysis, but only through an openness to the way that an understanding of being comes to prevail. (See Jean-Luc Marion's analysis in the final chapter of this volume.)

2

Reflection on religion after metaphysics, then, needs to be understood in terms of thought about the place of religion in an age where the understanding of being that legitimized certain traditional modes of conceptualizing the sacred and the divine is called into question. In thinking about the important changes in the forms of existence that once supported metaphysical theology, the natural starting point is Nietzsche's work, and his account of the history of nihilism and the death of God.

Nietzsche's declaration of the death of God, as Robert Pippin notes, "has come to represent and sum up not just the unbelievability of God in the late modern world, but the 'death' of a Judeo-Christian form of moral life, the end of metaphysics, or the unsuccessful attempt to end metaphysics, or even the end of philosophy itself" (see p. 7 below). Pippin argues, however, that the central focus of Nietzsche's claim is a certain "loss of desire," which has rendered us "pale atheists," unable even to long for the God that is absent. In the face of the widespread pale atheism that characterizes the modern age, the challenge for us after the death of God is, on this view, that of inspiring enough desire and longing to sustain life itself.

For Gianni Vattimo, on the other hand, the death of the onto-theological God needs to be understood in terms of the impossibility of believing in an objective truth or a uniquely valid language or paradigm for understanding the world. Without this metaphysical belief in an objective and universal foundation – that is, with the end of metaphysics – Vattimo argues that there is now room for a "truce" between philosophy, religion, and science. This, in turn, leaves us free to respond to the core of the Judeo-Christian message.

Richard Rorty agrees with Vattimo in reading the end of onto-theology as the end of a certain metaphysical universalism in religion, thus taking religion out of the "epistemic arena" (p. 40). But in contrast to Vattimo, Rorty argues that religion remains a kind of "unjustifiable nostalgia," without which, Rorty hopes, we can eventually learn to live.

Charles Taylor, rather than seeing in our history a uniform and inevitable progress of secularization, argues that the contemporary West is characterized by the progressive fracturing of a unified understanding of being into a multiplicity of "world structures." The predominant world structures tend to "occult or blank out the transcendent" (p. 66), and thus marginalize religious practices and modes of discourse. Taylor argues that the marginalization of religious practices, however, is based on an "over-hasty naturalization" which, when recognized as such, should yield to a more open stance toward religious forms of life.

It should be apparent by now that there is considerable room for disagreement over the nature of the death of the philosopher's God and the direction in which Western culture is moving. As the next set of essays demonstrates, there are also sharply contrasting views of what was wrong with the metaphysical account of God.

Some of the authors see the failure of onto-theology in the way it strips the divine of all personal attributes, thereby turning God into the God of the philosophers. If God is made the transcendental ground of the world and of all intelligibility, the divine no longer is able to have the kind of presence within the world necessary to give our lives worth. On this reading of the onto-theological tradition, the challenge facing a religion after onto-theology is that of reviving the possibility of having a direct relation to the divine. The next two chapters in the volume explore this vision of a non-onto-theological God as the basis for responses to contemporary pragmatic dismissals of religion, typified by Rorty's chapter. Mark Wrathall reviews Heidegger's diagnosis of the ills of contemporary technological society in terms of the reduction of all the things which once mattered to us or made demands on us to mere resources. Heidegger believes that the only hope for salvation from the dangers of technology is a life attuned to the fourfold of earth, sky, mortals, and divinities. A relation to the divine, on the

Heideggerian account, is thus not just a matter of personal preference, but a necessary part of a life worth living in the technological age. Hubert Dreyfus explores the Kierkegaardian response to the nihilism of the present age. Unlike Heidegger, Kierkegaard accepts the futility of resisting the nihilism apparent in the levelling of all meaningful distinctions, because he sees it as the inevitable consequence of the onto-theological tradition. But rather than seeing this as destroying the possibility for an authentic relationship to the divine, Kierkegaard sees it as clearing the way for us to confront our despair at being unable to unify the seemingly contradictory factors in human existence. Christianity, according to Kierkegaard, has shown us the only way to get the factors together and thus escape from despair: namely, by "responding to the call" of a "defining commitment" (p. 96). In this way, Dreyfus argues, "Kierkegaard has succeeded in saving Christianity from onto-theology by replacing the creator God, who is metaphysically infinite and eternal, with the God-man who is finite and temporal" (p. 101).

Rather than seeing the failing of onto-theology in terms of its failure to admit the possibility of encountering God within the world, Peperzak and Caputo understand the limitations of onto-theology in terms of a reduction of God to a being about whom we could come to have a pretension of theoretical clarity. That is, onto-theology obstructed access to an authentic experience of the divine by making God a being who could be understood, whose nature could be categorized, and whose existence could be proved. The hope for religion after onto-theology is, for these authors, to recognize that God has a kind of majesty and incomprehensibility that we do not find in intra-worldly beings. God, Peperzak notes, is "the One who cannot be caught by any categorical or conceptual grasp" (p. 107). While agreeing that the onto-theological attempts at trying to get a conceptual grasp of God "have (at least partially) failed," Peperzak sees the work of Levinas as a basis for a "retrieval of the onto-theo-logical project" (pp. 110, 112) of thinking God simultaneously as a person to whom we can relate and as that which makes all relations possible – in Heideggerian terms, that is, to think God simultaneously as a being and Being. Caputo argues that, after onto-theology, we can engage in a phenomenology of the experience of God, which, he argues, is a phenomenology of the experience of the impossible. The failing of onto-theology, Caputo suggests, was that it was unable to entertain the possibility of the impossible, and thus it "tended to keep a metaphysical lid on experience" (p. 129). The end of onto-theology thus holds out the promise of an authentic relationship to an incomprehensible God.

Of course, in a volume by philosophers on the topic of religion after onto-theology, the nature of post-metaphysical philosophy is at least as much in issue as the nature of post-metaphysical religion. And, not surprisingly, a recurring theme in many of the chapters is the question of the kind of philosophical inquiry appropriate to post-onto-theological religious experience. The last essays in this book address this problem directly. Leora Batnitzky reviews the work of Leo Strauss and Emmanuel Levinas in terms of their efforts to articulate the relation between philosophy and revelation. If the revelation contained in the Bible "is not concerned with the onto-theological status of God" (p. 155), then the philosophical appropriation of the revelation cannot be understood as articulating the metaphysical essentialism implicit in the revelation. Instead, Batnitzky suggests that the task for us is to think through the possibilities for a philosophical but non-metaphysical account of ethics and politics – an account which must be grounded in the revelation if it is to "defend morality to humanity at large" (p. 155).

In the final chapter, Marion brings us back to the general question of the possibilities available for thought at the end of metaphysics – a central issue which, more or less self-consciously, motivates every other chapter in this volume. Marion explores the nature of Heidegger's critique of metaphysics, and his enduring effort to think through the end of metaphysics. Heidegger, Marion argues, opens the horizon of, but hesitates before the possibility of, overcoming metaphysics in and through a thought of the donation – the giving of a clearing by "something other than being" (p. 183). It is this opening that, Marion argues, needs to be pursued if there is to be a "radical overcoming" of metaphysics.

NOTES

1. Rudolf Carnap, "The Elimination of Metaphysics Through Logical Analysis of Language," in *Logical Positivism*, ed. A. J. Ayer (Glencoe, Ill.: Free Press, 1959), p. 80.
2. Martin Heidegger, "Introduction to 'What is Metaphysics?,'" in *Pathmarks*, ed. William McNeill (Cambridge: Cambridge University Press, 1998), p. 288.
3. See "Nihilism as Determined by the History of Being," *Nietzsche*, vol. IV, ed. David Farrell Krell (New York: Harper & Row, 1982), pp. 210–11.
4. In *Identity and Difference*, trans. Joan Stambaugh (University of Chicago Press, 1969).
5. Heidegger, *Schelling: Vom Wesen der menschlichen Freiheit, Gesamtausgabe*, vol. XLII (Frankfurt-on-Main: Klostermann, 1988), p. 88.

CHAPTER 2

Love and death in Nietzsche

Robert Pippin

Phoebus is dead, ephebe. But Phoebus was
A name for something that never could be named.
There was a project for the sun and is.

There is a project for the sun. The sun
Must bear no name, gold flourisher, but be
In the difficulty of what it is to be.
(Wallace Stevens, "Notes Towards a Supreme Fiction:
It Must be Abstract," *The Collected Poems*
[New York: Vintage, 1990], p. 381)

Section 125 of Nietzsche's *The Gay Science* is justifiably famous; it is perhaps the most famous passage in all of Nietzsche.[1] In it, Nietzsche introduces a character, *der tolle Mensch*, the crazy man, who proclaims that God is dead, that we all collectively have killed him, and that all must bear the burden of guilt (for centuries) for this horrible murder. Like other famous images in philosophy, like Plato's cave or Descartes's evil genius or Kant's island of truth surrounded by seas of illusion, the passage has taken on a life of its own quite independent of its place and function in what may be Nietzsche's most beautiful and best-thought-out book. It has come to represent and sum up not just the unbelievability of God in the late modern world, but the "death" of a Judeo-Christian form of moral life, the end of metaphysics, or the unsuccessful attempt to end metaphysics, or even the end of philosophy itself.

Yet the passage is also quite mysterious and suggests a number of interpretive problems. The very idea of a *death* or *end* to a form of life (rather than a refutation or enlightenment) is worth considerable attention in itself, but the literary details of this little drama are even more striking.[2] The announcement is made by a crazy man who carries a lantern in the daylight, seeks a God who he clearly knows does not exist, and after proclaiming that the time for such an announcement is not right and that he will not be understood, promptly begins his prophetic activity anew and with more

7

intensity, breaking into churches and screaming his message. (He is clearly crazy, but in what sense is he crazy?[3])

The announcement itself suggests a kind of insanity. On the face of it, the announcement that "God is dead" is, even metaphorically, opaque. If there had been a *god*, we could not have killed him. If we could have killed him, he could not have been a god. If "God" existed only as a constructed object of belief, a kind of collective "illusion" in Freud's famous claim, then exposing this illusion might be unsettling and make for much anxiety; and afterwards, it might be impossible to return to the same illusion, but the content of such unease could not be about a "death," or, especially, *guilt* at having "caused" it, even if one reads the claim metaphorically. (One interpretation might be "*we* destroyed the old illusion that there was a god." If that were the literal meaning, the only guilt relevant would have to be guilt at having allowed ourselves to be so deceived, and could not be guilt at ending the delusion.) Indeed, Nietzsche himself provides, in his own voice, not the voice of a persona, a much simpler gloss on the claim and one far different in tone. He explains in section 343 that "The greatest recent event – that 'God is dead'" should simply be taken to mean "that the belief in the Christian God has become unworthy of belief."[4]

So, the oddness of the language in section 125 itself, and Nietzsche's own very different gloss (especially since the theme of the later passage in Book 5 is "cheerfulness," not guilt), directs our attention to the contrasting uncheerful, indeed morbid, tone of the first passage, the famous *locus classicus* often cited as Nietzsche's own "belief" that "God is dead." (Cheerfulness [*Heiterkeit*] is the important issue here because the most important interpretive question at stake is the possibility of a "joyous science" [*fröhliche Wissenschaft*] and so not nihilism and guilt.) But it would seem that Nietzsche is trying most of all to draw attention to, rather than express or identify with, the "melancholic" tone, both of the announcement and perhaps of the coming culture of melancholy – the tone appropriate to the belief that a kind of death has occurred, that we were responsible, and that this death results only in some unbearable, frightening absence. So one extraordinary feature of the history of the reception of the passage is that what seems clearly to be a kind of symptom of a modern pathology, for which Nietzsche *wants* a diagnosis, is often taken as *the diagnosis* of the modern "orientation" or mood itself! Indeed, I have tried to show elsewhere that Nietzsche is here anticipating Freud's famous distinction between mourning and melancholy in reaction to a loss or trauma, suggesting that the madman's madness is this kind of melancholic obsession with what has been lost, complete with its narcissistic assumption of grandiose responsibility, lurid details of murder and blood and guilt, and repetitive compulsion.[5]

Freud famously contrasts the genuine work of mourning, in which the loss of a loved one, or a disappointed expectation or rejection, is finally acknowledged (something that also presupposes that the genuine separateness of the person or the independence of the world is also acknowledged), so that one's libido can be redirected then to other such objects; and the absence of such work for the melancholic, whose world is so narcissistic that he believes that *he* could not have been left, even while, also out of such narcissism, he also believes that he must have been somehow responsible for the loss. Both reactions deny the separateness and independence of the other and so deny the other's death, preserving in unovercomeable grief (which Freud points out must be as constantly and repetitively exhibited and staged as the madman's) a kind of morbid living presence of the other and the continuing importance of the subject. It is this pathology, perhaps the typical pathology of a "modernist" culture of melancholia (Dostoevsky, Musil, Kafka, Beckett), likewise inspired by a type of narcissism, that Nietzsche precisely wants to avoid with his *gaya scienza*. (Nietzsche's name for such an illness is as often "romanticism" as melancholy. He links both in some of his remarks on Brahms and Wagner, saying of the former that "his is the melancholy of incapacity; he does *not* create out of an abundance; he *languishes* for abundance"[6] and that it is when Brahms "mourns" for himself that he is "modern." This distinction between desire as a lack – and the death of God as a new lack – and desire as abundance, excess – and so the death of God as freeing such generosity – will emerge frequently in what follows.)

The most significant feature of the passage, for our purposes in this volume, concerns what Nietzsche appears to think the appropriate response to this announcement should be. In setting the context for the announcement, especially the audience to whom it is made, Nietzsche goes out of his way to suggest that what we normally regard as "atheism" is far too simplistic a description of what it would be truly to "incorporate" this truth. The opening passage describes, as the madman's audience, a group of people who "did not believe in God" and, when they hear the madman proclaim that he seeks God, jeer sarcastically and joke, "Has he got lost?" "Did he lose his way like a child?" "Is he hiding?" "Is he afraid of us?" "Has he gone on a voyage?" But if the madman is mad, these jeering atheists are clearly portrayed, as they are elsewhere in Nietzsche, as thoughtless, smug, self-satisfied boors. In other passages, Nietzsche's Homeric epithet for such atheists is "*pale* atheists," suggesting this lack of vitality or even sickness.

(Thus we need to understand why, if the death of God signals a general end to the possibility of transcendence, religion, morally significant truth, and so forth, the successor culture would *not* simply have to be a culture of such pale [joking, ironic] atheists.)[7] If Nietzsche wants to suggest that the madman is pathologically wrong to treat the absence of God as a loss, wrong to take on the burden of a self-lacerating guilt, he seems just as dissatisfied with these village atheist types who are too easily satisfied with a secular materialism and so do not understand the aspirations and ideals Nietzsche elsewhere treats as "a condition of life."

So my question will be, why does Nietzsche treat these self-satisfied atheists this way? What are they missing? What does Nietzsche want us to understand by his rejecting both the notion of a now absent God and the stance of what appears to be straightforward, Enlightenment atheism? In his own terms, this means understanding why a life guided by the "old values" is just as impossible as a life guided by "no values," or why a "transvaluation," an "*Umwertung*," of all values is what is now necessary and what it would be like.

This question already reflects Nietzsche's earlier way of posing it in *The Birth of Tragedy*: the unbelievability of monotheism in no way necessarily ushers in the age of a-theism, the anti-religion of "last men." (In *The Birth of Tragedy* a modern "polytheism" still seemed possible to Nietzsche.) That dogmatic anti-dogma (atheism) is hard to understand as a way of life, he often suggests, as in this evocative passage from *The Gay Science*:

> We are, in a word – and it should be our word of honor – good Europeans, the heirs of Europe, the rich, well-endowed, but also over-rich, obligated heirs of centuries of European spirit: as such also those who have grown up and away from Christianity, and just because we have awakened from it, because our forebears were Christians from an unreflective sense of the righteousness of Christianity, who willingly for their faith sacrificed blood, position and fatherland for it. We – do the same. But for what? For our lack of faith? For a kind of disbelief? No, you know better than that, my friends. The hidden *yes* in you is stronger than all the no's and perhaps from which you and your age are sick; and if you have to sail the seas, you wanderer, something also compels you to do so – a faith![8]

Nietzsche's most comprehensive term for the historical and psychological situation that in the present age requires this "transvaluation of values" after "the death of God" is "nihilism." But here again the surface meaning of these claims about what necessitates a transvaluation has suggested many different sorts of provocations and so raises questions about how Nietzsche wants us to understand at the most general level the conditions possible now (without "God," in all senses of the term) for the success of that activity he seemed to treat as identical to a distinctly human living: esteeming (*schätzen*), valuing. ("Man," Zarathustra says, means "esteemer."⁹)

On the one hand, the problem of nihilism can look like a problem of knowledge, or at least reasonable belief. What had once seemed known, or worthy of belief, now seems a "lie," "unworthy of belief." A typical version of this view of nihilism as a crisis of knowledge or reasonable belief is the following from the *Nachlass*:

> What has happened, at bottom? The feeling of valuelessness was reached with the realization that the overall character of existence may not be interpreted by means of the concept of "aim," the concept of "unity," or the concept of "truth." Existence has no goal or end; any comprehensive unity in the plurality of events is lacking; the character of existence is not true, is *false*. One simply lacks any reason for convincing oneself that there is a *true* world.¹⁰

Such calmly cognitivist terms suggest an anthropologist watching the disenchanting enlightenment of a primitive tribe, and so appeal to such double-edged enlightenment as the best explanation for how we have come to be the first civilization that must live self-consciously without any confidence that we "know" what civilized life is for, without "the truth."¹¹

On the other hand, especially when Nietzsche is trying to draw a distinction between what he calls a passive and an active nihilism, what we have come to claim to know or to believe, while important, is not the whole or the chief issue. "Active" nihilism is interpreted as a "sign of increased *power* of the spirit"; "passive" nihilism as "decline and recession of the *power* of spirit."¹² In passages like these, Nietzsche is more likely to say that nihilism results when we are threatened with the impossibility of willing at all, of fulfilling the conditions necessary for decision and commitment – "value." We choose instead to try to regard ourselves as *willing* "nothing," as bravely insisting on such an absence, and so are able to construe the realization as a result of our "active" self-enlightenment, righteousness, and honesty, and not a passive, merely endured fate. Indeed, many of the passages that seem to appeal to worthiness of belief alone as the source of the crisis conclude by suggesting instead that nihilism is at bottom a matter of *strength or weakness of will*. The "feeling of valuelessness" passage just quoted above concludes by saying that the categories "which we used to project some value into the world, *we pull out* again; so the world looks *valueless*."¹³

The force of these passages suggests a familiar skeptical attitude about the practical implications of any such putative intellectual enlightenment. For one thing, the emerging modern consensus in European high culture about the disenchantment of nature, skepticism about teleology, and a spreading atheism are all, on their own, as assertions about the facts, motivationally or practically inert. This is so because, according to Nietzsche, contra the cognitivist formulations, it is extremely unlikely that belief in any such first principle of value or objective moral order originally or subsequently played any decisive role in commitment to a value or in keeping faith with it. The justifiability of a belief is, in itself, not one of the practically necessary conditions of value (although, as we shall see, in special circumstances it may become so). He is quite explicit about this in *The Gay Science*:

> The mistake made by the more refined among them [among the modern historians of morality] is that they uncover and criticize the perhaps foolish opinions of a people about morality, or of humanity about all human morality – opinions about its origin, religious sanction, the superstition of free will, and things of that sort – and then suppose that they have criticized the morality itself. But the value of a command, "thou shalt" is still fundamentally different from and independent of such opinions about it and the weeds of error that may have overgrown it – just as certainly as the value of a medication for a sick person is completely independent of whether he thinks about medicine scientifically or the way old women do. Even if a morality has grown out of an error, the realization of this fact would not as much as touch the problem of its value.[14]

For another thing, claims about value do not, for Nietzsche, report the discovery of moral facts, but express, enact, and partially realize a commitment. Accounting for – giving a genealogy of – such commitments (and the various conditions necessary for these to serve as ways of life) can never be completed by an inventory of theoretical beliefs; something else must always be added. It has seemed to many modern philosophers that such an addition must be a kind of *subjective* reaction – an outpouring of sympathy, a recoil in pain, the stirring of a passion – and therewith an imposition or projection of a "value" as an embrace or rejection of some situation. This is not Nietzsche's position, but for now we need only note that while we can base reasons to act or to undertake commitments on such beliefs, the strength or weakness of the theoretical claim about "what there is" is not itself an *independent* factor in such commitments, in such acts of valuing. Acting is *negating* what there is, and so presumes some sort of experience where some state of affairs becomes unacceptable, not merely noted; it is experienced as something-that-must-be-overcome. Acting in the light of this unacceptability is "acting for a value," and what we are in effect looking for is the source and meaning of such unacceptability in the absence of any notion of a natural completion or telos, natural law, common human nature, or some objective ideal or divine legislator. (This is partly the problem with our pale atheists. They dogmatically believe that the absence of

God in itself *matters*; that a "faith" of sorts can be made of this denial. It mattering to them, their *being* atheists, is a reflection of some other lack or need or fear unthought by the atheists.)

Since whatever else nihilism and the death of God involve, then, they involve this problem of value, what *does* "touch the problem" of value? The passages we have been citing suggest strength of will, resolve, power, and courage; they focus on the problem of strong and weak will, and have long been part of the canon of quotations cited in "existentialist" readings of Nietzsche (of a Kierkegaardian "leap" or Sartrean "condemned to freedom" variety.)[15]

This duality (treating nihilism as a problem either of belief or of will power) is of a piece with a more familiar, very general tension in interpretations of Nietzsche: that is, the tension between those who focus on a doctrinal Nietzsche, with radically new answers to traditional problems, and those who insist on a wholly rhetorical, much more literary Nietzsche, fiercely resistant to all doctrine. According to this latter Nietzsche, civilizations should be understood as collectively projected and sustained fantasies of value and importance, fantasies that have an essentially psychological origin[16] and a kind of organic "life" and "death" in unceasing repetitions, periodically requiring some new master rhetorician and fantasy maker. Every so often, as a matter of luck, some such value-legislator, a Sophocles, Socrates, St. Paul, Goethe, or Nietzsche, is found. And so too the familiar dialectic in understanding Nietzsche: the doctrinalists or naturalists or metaphysicians of the will to power look too close to the dogmatists Nietzsche clearly sweepingly rejects (they still evince a naïve confidence in the value of truth); the philosopher of will and rhetoric looks like a doctrinalist *malgré lui*, not able to keep from asserting a doctrine about rhetoric and rhetoricality.

What I want to suggest at this point is that we treat the phenomenon of nihilism in a way closer to Nietzsche's images and figures and tropes, many of which were cited at the outset here: images of death, decay, illness, the absence of tension, a "sleep" of the spirit (he sometimes claims that what is needed now is an ability to dream without having to sleep), and perhaps the most intuitive metonymy of failed desire – boredom. These images suggest that the problem of nihilism does not consist in a failure of knowledge or a failure of will, but a *failure of desire*, the flickering out of some erotic flame. Noting how often and with what significance Nietzsche refers to life and the "perspective of life" as the issue of an erotic striving, what makes possible the origination of such a wanting, what sustains it and the sacrifices it calls for, and so forth, casts a completely different light on the nature of the "death of God" or nihilism crisis and on what Nietzsche regards as a possible way out of it. It frames all the issues differently, especially since the failure of desire can be baffling, quite mysterious, not something that, in some other sense, we ever "want" to happen, as mysterious as the issue of how one might address such a failure.

This is not an easy case to make because Nietzsche is famous as a philosopher of "the will," and as oriented everywhere by the unavoidability and severity of human conflict. The primary phenomenon for a Nietzschean is supposed to be such basic conflict and struggle for power, and so the eternal unavoidability of an exclusive disjunction: either being subject to the will of others, or subjecting them to one's will. This is supposed to be the ur-phenomenon out of which various reactive institutions, like the Christian religion and morality, grow and which they express (Christianity being essentially a slave revolt against Roman power), and which modern institutions, like liberalism, hypocritically ignore. Modern liberalism and socialism assume that the growth of technological power over nature and the spread of intellectual enlightenment, especially enlightenment about the death of God and the futility and eventually unbearable expense of sectarian war, will make men milder, enhance the possibility of overlapping consensus and compromise, and so forth. By contrast, Nietzsche is taken to hold that this is a fatuous delusion, that it is far more likely that there will be massive and voluntary subordination and more subtle, less visible oppression than consensus (a herd society), and that whatever mildness ensues will just be the result of such sheeplike submission to the power of the herd itself.

But even the surface of these claims is suspiciously simplistic. One seeks power to effect an end one cares about; victory in a conflict is struggle and victory for the sake of something one cares about, and there is no more a priori entitlement, in Nietzsche's philosophical universe, to assume that one by nature cares about "maximizing power" (whatever that is supposed to mean; whatever counts as "maximizing power") than there is to assume that one by nature cares about avoiding a violent death, or about having as commodious a life as possible, or about being recognized as an equal, and so forth. The famous will to power is always applied purposively, for the sake of some end, and these ends reflect a striving, negation, and simple desire not at all reflected in the official Nietzsche (the philosopher of the will).

But these erotic images are well known in the textual or actual Nietzsche, and they make clear how much closer he stands to his great opponent, Plato, than to Hobbes or Machiavelli (who both accept a modern and so naturalistic account of the pulls and pushes of the passions). Indeed, these images occur quite prominently, at the beginnings of all three of Nietzsche's best-known books. "Truth is a woman," and philosophers are clumsy lovers;[17] Zarathustra "goes under" because "he loves man";[18] "where your treasure is, there will your heart be also."[19] And there are the rich associations of *The Gay Science*, *Die fröhliche Wissenschaft* itself, *gaya scienza*, with its evocation of the *gai saber*, *troubadours*, or warrior-poets who produce essentially lyrics or love poems, whose main claim to knowledge was of erotics.[20] (All such that Nietzsche is also inherently claiming as his subject the one thing Socrates ever claimed to know something about – eros.) In fact, the *Gay Science* as a book is so important because it represents the first concentrated presentation of some affirmative post-philosophical activity, after Nietzsche had abandoned the so-called "romantic" fantasy of a Wagnerian revival. There is now to be some new form of reflective engagement with the world and others; the question at issue in such engagement is always the question of value, but at the heart of that question is the erotic issue, and all of this somehow is what the *gai saber* knows. A gay science, in other words, is a new way of thinking about value, a new kind of thinking activity and therewith valuing, but one intelligible only if we understand its unique goal, and why that goal has become important, why we now strive for it.

Some of the erotic images repeat, become like motifs in Nietzsche's work. In *Thus Spoke Zarathustra*, Zarathustra announces the advent of nihilism as an erotic problem. "Alas the time is coming when man will no longer shoot the arrow of his longing beyond man, and the string of his bow will have forgotten how to whir."[21] In the preface to *Beyond Good and Evil*, he notes that our long struggle with, and often opposition to and dissatisfaction with, our own moral tradition, European Christianity, has created a "magnificent tension of the spirit the like of which had never yet existed on earth: with so tense a bow we can now shoot for the most distant goals." But, he goes on, the "democratic enlightenment" also sought to "unbend" such a bow, to "bring it about that the spirit would no longer experience itself so easily as a 'need.'"[22] This latter formulation coincides with a wonderfully lapidary expression in *The Gay Science*. In discussing "those millions of young Europeans who cannot endure their boredom and themselves," he notes that they would even welcome "a craving to suffer" and so "to find in their suffering a probable reason for action, for deeds." In sum: "neediness is needed!" ("Not ist nötig."[23]) (One of his most striking formulations of the death of desire occurs in *Ecce Homo*, when he notes what is happening to us as "one error after another is coolly placed on ice; the ideal is not refuted – it freezes to death."[24])

Attending to this erotic problem in Nietzsche should also help free us from the grip of the image that has probably the greatest hold on the imagination of Nietzsche's modern readers, the image of a world discovered to be intrinsically valueless, without God, thereby calling for the spontaneous creation and injection of value by creative subjects, and thereby provoking a kind of crisis of conscience (nihilism), despair that we, the frail, finite creatures that we are, could do that without the traditional props (nature, revealed law, Truth, etc.). (This is the most frequent combination of the cognitive and volitional elements noted above.) But from the "erotic" point of view, all such considerations of what Nietzsche is after start much too far downstream. Rendering a possible state of character or society actually valuable would be being able somehow to render it desirable. It would be to be able to create a longing for such an object, or to find others in whom a possible spark of such longing could be found and fanned. Such a possibility is hard to imagine, since no subject, however strong-willed, could simply inject such *erotic* value "into" the world from a position "outside it" like this. Any such desire can only be found and inspired and sustained *in* a certain sort of world, a world where already some intense dissatisfaction can be balanced by an aspiration at home in that very world; a world, in other words, lovable enough to inspire as well as frustrate.[25] Consider this summation of the issue (a passage that also renders pretty irrelevant most of Heidegger's *Auseinandersetzung* with Nietzsche as well as the subjectivist/projection, neo-Humean readings of Nietzsche on value):

The whole pose of "man *against* the world," of man as a "world-negating" principle, of man as the measure of the value of things, as judge of the world who in the end places existence itself upon his scales and finds it wanting – the monstrous insipidity of this pose has finally come home to us and we are sick of it. We laugh as soon as we encounter the juxtaposition of "man *and* world," separated by the sublime presumption of the little word "and."[26]

Passages about eros and about the worldliness of eros have not, of course, been wholly ignored, but, as alluded to above, they are often folded into a general discussion of Nietzsche's views on the body, his supposed naturalism, and what he often refers to as the problem of instincts. And there is no particular reason not to see this emphasis on constant, powerfully motivating, human longing (or the enervating experience of its failure) as an aspect of what Nietzsche talks about elsewhere as instinctual forces (or their absence). He began his career in *The Birth of Tragedy* apparently positing elemental longings or drives, either for the destruction of form and individuation, and for a self-less, Dionysian indeterminacy, or a longing for determinacy, form, and clarity. He notes also a longing for an "animal" forgetfulness that required millennia of pain and training to overcome, such that we could have new longings and become animals capable of keeping promises; he describes an unavoidable, instinctual striving to render suffering meaningful, and so forth; not to mention that apparently elemental drive – the will to power.

But a wholly naturalistic account would be much too hasty here. The very multiplicity and range of the different possible drives appealed to, and the fact that Nietzsche's accounts of prevolitional drives and instincts are often as much historical as organic (tied essentially to a specific historical self-understanding), indicate already that the basic question for him has remained interpretive, a question about meaning; the basic response a matter of *Bildung* or culture, not causality. (So, any question about some presumed Nietzschean ultimate explainer, like *Macht*, or power, must always leave room for the prior and decisive question of what counts as having power or exercising it.) For example, Nietzsche notes in *The Gay Science*, section 334 that all love has to be *learned*. "Even those who love themselves will have learned it in this way; for there is no other way. Love too has to be learned." (He does not mention here what he stresses in *Schopenhauer as Educator*, a difficulty that suggests a tragic pathos to this position.)

It is hard to create in anyone this condition of intrepid self-knowledge because it is impossible to teach love; for it is love alone that can bestow on the soul, not only a clear, discriminating, and self-contemptuous view of itself, but also the desire to look beyond itself and to seek with all its might for a higher self as yet still concealed from it.[27]

The thought itself beginning to emerge throughout these passages is paradoxical – that we can desire, long, strive (suffer from some burden of "excess," of too much meaning, too many possibilities), without knowing or ever finding what would satisfy that longing, without the experience of a determinate or natural lack or gap that cries out for satisfaction. We "learn" in some sense to want and feel in some way, but it is forever impossible to formulate what would ultimately satisfy such a polymorphic longing, relieve the distress caused by such a burden. On the other hand, what Nietzsche is getting at is all phenomenologically quite familiar, as familiar as the *essential* ambiguity of the great "quest" objects of modern literature and the irony of those quests, those hopes for resolution and completion and redemption:

Quixote's adventure and windmills, Tennyson's Holy Grail, Emma Bovary's desperate romance, the White Whale, the Ring of the Nibelung, Godot, K's trial, Pynchon's V, and so forth.

But this multiply realizable interpretive activity, I should hasten to add, is not at all a reflective activity directed *at* some brute, somatic event that we can isolate, whose simple causes we can investigate. While there *are* clearly desires provoked exogenously by natural objects, clear that the world in its cold and heat and weather and scarcity provokes a very determinate dissatisfaction with and so a desire to overcome these natural limitations, clear that there are fixed human drives, there is another level, the one Nietzsche is interested in, on which human existence is plagued by a deeper, categorically different dissatisfaction, and so a longing that is not just such a *response to a lack*. (In the familiar words of parents everywhere: we "*make ourselves miserable*," and could, in a sense, *stop* doing so. But that would be to live like last men. There is no argument in Nietzsche that we should not so live, and Nietzsche seems more interested in the question of "under what conditions" his interlocutors would find such a life shameful rather than successful.) So, at this level, such dissatisfactions cannot be said to have simple causes or determinate objects. Rather we continue to try to express a dissatisfaction we also cannot pin down and so cannot satisfy, even though without this self-induced dissatisfaction, we *would* be last men, for that (that absence of such dissatisfaction or the self-contempt he had said springs from "love") is precisely their state. They are, in other words, *happy*. Such dissatisfaction exists, then, in a very mediated sense, only "because of us," because of what we will not settle for, not because of our nature or transactions with the world. Such a desire "for more" is nothing but our determinate expression of a dissatisfaction, and yet that determinacy can never be fixed with certainty and can no longer be tied to transcendent aspirations. Thus, from *The Gay Science*, "when a strong stimulus is experienced as pleasure or displeasure, this depends on the *interpretation* of the intellect which, to be sure, generally does this work without rising to our consciousness."[28] And especially in *Human, All Too Human*: "Since we have for millennia looked upon the world with moral, aesthetic, and religious demands... the world has gradually *become* so remarkably variegated, terrible, soulful, meaningful, it has acquired color – but we have been the colorists."[29]

There *is* a gap, an experience of not-being something or other, but *we* open up that possibility and hold it open by means of these expressions of dissatisfaction, even though we obviously do not do so in some individual, intentional, volitional sense. There *isn't*, say, a legitimate authority or distributive justice problem waiting to be found by philosophers. There is such a problem only if philosophers find a way of picturing "life" in such a way that life is lacking without addressing such problems. They don't impose such a view onto life, because there isn't, properly speaking, a life to lead without such a yearning. In the language of the classical German philosophical tradition, we would call this dissatisfaction and longing a "self-negation," that is, a dissatisfaction *due to us*, a *refusal* on our part ever to rest content, rather than a reaction to a natural lack. (Even righteous subjection to the moral law in Kant, for example, becomes an object of striving, a matter of possible perfectibility, but only because, as Kant says, we are the "authors" of such a law; we subject *ourselves* to its constraint.)

Human experience, I think Nietzsche is trying to suggest with his somatic and erotic images, is at its core, at a level deeper than everyday dissatisfactions and desires, a great longing, even though not a determinate lack that must be filled. The odd and somewhat mawkish image Nietzsche often uses to make this point is that of a bee or hive overloaded with honey. The image suggests desires well beyond any need, or a surfeit or abundance of desires (one might even say, desires for ever "more," for "excess" meaning) that can be communicated and shared.[30] (In this sense, although Nietzsche would often poke fun at Kant's account of aesthetic pleasure, it could fairly be said that one source for this image of desire in excess, not responsive to a missing fulfillment or need, but a surplus outside any calculability, is the post-Kantian understanding of aesthetic experience as preconceptual and sensual, but not "interested" desire satisfaction.) The generosity and even potential frivolity in decorating, beautifying, etc., even at the expense of prudence and sober self-interest, is, Schiller maintained, the first manifestation of a desire that exceeds any logic of calculation. Consider from Schiller's letters:

Not content with what simply satisfies Nature and meets his need, he demands superfluity; to begin with, certainly, merely a superfluity *of* material, in order to conceal from his desires their boundaries, in order to assure his enjoyment beyond the existing need, but soon a superfluity *in* the material, an aesthetic supplement, in order to be able to satisfy his formal impulse also, in order to extend his enjoyment beyond every need.[31]

In the *Nachlass*, Nietzsche tries frequently to distinguish his position from what he considers the neediness and non-aesthetic status of "romanticism."

Is art a consequence of *dissatisfaction with reality*? Or an expression of *gratitude for happiness enjoyed*? In the former case, *romanticism*; in the latter, aureole and dithyramb (in short, art of apotheosis): Raphael, too, belongs here; he merely had the falsity to deify what looked like the Christian interpretation of the world. He was grateful for existence where it was *not* specifically Christian.[32]

And this distinction between romanticism (and romantic pessimism, Schopenhauer, Wagner) and what he favors, "art of apotheosis," is said to be based on a "fundamental distinction." "I ask in each individual case 'has hunger or superabundance become creative here?'" and he affirms an art he says is based on "gratitude and love," not hunger.[33] "The full and bestowing" is what he affirms, not "the seeking, desiring."[34] (He makes the same distinction in *The Gay Science*, distinguishing between two kinds of sufferers: those who suffer from "over-fullness of life," and romantics, "who suffer from the *impoverishment of life*."[35])

As noted above, part of Nietzsche's "experiment" is to suggest that such an "excess" erotic insistence can come to seem as ennobling as the equally "useless" impulse for aesthetic production; indispensable in a life being human, but which, paradoxically (*the same paradox* we have been encountering all along), cannot be undertaken *for* that reason, because we "need" it "in order to be" human.

That human nature is such as to deny *itself* satisfaction (in an evolutionary metaphor, human beings have evolved to be beyond a natural niche or function; everything about them that is distinctly human is evolutionary excess, waste) is a theme that resonates with many philosophers whom Nietzsche would disown, but who form an exclusive club. It is the founding thought of a decisive strand of modern philosophy – Rousseau's thought – and thanks to Rousseau it shows up in Kant's account of our "unsocial sociability" (*ungesellige Geselligkeit*), in Hegel's account of the non-natural (or "excessive") claim of the other for recognition, and in Marx's famous account of the social (not natural) significance of organized labor. It shows up for different reasons in Freud's account of the harshness of the repression of natural (essentially Oedipal) desire and so our self-division (the self-division that makes us human allows it to be said that we lead lives, rather than merely exist or suffer our existence). (Hegel also says in his *Aesthetics Lectures* that human existence itself is a self-inflicted wound, but one which we can also "heal" ourselves.[36]) The somewhat mythic picture here is straightforward: the natural world is a world without genuine individuality (just mere particularity, in Hegel's language); it is formless, brutal, chaotic, and indifferent, and to live a human life is (and essentially is *only*) to *resist* this, to *make* oneself anything other than this, all because we will not accept it and have found a way to provoke such dissatisfaction in others and for posterity. (Individuality is always a kind of fragile, unstable, threatened *achievement*, not an original state of being.[37]) We know in other words where we don't want to be, what would be a kind of spiritual death, without knowing in effect where to go. (And again, it all also means that we *can* cease to resist, become "last men" because barely human at all once this tension is lost.)

The best example of what I have been talking about occurs in section 300 of *The Gay Science*. Nietzsche first claims that necessary preconditions for modern science were the "magicians, alchemists, astrologers and witches," because their "promises and pretensions" "*had to create (schaffen mussten)* a thirst, a hunger, a taste for hidden and forbidden powers," and that much more had to be promised than could be delivered so that this frustration would sustain the scientific enterprise until much later the promise could be fulfilled in the "realm of knowledge." Then, in comments on religion he goes on, or goes so far, as to say that man had to *learn* even to "experience a hunger and thirst for himself," and so to learn to "find satisfaction and fullness in himself." Religious ways of life, in other words, gave this surfeit of human desire a form and a goal; it did not respond to, but opened up, the experience of a gap between me and myself, made it possible for me to experience myself as somehow dissatisfying so that I had to become a self, become who I am. And all this just as astronomy does not do better what astrologers attempted; it realizes a desire to know about the stars that had to be originated and sustained, rather than responded to. His next remark is the most elliptical and, as is usual with Nietzschean imagery like this, it creates the very thing it describes; an aspiration to more meaning:

Did Prometheus have to fancy (*wähnen*), first that he had stolen the light and then pay for that – before he finally discovered that he had created the light by coveting the light and that not only man but also the god was the work of his own hands and had been mere clay in his hands? All mere images of the maker – no less than fancy, the theft, the Caucasus, the vulture, and the whole tragic *Prometheia* of all seekers after knowledge. (*GS* §300)

Prometheus created the light by coveting it is the phrase that says it all; the incapacity to rest content, the impulse to give away, is treated by Nietzsche as a kind of luxurious magnanimity and generosity of spirit. The dissatisfaction Prometheus felt was not the occasion of this generosity but its result, and the determinate meaning of what happened, the injustice of Zeus, the meaning of his suffering represent extensions and consequences of the kind of dissatisfaction that he opened up and held open; the excess meaning he creates by his act and that he promises to be able to explain.

One can easily lose one's hold on these suggestions; looking at things "from the point of view of life" can look as if it makes what we want, perhaps arbitrarily and accidentally want, a condition of what we accept as valuable, and that can seem like wishful thinking. And we seem to be sliding back to some version of the radical rhetorical reading, with meaning and value originally projected or imposed. Moreover, other philosophers, notably Hegel, also began with the assumption that "the religion of modern times is 'God is dead.'"[38] Hegel was happy enough to concede that modern bourgeois life, with its distributed subjectivity (or radically divided labor and mundane preoccupations), is *prosaic* (his most frequent characterization in the *Aesthetics* lectures), without any possible heroism, so devoid even of beauty, so "liberated" from natural sensibility as to render art itself marginal, no longer of world-historical significance, and religion a merely civic experience. But one can understand Hegel as having also wagered that the realization of freedom embodied in modern law and modern social institutions like the family and market economy was, one might say, consolation enough; that allegiance (or erotic attachment) to this ideal was psychologically and socially sufficient to sustain and reproduce a form of life. One way of summarizing what we have been discussing is to note simply that Nietzsche thought that a bad wager; that the evidence was everywhere that the ideal had become a self-serving venality, and illusions about it had helped produce widespread chronic social pathologies. So far, though, in the passages we have looked at, he seems simply to be painting an alternative anti-bourgeois picture (of nobility, hierarchy of rank, courage, and so forth) and assuming that we could "choose" it instead.

But we need to remember that the theme in these passages is eros, not will or spontaneous creativity, and that such attempts to inspire a kind of longing, to break the hold of need and fear and inspire a kind of reckless generosity (e.g. like Prometheus), can fail, and that it is very hard to understand what kind of erotic promises will get a grip and why. It is also one of the reasons that there is little in the way of a programmatic response to nihilism in Nietzsche's texts. The failure of desire and its experiential manifestations in everyday life – boredom, loneliness, and fatigue – are very hard to diagnose, and extremely hard to respond to. (The pathos of romantic failure, the ever-possible sudden disappearance of desire, the role of illusion in sustaining any such romantic desire, and the total impossibility of any rational translation of desire into a calculus of mutual satisfaction are major metaphorical variations on the theme of eros throughout Nietzsche's writings.[39]) And again, sometimes, the extraordinarily enigmatic metaphors and images used by Nietzsche – the eternal return of the same, the spirit of gravity, the pale criminal, a Zoroastrian prophet, a gay science – all seemed mostly to provoke what he has said we need: "neediness" itself; the *expectation* of meaning, and therewith alone the sustenance of a "noble" human desire, a new kind of victory led by Nietzsche over our present "weariness with man."

But, in the small amount of space left in this chapter, it is possible to note several guideposts in any further reflection on Nietzsche and the problem of desire. There is, for example, a strict condition that he places on any such new engagement with the world, one that right away should dampen enthusiasm for a radically aesthetic or rhetorical reading. The second paragraph of *The Gay Science* contains a great contempt for "the majority" who do not have an "intellectual conscience," who

[do] not consider it contemptible to believe this or that and to live accordingly, without first having given themselves an account of the final and most certain reasons pro and con, and without even troubling themselves about such reasons afterward.[40]

He is describing here a historical situation peculiar to "us," an aspect of what we have inherited from the Socratic and modern Enlightenment, but without which we cannot now live, even though it might have been otherwise. An earlier formulation from *Daybreak* makes the historical point clear while returning directly to the erotic images. Nietzsche notes that "our passion," "the drive to knowledge,"

has become too strong for us to be able to want happiness without knowledge [or to be able to want the happiness] of a strong, firmly rooted delusion; even to imagine such a state of things is painful to us! Restless discovering and divining has such an attraction for us, and has grown as indispensable to us as is to the lover his unrequited love, which he would at no price relinquish for a state of indifference – perhaps, indeed, we too are *unrequited* lovers.[41]

In fact, the possibility of such an unrequited love, especially the possibility of sustaining it, turns out to be one of the best images for the question Nietzsche wants to ask about nihilism and our response. It is as consummate and all-encompassing a summation of Nietzsche's chief question as any other offered. It suggests exactly the position that Nietzsche's last men would find baffling and contemptible – always wanting more, in excess of what can be achieved, for which no useful reason can be given – and that Nietzsche clearly affirms as noble, beautiful, or in the classical sense, *kalos k'agathos*. However, it also immediately suggests an escape from one archetypal modernist pathology into another, from Dostoevskian melancholy to Proustian hysteria, in which it is only the unsatisfiability of a desire that sustains desire and therewith life itself, a libidinal cathexis to life and life's project's.[42] Just as one could quote Freud's classic account of melancholy to explain the madman's pathos, these remarks about endless erotic striving bring to mind a typical analytic definition of hysteria as in Juan-David Nasio's book, *Hysteria from Freud to Lacan*: "the hysteric unconsciously invents a fantasy scenario designed to prove to himself and to the world that there is no pleasure except the kind that is unfulfilled."[43]

In his own language, given this unavoidable intellectual conscience and the impossibility of living whatever lie seems most beautiful or pleasing, the question he wants to ask is: what is the alternative to "last man" contentment, itself quite a consistent turn to a "this-worldly" form of life? By "alternative," we mean not only an engagement we can care about, but one which also looks like some form of this-worldly dissatisfaction, provoked by some not-being that we strive to cancel, to overcome, a form of self-overcoming without asceticism or transcendence. We want a picture of striving without the illusion of a determinate, natural lack that we can fill. To anyone with an intellectual conscience, it will have to feel as if there just can be no human whole, not as proposed by Plato or Aristotle or Christianity or Schiller or Hegel, and so forth, and yet it can't just "not matter" that there can be no such harmony or completion, because all of the ways we have come to think about such desire start out from these assumptions about caused needs or an incompleteness that we strive to complete. The "last men" are atheists, scientific secularists, antimetaphysicians, and naturalists in ethics. (They look, that is, like many of the standard interpretations of Nietzsche.) But they provoke only contempt in Nietzsche. (Contrary to his remarks about the last men, there is always detectable a grudging admiration in Nietzsche for ascetics, priests, Platonists, and so forth. They "made life interesting," made it *life*, inspired and sustained desire.) Is there an *other* way, then, of thinking about this activity?[44]

This is a hard question to answer, not only because it is so abstract, but because it is the sort of question addressed more regularly by modern, romantic, and confessional poetry than by philosophy. Sometimes, many times actually, Nietzsche suggests that a good deal of the answer depends on *him*, on whether he can portray the heroism and beauty of such futile attempts well enough, can inspire a sense of nobility not dependent on guarantees, payoffs, natural completions, benefits, and probabilities. Looked at broadly, though, the historical answer to Nietzsche's question is clearly negative; the experiment with him at the center did not take; his "truth" could not be successfully incorporated. He did not become a new Socrates, and his cultural and historical impact has been much more as a kind of "dissolving fluid," a value-debunker, an immoralist, than as any prophet for a new form of life.

So, while Nietzsche may have avoided the melancholy of someone inter-
minably mourning the death of God, only to have retreated into a hysterical
fantasy, convinced that all life is like Tantalus' plight, or, to use his earlier
term of art, simply tragic, the positive, erotic side of the project he proposes
is also on view, and remains suggestive, tantalizing in the way he probably
intends. This is the last erotic "guidepost" I want to mention, and it can
only be mentioned here. At section 276 of *The Gay Science*, he writes:

I, too, shall say what it is that I wish from myself today, and what was the first
thought to run across my heart this year – what thought shall be for me the reason,
warranty and sweetness of my life henceforth. I want to learn more and more to
see as beautiful what is necessary in things; then I shall be one of those who makes
things beautiful. *Amor fati*: let that be my love henceforth! I do not want to wage
war against what is ugly. I do not want to accuse; I do not even want to accuse
those who accuse. *Looking away* shall be my only negation. And all in all and on
the whole: some day I wish to be only a Yes-sayer.[45]

NOTES

1. Nietzsche, *The Gay Science* (*GS*), trans. Walter Kaufmann (New York: Vintage,
   1974).
2. Nietzsche is obviously suggesting that this "death" is not rightly understood as
   the inability to believe a proposition. (And, if that is so, if the phenomenon is
   more like what the religious call "losing faith," then the original, being religious
   or having faith, cannot be originally and solely a matter of belief.)
3. There is, of course, a "romantic" sense of craziness, in which it is the unusual
   depth or profundity of the insight itself that drives one crazy, a successor notion
   to the mythic belief that God may not be viewed by humans. His absence
   apparently cannot be borne either, on such a romantic view. (It is also a view
   of Nietzsche's own insanity that has long fascinated French scholars. I discuss
   these aspects of the passage in "Nietzsche and the Melancholy of Modernity,"
   Social Research, vol. 66, no. 2 [Summer, 1999], pp. 495–520. This introductory
   section is a summary of some aspects of that paper.)
4. *GS*, p. 279, translation modified.
5. See "Nietzsche and the Melancholy of Modernity."
6. Nietzsche, *The Case of Wagner*, in *Basic Writings of Nietzsche*, trans. Walter
   Kaufmann (New York: The Modern Library, 1968), p. 643.
7. I acknowledge here a debt to Irad Kimhi for several valuable conversations
   about this problem in particular.
8. *GS*, section 377, p. 340, translation modified.
9. *Thus Spoke Zarathustra* (*TSZ*), trans. Walter Kaufmann (New York: Viking,
   1966), p. 59. I have discussed the relevance of this problem to the problem of
   philosophers as a "post-metaphysical," even post-philosophical, type in "The
   Erotic Nietzsche: Philosophers Without Philosophy," forthcoming in a volume
   of conference papers to be published by the University of Chicago Press. I rely
   there on many of the same quotations and analysis as here.

10. Nietzsche, *The Will to Power* (*WP*), trans. Walter Kaufmann (New York: Vintage, 1968), section 12A, p. 13.

11. One reason why Nietzsche's thought has become more and more relevant: the fact that "the West" now lives for the first time since the advent of political modernity without either the specter or the beacon (depending on one's point of view) of any revolutionary aspiration.

12. Nietzsche, *WP*, section 22, p. 17.

13. *Ibid.*, p. 13 (my italics). This is like a passage from *The Twilight of the Idols*: "Whoever does not know how to lay his will into things, at least lays some meaning into them: that means that he has faith that they already obey a will" (*Twilight of the Idols* [*TI*], trans. R. J. Hollingdale [Baltimore: Penguin, 1968], ch. 1, p. 24); and compare, "That it is the measure of strength to what extent we can admit to ourselves, without perishing, the merely *apparent* character, the necessity of lies" (*WP*, section 15, p. 15) and "It is a measure of the degree of strength of will to what extent one can do without meaning in things, to what extent one can endure to live in a meaningless world *because one organizes a small portion of it oneself*" (*WP*, section 585, p. 318).

14. Nietzsche, *GS*, section 345, p. 285.

15. Moreover, that there are no practical consequences, and hardly any nihilistic consequences, from any intellectual disillusionment is itself an important claim that Nietzsche wants to make and defend directly. Anyone who thinks that some sort of action would therewith be required or rendered impossible is himself willing that consequence, creating it, not inferring it. As he says frequently throughout his published and unpublished works: "One interpretation has collapsed; but because it was considered *the* interpretation it now seems as if there were no meaning at all in existence, as if everything were in vain" (Nietzsche, *WP*, section 55, p. 35).

16. For a more detailed discussion of the category of "psychology" as employed by Nietzsche, see my "Morality as Psychology; Psychology as Morality: Nietzsche, Eros, and Clumsy Lovers," in *Nietzsche's Postmoralism: Essays on Nietzsche's Prelude to Philosophy's Future*, ed. Richard Schacht (Cambridge University Press, 2001), pp. 79–99.

17. *Beyond Good and Evil* (*BGE*), trans. Walter Kaufmann (New York: Vintage, 1989), p. 1.

18. *TSZ*, pp. 10, 11.

19. *On the Genealogy of Morals*, in Nietzsche, *Ecce Homo/On the Genealogy of Morals* (*OGM*), trans. Walter Kaufmann (New York: Vintage, 1989), p. 15.

20. See my "Gay Science and Corporeal Knowledge," *Nietzsche-Studien* 29 (2000), pp. 136–52.

21. Nietzsche, *TSZ*, p. 17.

22. *BGE*, p. 2.

23. Nietzsche, *GS*, p. 117.

24. *OGM*, p. 284. Trying to "refute" an ideal is called an "idealism" (a faith in the autonomy of ideals) and is rejected.

25. See on this topic the discussion by Jonathan Lear, *Love and its Place in Nature* (New York: Farrar, Straus, and Giroux, 1990), pp. 132–55.

26. Nietzsche, *GS*, pp. 286.

27. Nietzsche, *Untimely Meditations*, trans. R. J. Hollingdale (Cambridge University Press, 1983), p. 163.

28. Nietzsche, *GS*, p. 184.

29. Nietzsche, *Human, All Too Human*, trans. R. J. Hollingdale (Cambridge University Press, 1986), p. 20, translation modified.

30. Compare this passage from *The Twilight of the Idols*. "The genius in work and deed is necessarily a squanderer [Verschwender]: that he squanders himself, that is his greatness. The instinct of self-preservation is suspended, as it were; the overpowering pressure of outpouring forces forbids him any such care and caution. People call this "self-sacrifice" and praise his "heroism," his indifference to his own well-being, his devotion to an idea, a great cause, a fatherland: without exception, misunderstandings. He flows out, he overflows, he uses himself up; he does not spare himself – and this is a calamitous, involuntary fatality, no less than a river's flooding the land. Yet because so much is owed to such explosives, much has also been given them in return: for example a higher kind of morality. After all, that is the way of human gratitude: it *misunderstands* its benefactors" (ch. IX, p. 98) (translation modified).

31. Friedrich Schiller, *On the Aesthetic Education of Man in a Series of Letters*, trans. Reginald Snell (New York: Unger, 1965), p. 132. Cf. especially the perceptive use made of Schiller by Volker Gerhardt in "Zu Nietzsches frühem Programm einer ästhetischen Rechtfertigung der Welt," in *Pathos und Distanz* (Stuttgart: Reclam, 1988), especially p. 67.

32. Nietzsche, *WP*, section 845, p. 445.

33. *Ibid*., section 846, pp. 445–6.

34. *Ibid*., section 843, p. 445.

35. Nietzsche, *GS*, section 370, p. 328. See also the Second Edition Preface to *GS*, where Nietzsche distinguishes a philosophy based on need from one that understands itself as simply a "beautiful luxury," the "voluptuousness of a triumphant gratitude" (pp. 33–4).

36. G. W. F. Hegel, *Aesthetics: Lectures on Fine Art*, trans. T. M. Knox (Oxford University Press, 1991), p. 8.

37. Cf. chapter 6 of Lear, *Love and its Place in Nature*. I consider this position on individuality (as a social and psychological achievement) an essential theme in post-Kantian German philosophy. See my "What is the Question for Which Hegel's 'Theory of Recognition' is the Answer?'," *European Journal of Philosophy* 8 (2) (August, 2000), pp. 155–72.

38. "Glauben und Wissen," *Werke*, vol. II (Frankfurt: Suhrkamp, 1970), p. 432.

39. See my "Morality as Psychology; Psychology as Morality: Nietzsche, Eros, and Clumsy Lovers," and "Deceit, Desire, and Democracy: Nietzsche on Modern Eros," *International Studies in Philosophy* 32 (3) (March, 2000), pp. 61–70.

40. Nietzsche, *GS*, p. 76.

41. Nietzsche, *Daybreak*, trans. R. J. Hollingdale (Cambridge University Press, 1982), p. 184.
42. Proust is relevant in another sense too. The "death of God," let us say, does not for Proust occasion a kind of melancholy or despair that the narrative structure without which a self, an identity, would not be possible has lost all authority. The problem is rather an excess of meaning; there are too many possible, possibly authoritative narratives, one of the reasons why Marcel has such a tough time starting to write.
43. This possibility was suggested to me in a commentary on an earlier version of this chapter by Eric Santner. I owe the reference to Nasio's book to Santner: *Hysteria from Freud to Lacan: The Splendid Child of Psychoanalysis* (Northvale, N.J.: J. Aronson, 1997), p. 5. I would want ultimately to be able to show that the situation Nietzsche describes is more fruitfully understood as much more like Schiller's picture of "useless" and "excess" aesthetic experience (unsatisfiable because not a lack or a need) than Freud on hysterics, but that must remain a promissory note.
44. What determines whether this sense of our own eros is dispiriting and enervating and hopeless, simply tiring, or a great field of possibilities, inspiring, or, in one of his favorite terms for it, "innocent," is a central question. (To see being itself as innocent is to see this surfeit and endlessness not as morally dispiriting, but as *not morally anything*. It would be to be able to think of it as the mere play of an innocent child, Heraclitus, *pais paizon*, in such a way that to "blame" the world would feel like blaming an innocently destructive and disruptive child.)
45. Nietzsche, *GS*, p. 223.

CHAPTER 3

After onto-theology: philosophy between science and religion

Gianni Vattimo

The twentieth century seemed to close with the end of the phenomenon that has been called secularization. If, just to draw a superficial parallel, the nineteenth century seemed to end with the triumph of science and technology (think of the spirit of the *belle époque*, though overly mythologized, which already bore the signs of a spleen that burst into view in the *Kulturkritik* of the first decades of the twentieth century), so the twentieth century, the old millennium, seemed to end with the renewal of religion. To be sure, religions (I am thinking primarily of the great Abrahamic religions, and among them especially Christianity and Islam) are not being reborn today. Their new visibility has to do, at least in Europe, with the weight of religious factors in the fall of communist regimes, and the dramatic nature of many ecological problems (broadly defined, ranging from environmental pollution to genetic manipulation) that have risen from the application of the life sciences. In other words, while religions (in accordance with the Enlightenment and positivist view) were seen for decades as residual forms of experience, destined to diminish with the imposition of "modern" forms of life (technical and scientific rationalization of social life, political democracy, and so on), now they appear once again as possible guides for the future. The authority by which the Pope and other representatives of the world religions speak on the international stage cannot be explained by the new ability they have to talk to multitudes through the mass media. The "end of modernity," or in any case its crisis, has brought about the dissolution of the main philosophical theories that claimed to have done away with religion: positivist scientism, and Hegelian – later, Marxist – historicism. Today there are no good philosophical reasons to be an atheist, or in any case, to dismiss religion.

In modernity, atheistic rationalism has taken two forms that have often been blended: the belief that in the experimental sciences of nature lies an exlusive claim to the truth, and faith in the progress of history toward a condition of full emancipation. These two kinds of rationalism have often been mixed, for example, in the positivist conception of progress. Each perspective assigned only a provisional place to religion, which was regarded as an error destined to be dismissed by scientific rationality, or a moment to be overcome by reason's self-unfolding toward fuller and truer forms of self-consciousness. Today, both belief in the objective truth of the experimental sciences and faith in the progress of reason toward full transparency appear to have been overcome.

By now, all of us are used to the fact that disenchantment with the world has generated a radical disenchantment with the very idea of disenchantment. In other words, demythification has finally turned against itself, thereby acknowledging that the ideal of the elimination of myth is a myth too. Yet it is not altogether clear whether this means that, having eliminated all myths, we shall easily get rid of the myth of demythification too, moving then toward new stages of rationality. This is how Richard Rorty seems to conceive of this process, though in different terms, when defining our epoch as a post-philosophical one, analogous to the post-religious epoch that followed the triumph of the Enlightenment in the eighteenth century. One could object to Rorty that his belief is still underlined by a subtle historicist faith in the linearity and irreversibility of progress: we overcame religion in the past, and now we shall overcome philosophy, according to a linear course of development. However, if we were not de facto placed before the visible renewal of religion as a social and cultural phenomenon, this "logical" objection would have no value. My point is not to embrace again a historicist faith in the rationality of the real, by putting forth the argument that if religions "win," then it means that they must be true. Rather, it is to be able to hear the "signs of the times," to use an expression from the Gospels: once the social and political renewal of religion is associated with the crisis of the rationalist ideologies that in modernity were the basis of atheism, these signs acquire an extraordinary meaning. This ensemble of phenomena is not limited to the ethnic-religious wars fought all over the world (and which cannot be explained exclusively in economic terms), or to the extraordinary authority recently acquired by the great religious leaders vis-à-vis political figures. This picture is also partly informed by the new permeability of contemporary philosophy to myth, and to the substance of religious traditions.

Today (continental) philosophers speak increasingly, and without providing explicit justification, about angels, redemption, and various mythological figures. This is a practice that, as far as classical mythology is concerned, is clearly promoted by psychoanalysis. Jungian psychoanalysis, in particular, speaks explicitly of a new polytheism; but even in classical

Freudian theory, the relation with mythological figures cannot be conceived merely as a recourse to metaphors that must be reduced finally to their "proper meaning." Other sources for the philosophical recovery of mythical and religious terminology are thinkers such as Rosenzweig and Benjamin, though with them (at least insofar as the former is concerned) this recovery was explicitly justified on theoretical grounds. Instead in today's culture these concepts, figures, and metaphors are used widely, taken for granted, and implicitly justified by the fact that the relation of philosophy with poetry is no longer conceived in antagonistic terms, or by the destruction of the boundary between metaphor and its "proper meaning," which seems to be the main consequence of the end of metaphysics announced by Heidegger. At the very end, the introduction of mystic and religious terms in philosophy, without an explicit theoretical elaboration, seems justified, albeit implicitly, by the new relationship that philosophy (especially after Heidegger) claims to establish with poetry, and with aesthetic experience more generally.

In sum, we see in our social and political life the renewed authority of the world religions, a renewal that has its basis in the actual importance of religion in bringing down communism, and in the emergence of broadly defined "apocalyptic" issues, such as those linked to fundamental resources for life – genetic manipulation and so on. At the same time, in literate culture, that is, in philosophical and critical reflections (including literary criticism), the new, pervasive presence of mythical and religious themes and terminologies depends perhaps on the new legitimacy granted to metaphorical discourse by the end of metaphysics. I employ metaphor here in the sense intended by Nietzsche in his great youthful fragment, "Über Wahrheit und Lüge in aussermoralischen Sinn."[1]

Recall that in this text Nietzsche conceives of all knowledge of the world in metaphorical terms:[2] we meet a thing in the world and form an image of it in our mind – the first metaphor, that is, transposition; then we invent a sound to point to that image – the second metaphor; and so on. Thus all language is metaphorical. Yet why is it that at a certain point in time the distinction is made between metaphors and "proper" terms? It is, Nietzsche argues, because an individual or group imposes its own metaphors upon all the others as the only legitimate, acceptable, and true ones. Thus the nation-state speaks a language, whereas dialects are "only" dialects. In stating universally valid propositions, reason speaks primarily the language of "proper" terms, while private languages – including the language of poetry, myth, and so on – are reduced to the status of "pure metaphors."

This argument of Nietzsche's, to some extent, can be found in Heidegger as well. One may say that on the basis of his thought, the distinction between metaphor and proper meaning is less the effect of an authoritarian imposition of a certain language by a group than the imposition of a claim to objectivity which, for Heidegger, is today advanced by the language of experimental science. According to Heidegger, the truth may be thought in terms of correspondence between proposition and thing, but only within a preliminary opening (*Offenheit, Weltoffenheit*), which in turn is not guaranteed by any verifiable correspondence (which would require another opening, and so on ad infinitum). The opening (we might also speak, for clarity's sake, of a paradigm) within which scientific propositions are verified or falsified cannot lay claim to the authority of the "proper meaning": it is a metaphor, and must be recognized as such. However, for Heidegger, it is not as the result of a causal game of forces that the various metaphorical languages have imposed themselves as true and proper, nor can their relationship be arbitrarily modified. In other words, the fact that the language of scientific objectivity and of the experimental method rules as the exclusive truth of modernity is not the effect of a pure game of forces, which could be changed by a human decision. The event of being (*Ereignis*) on which the multiple openings depend (that is, the coming to the domination of the metaphorical systems) is a game of *Übereignen* and *Ent-eignen* (transpropriation and disappropriation). But there is still, fundamentally, a sort of "property" or authenticity (*Eigentlichkeit*), which coincides with the history of being (though this genitive has not only a subjective sense, but also an inseparable objective one).

I leave aside the many objections that could be raised to Heidegger's account. However, it is important to underscore that already here, in the difference between Nietzschean metaphors and Heideggerian events or "openings," there are the premises for further developing the argument I want to make, leading up to the theme of secularization. Metaphysics (or modernity, if you will) does not end because we have found a truer truth, which disavows it and finally offers us the true meaning of being. For Heidegger (I shall limit myself here to a few remarks), metaphysics ends when it reaches its highest peak in the universal mastery of technology and of the will to power. In fact, metaphysics is the forgetting of the ontological difference, the identification of true being with the present, quantifiable, and verifiable objectivity. In late modernity, this is analogous to the objectivation of the whole by a subject who, through techno-science, actively constructs the world rather than letting it be. In the end, however, even the constructivist subject becomes pure, manipulable material, according to a dizzy circularity that belongs to the "total organization" of which Adorno spoke (which, for Heidegger, is the *Ge-stell,* the ensemble of *stellen*). Metaphysics confutes itself precisely insofar as it establishes itself universally. It somewhat resembles Nietzsche's God, who dies when the faithful, in order to respect his command not to lie, unmask him as a lie that can no longer be maintained and is no longer necessary. Metaphysics, having started with the idea that truth is objectivity, ends up with the "discovery" that objectivity is posited by the subject, who in turn becomes a manipulable object. The effect of all this is that metaphysics disavows itself precisely when it fulfills itself, reducing all being to objectivity. From this moment on, we can no longer think of being as an object that is given before the eyes of reason – at least because, in doing so, we would deny that our very existence – made up of projects, memories, hopes, and decisions – is "being" (since it is never pure "objectivity").

This process is correctly referred to as the history of nihilism. As Nietzsche writes in the *Götzendämmerung*, "the real world has become a fable."[3] In other words, we all know by now – though this, too, is not objective knowledge – that what we call reality is a game of interpretations, none of which may claim to be a pure and objective mirror of the world, that is, a privileged knowledge of the "proper" meaning which would reduce all other senses to the status of poetic or mythical metaphors.

This is the background against which, in today's culture, a kind of peace – or at least a truce – is established between philosophy, science, and religion. In Italy, we have a proverb that says "with the saints in church, with the knaves in the tavern." For us, here, this means that there are many languages, many "language games," for experiencing the world, each of which has legitimacy, provided it respects the boundaries of its own rules. Just as the rules of religious or ethical language differ, so different sciences have their specific methods for the verification and falsification of statements. But can we really be satisfied with this "liberalization," given, after all, that it corresponds all too well to the specialization and division of labor characteristic of modernity? Is it true that the liberal and pluralistic perspective forgoes the recognition of a privileged, objectively true language? Let me make an observation that should give us food for thought. We know many philosophies that speak of myth, but not many myths that speak of philosophy. What I mean is that, according to the liberal and pluralistic perspective, there is still a discourse which distributes the roles in the play, and assigns to other discourses their proper roles: it is precisely the philosopher's discourse (Nietzsche and Heidegger, but also Foucault, Putnam, Rorty, Goodman, and the theories of the paradigms) that advances a theory of the interpretive character of every truth. In turn, is the thesis concerning truth as interpretation – that is, the idea that every statement can only be verified or falsified within a horizon (opening, paradigm, language) which in its turn cannot be verified – an objective description of a state of affairs?

It seems to me that here we must complete Nietzsche's nihilism with Heidegger's ontology, at least in the sense I have suggested this ontology might be interpreted. The thesis concerning truth as interpretation is nothing but an interpretation – namely, a response to a message which comes from the history of our culture as reconstructed by Nietzsche and Heidegger, and more or less explicitly by the other philosophers I have mentioned above (for example, consider Rorty's great book, *Philosophy and the Mirror of Nature*[4]). This reconstruction is already an interpretation, though not an arbitrary one, insofar as it claims to be a reasonable way of placing oneself in the late-modern condition of existence. Its good reasons include: the end of Eurocentrism (which saw history as a linear process in which Europe and its culture were the most advanced stage); the multiplication of scientific languages which cannot be reduced to a unity (for example, the non-Euclidean geometries); the discovery by psychoanalysis of the "secondary" nature of consciousness (thus it becomes impossible to conceive of an ultimate evidence in the manner of the Cartesian Cogito); the increasing difficulty of linking together the entities of which physics speaks with the things of our daily experience (so that even physics seems to have become an agent of de-realization – *Entwirklichung*, *Entrealisierung*); and even the rise of the democratic state, which removes any possibility of grounding politics and the law upon rigid rational schemes.

My thesis – or better, hypothesis – is that if philosophical pluralism takes its status as an interpretation seriously, it encounters once again the Western religious tradition, namely, the Judeo-Christian tradition. Nihilism does not open the dialogue between philosophy and religion only in the sense that in the absence of the great atheist rationalist systems of the eighteenth and nineteenth centuries (the Enlightenment, historicism, positivism, and Marxism) there are no longer good philosophical reasons to be atheists. If we were to confine ourselves to this type of liberalism, we would really find ourselves in a general condition of irrationalism, where, according to Feyerabend's famous expression, everything goes – within its own limits (but who sets these limits?). By contrast, we get to truth as interpretation by responding to the history that Heidegger calls the history of being, and which it seems reasonable to read as a history of weakening.

If today the world is given to us as a game of interpretations, this is not because we have understood – more acutely than Aristotle, Parmenides, and Descartes – that things are objectively so. Rather, it is because being itself, which is never a pure object placed before us, the subjects, gives itself in a less peremptory, weakened form. Does such a thought have any sense? It seems to me that it is a way of "translating," in terms that are themselves weak, the core of the Judeo-Christian message. This message speaks of an occurrence of being, which has a history, and this history is the history of creation (God creates a being other than himself, a being who is free even to deny God) and of salvation (God becomes man in abasement and humiliation, and dissolves his own transcendence – the event that St. Paul calls *kenosis*).

To sum up the argument in a rather provocative fashion: the history of being is the history of nihilism, *that is*, the *same* history of salvation that we have come to know from the Bible. Here the risk of irrationalism of the liberal and pluralistic perspectives encounters a limit: nihilism is not just the unleashing of an interminable conflict where there are no good reasons, only forces that impose themselves with more or less violence. In the game of interpretations, it is possible to distinguish between valid and arbitrary interpretations, and the criterion for doing so is precisely the weakening of strong structures, of the peremptoriness of objectivity, of sovereign will, of the overpowering force that arbitrarily establishes what is truth and what is a lie. We have not completely lost reality in the fable, for reality is the history of the dissolution of the real as peremptory objectivity, or to use a religious term, the history of secularization.

Indeed, secularization is not merely the dissolution of the sacred, the estrangement from the divine, the loss of religiosity – as it is usually conceived – a path to be retraced in reverse by believers in order to recover the truth of the original biblical message.

Secularization is, more fundamentally, an essential aspect of the history of salvation, as other modern philosophers saw, and long before them too, Joachim of Fiore. If the Bible speaks of being as an event, and of God as the one who abandons his own transcendence, first by creating the world, and then by redeeming it through the Incarnation and the Cross – through *kenosis* – then the desacralizing phenomena characteristic of modernity are the authentic aspects of the history of salvation. To quote another Italian saying: "Thank God I am an atheist." Biblical revelation liberates us from "natural religion," superstitions, and the idea of the divine as a mysterious power which lies absolutely beyond our comprehension and therefore is irrational, and to which we would have to succumb, accepting quietly the most varied dogmatic and moral disciplines imposed by the authority of churches.

How, then, are we to configure the relation between philosophy, religion, and science alluded to in the title of this chapter? Philosophy is not reducible to religion; rather, it has to rethink itself as the secularization *in actu* of the religious message of the West. Philosophy finds in the common thread of reducing the peremptoriness of being the criterion for looking at the sciences and technologies that depend on it. These – the technologies that make existence easier, and the more specialized and fragmented fields of knowledge that cannot be reduced to a unitary image of the real – no longer appear as mere tools contrived by man to attain an ever more secure survival in the midst of nature. Rather, they too must be interpreted as moments of a history of emancipation that goes beyond the purely biological sphere, and perhaps may be called a history of spirit.

NOTES

1. Translated as "On Truth and Lies in a Nonmoral Sense," in *Philosophy and Truth: Selections from Nietzsche's Notebooks of the Early 1870's*, trans. Daniel Brazeale (Atlantic Highlands, N.J.: Humanities Press, 1979), pp. 79–97.
2. *Ibid.*, p. 82.
3. See Friedrich Nietzsche, *Twilight of the Idols*, trans. Duncan Large (New York: Oxford University Press, 1998), p. 20.
4. (Princeton University Press, 1981).

CHAPTER 4

Anti-clericalism and atheism

Richard Rorty

Some day, intellectual historians may remark that the twentieth century was the one in which the philosophy professors began to stop asking bad questions – questions like "What really exists?" "What are the scope and limits of human knowledge?" and "How does language hook up with reality?" These questions assume that philosophy can be done ahistorically. They presuppose the bad idea that inspection of our present practices can give us an understanding of the "structure" of all possible human practices.

"Structure" is just another word for "essence." The most important movements in twentieth-century philosophy have been anti-essentialist. These movements have mocked the ambitions of their predecessors, positivism and phenomenology, to do what Plato and Aristotle had hoped to do – sift out the changing appearances from the enduringly real, the merely contingent from the truly necessary. Recent examples of this mockery are Jacques Derrida's *Margins of Philosophy*[1] and Bas van Fraassen's *The Empirical Stance*.[2] These books stand on the shoulders of Heidegger's *Being and Time*,[3] Dewey's *Reconstruction in Philosophy*,[4] and Wittgenstein's *Philosophical Investigations*.[5] All these anti-essentialist books urge us to fight free of the old Greek distinctions between the apparent and the real, and between the necessary and the contingent.

One effect of the rise of anti-essentialism and of historicism is insouciance about what Lecky famously called "the warfare between science and theology." A growing tendency to accept what Terry Pinkard calls "Hegel's doctrine of the sociality of reason," and to abandon what Habermas calls "subject-centered reason" for what he calls "communicative reason," has weakened the grip of the idea that scientific beliefs are formed rationally, whereas religious beliefs are not. The anti-positivist tenor of post-Kuhnian philosophy of science has combined with the work of post-Heideggerian theologians to make intellectuals more sympathetic to William James's claim that natural science and religion need not compete with one another.

These developments have made the word "atheist" less popular than it used to be. Philosophers who do not go to church are now less inclined to describe themselves as believing that there is no God. They are more inclined to use such expressions as Max Weber's "religiously unmusical." One can be tone-deaf when it comes to religion just as one can be oblivious to the charms of music. People who find themselves quite unable to take an interest in the question of whether God exists have no right to be contemptuous of people who believe passionately in his existence, or of people who deny it with equal passion. Nor do either of the latter have a right to be contemptuous of those to whom the dispute seems pointless.

Philosophy resembles music and religion in this respect. Many students – those who walk out of the final examination in Philosophy 101 determined never to waste their time with another philosophy course, and unable to understand how people can take that sort of thing seriously – are philosophically unmusical. Some philosophers still think that this attitude toward the discipline to which they have devoted their lives is evidence of an intellectual, and perhaps even a moral, flaw. But most are by now content to shrug off an inability to take philosophical issues seriously as no more important, when evaluating a person's intellect or character, than an inability to read fiction, or to grasp mathematical relationships, or to learn foreign languages.

This increased tolerance for people who simply brush aside questions that were once thought to be of the highest importance is sometimes described as the adoption of an "aestheticist" attitude. This description is especially popular among those who find such tolerance deplorable, and who diagnose its spread as a symptom of a dangerous spiritual illness ("skepticism" or "relativism" or something equally appalling). But the term "aesthetic" in such contexts presupposes the standard Kantian cognitive–moral–aesthetic distinction. That distinction is itself one of the principal targets of anti-essentialist, historicist, philosophizing.

Kantians think that once you have given up hope of attaining universal agreement on an issue you have declared it "merely a matter of taste." But this description strikes anti-essentialist philosophers as just as bad as the Kantian idea that being rational is a matter of following rules. Philosophers who do not believe that there are any such rules reject Kantian pigeonholing in favor of questions about what context certain beliefs, or practices, or books can best be put in, for what particular purposes. Once the Kantian trichotomy is abandoned, the work of theologians like Bultmann and Tillich no longer looks like a reduction of the "cognitive" claims of religion to "merely" aesthetic claims.

In this new climate of philosophical opinion, philosophy professors are no longer expected to provide answers to a question that exercised both Kant and Hegel: How can the worldview of natural science be fitted together with the complex of religious and moral ideas which were central to European civilization? We know what it is like to fit physics together with chemistry and chemistry together with biology, but that sort of fitting is inappropriate when thinking about the interface between art and morality, or between politics and jurisprudence, or between religion and natural science. All these spheres of culture continually interpenetrate and interact. There is no need for an organizational chart that specifies, once and for all, when they are permitted to do so. Nor is there any need to attempt to reach an ahistorical, God's-eye, overview of the relations between all human practices. We can settle for the more limited task Hegel called "holding our time in thought."

Given all these changes, it is not surprising that only two sorts of philosophers are still tempted to use the word "atheist" to describe themselves. The first sort are those who still think that belief in the divine is an empirical hypothesis, and that modern science has given better explanations of the phenomena God was once used to explain. Philosophers of this sort are delighted whenever an ingenuous natural scientist claims that some new scientific discovery provides evidence for the truth of theism, for they find it easy to debunk this claim. They can do so simply by trotting out the same sorts of arguments about the irrelevance of any particular empirical state of affairs to the existence of an atemporal and non-spatial being as were used by Hume and Kant against the natural theologians of the eighteenth century.

I agree with Hume and Kant that the notion of "empirical evidence" is irrelevant to talk about God,[6] but this point bears equally against atheism and theism. President Bush made a good point when he said, in a speech designed to please Christian fundamentalists, that "atheism is a faith" because it is "subject to neither confirmation nor refutation by means of argument or evidence." But the same goes, of course, for theism. Neither those who affirm nor those who deny the existence of God can plausibly claim that they have *evidence* for their views. Being religious, in the modern West, does not have much to do with the explanation of specific observable phenomena.

But there is a second sort of philosopher who describes himself or herself as an atheist. These are the ones who use "atheism" as a rough synonym for "anti-clericalism." I now wish that I had used the latter term on the occasions when I have used the former to characterize my own view. For anti-clericalism is a political view, not an epistemological or metaphysical one. It is the view that ecclesiastical institutions, despite all the good they do – despite all the comfort they provide to those in need or in despair – are dangerous to the health of democratic societies.[7] Whereas the philosophers who claim that atheism, unlike theism, is backed up by evidence would say that religious belief is *irrational*, contemporary secularists like myself are content to say that it is politically dangerous. On our view, religion is un-objectionable as long as it is privatized – as long as ecclesiastical institutions do not attempt to rally the faithful behind political proposals, and as long as believers and unbelievers agree to follow a policy of live-and-let-live.

Some of those who hold this view, such as myself, had no religious upbring-ing and have never developed any attachment to any religious tradition. We are the ones who call ourselves "religiously unmusical." But others, such as the distinguished contemporary Italian philosopher Gianni Vattimo, have used their philosophical learning and sophistication to argue for the rea-sonableness of a return to the religiosity of their youth. This argument is laid out in Vattimo's moving and original book *Credere di credere*.[8] His re-sponse to the question "Do you now once again believe in God?" amounts to saying: I find myself becoming more and more religious, so I suppose I must believe in God. But I think that Vattimo might have done better to say: I am becoming more and more religious, and so coming to have what many people would call a belief in God, but I am not sure that the term "belief" is the right description of what I have.

The point of such a reformulation would be to take account of our conviction that if a belief is true, everybody ought to share it. But Vattimo does not think that all human beings ought to be theists, much less that they should all be Catholics. He follows William James in disassociating the question "Have I a right to be religious?" from the question "Should everybody believe in the existence of God?" Just insofar as one accepts the familiar Hume/Kant critique of natural theology, but disagrees with the positivistic claim that the explanatory successes of modern science have rendered belief in God irrational, one will be inclined to say that religiosity is not happily characterized by the term "belief." So one should welcome Vattimo's attempt to move religion out of the epistemic arena, an arena in which it seems subject to challenge by natural science.

Such attempts are, of course, not new. Kant's suggestion that we view God as a postulate of pure practical reason rather than an explanation of empirical phenomena cleared the way for thinkers like Schleiermacher to develop what Nancy Frankenberry has called "a theology of symbolic forms." It also encouraged thinkers like Kierkegaard, Barth, and Levinas to make God wholly other – beyond the reach, not only of evidence and argument, but of discursive thought.

Vattimo's importance lies in his rejection of *both* of these unhappy post-Kantian initiatives. He puts aside the attempt to connect religion with truth, and so has no use for notions like "symbolic" or "emotional" or "metaphorical" or "moral" truth. Nor does he have any use for what he calls (somewhat misleadingly, in my opinion) "existentialist theology" – the attempt to make religiosity a matter of being rescued from Sin by the inexplicable grace of a deity wholly other than man. His theology is explicitly designed for those whom he calls "half-believers," the people whom St. Paul called "lukewarm in the faith" – the sort of people who only go to church for weddings, baptisms, and funerals (p. 69).

Vattimo turns away from the passages in the Epistle to the Romans that Karl Barth liked best, and reduces the Christian message to the passage in Paul that most other people like best: 1 Corinthians 13. His strategy is to treat the Incarnation as God's sacrifice of *all* his power and authority, as well as *all* his otherness. The Incarnation was an act of *kenosis*, the act in which God turned *everything* over to human beings. This enables Vattimo to make his most startling and most important claim: that "'secularization' ... [is] the constitutive trait of an authentic religious experience" (p. 21).

Hegel too saw human history as constituting the Incarnation of the Spirit, and its slaughter-bench as the Cross. But Hegel was unwilling to put aside truth in favor of love. So Hegel turns human history into a dramatic narrative that reaches its climax in an epistemic state: absolute knowledge. For Vattimo, by contrast, there is no internal dynamic, no inherent teleology, to human history; there is no great drama to be unfolded, but only the hope that love may prevail. Vattimo thinks that if we take human history as seriously as Hegel did, while refusing to place it within either an epistemological or a metaphysical context, we can stop the pendulum from swinging back and forth between militantly positivistic atheism and symbolist or existentialist defenses of theism. As he says, "It is (only) because metaphysical meta-narratives have been dissolved that philosophy has re-discovered the plausibility of religion and can consequently approach the religious need of common consciousness independently of the framework of Enlightenment critique."[9] Vattimo wants to dissolve the problem of the coexistence of natural science with the legacy of Christianity by identifying Christ neither with truth nor with power, but with love alone.

Vattimo's argument provides an illustration of how lines of thought drawn from Nietzsche and Heidegger can be intertwined with those drawn from James and Dewey. For these two intellectual traditions have in common the thought that the quest for truth and knowledge is no more, and no less, than the quest for intersubjective agreement. The epistemic arena is a public space, a space from which religion can and should retreat.[10] The realization that it should retreat from that sphere is not a recognition of the true essence of religion, but simply one of the morals to be drawn from the history of Europe and America.

Vattimo says that "now that Cartesian (and Hegelian) reason has completed its parabola, it no longer makes sense to oppose faith and reason so sharply" (p. 87). By "Cartesian and Hegelian thought" Vattimo means pretty much what Heidegger meant by "onto-theology." The term covers not only traditional theology and metaphysics but also positivism and (insofar as it is an attempt to put philosophy on the secure path of a science) phenomenology. He agrees with Heidegger that "the metaphysics of objectivity culminates in a thinking that identifies the truth of Being with the calculable, measurable and definitively manipulatable object of techno-science" (p. 30). For if you identify rationality with the pursuit of universal intersubjective agreement, and truth with the outcome of such a pursuit, and *if you also claim that nothing should take precedence over that pursuit*, then you will squeeze religion not only out of public life but out of intellectual life. This is because you will have made natural science the paradigm of rationality and truth. Then religion will have to be thought of either as an unsuccessful competitor with empirical inquiry or as "merely" a vehicle of emotional satisfaction.

To save religion from onto-theology you need to regard the desire for universal intersubjective agreement as just one human need among many others, and one that does not automatically trump all other needs. This is a doctrine Nietzsche and Heidegger share with James and Dewey. All four of these anti-Cartesians have principled objections to the pejorative use of "merely" in expressions such as "merely private" or "merely literary" or "merely aesthetic" or "merely emotional." They all provide reasons both for replacing the Kantian distinction between the cognitive and the non-cognitive with the distinction between the satisfaction of public needs and the satisfaction of private needs, and for insisting that there is nothing "mere" about satisfaction of the latter. All four are, in the words that Vattimo uses to describe Heidegger, trying to help us "quit a horizon of thought that is an enemy of freedom and of the historicity of existing" (p. 31).

If one stays within this horizon of thought, and so continues to think of epistemology and metaphysics as first philosophy, one will be convinced that all one's assertions should have cognitive content. An assertion has such content insofar as it is caught up in what the contemporary American philosopher Robert Brandom calls "the game of giving and asking for reasons."[11] But to say that religion should be privatized is to say that religious people are entitled, for certain purposes, to opt out of this game. They are entitled to disconnect their assertions from the network of socially acceptable inferences that provide justifications for making these assertions and draw practical consequences from having made them.

Vattimo seems to me to be aiming at such a privatized religion when he describes the secularization of European culture as the fulfillment of the promise of the Incarnation, considered as *kenosis*, God's turning everything over to us. The more secular, the less hierocratic, the West becomes, the better it carries out the Gospels' promise that God will no longer see us as servants, but as friends. "The essence of [Christian] revelation," Vattimo says, "is reduced to charity, while all the rest is left to the non-finality of diverse historical experiences" (p. 77).

This account of the essence of Christianity – one in which God's self-emptying and man's attempt to think of love as the only law are two faces of the same coin – permits Vattimo to see all the great unmaskers of the West, from Copernicus and Newton to Darwin, Nietzsche, and Freud, as carrying out works of love. These men were, in his words, "reading the signs of the times with no other provision than the commandment of love" (p. 66). They were followers of Christ in the sense that "Christ himself is the unmasker, and . . . the unmasking inaugurated by him . . . is the meaning of the history of salvation itself" (p. 66).

To ask whether this is a "legitimate" or "valid" version of Catholicism, or of Christianity, would be to pose exactly the wrong question. The notion of "legitimacy" is not applicable to what Vattimo, or any of the rest of us, does with our solitude. To try to apply it is to imply that you have no right to go to church for the weddings and baptisms and funerals of your friends and relations unless you acknowledge the authority of ecclesiastical institutions to decide who counts as a Christian and who does not, or no right to call yourself a Jew unless you perform this ritual rather than that.

I can summarize the line of thought Vattimo and I are pursuing as follows: The battle between religion and science conducted in the eighteenth and nineteenth centuries was a contest between institutions both of which claimed cultural supremacy. It was a good thing for both religion and science that science won that battle. For truth and knowledge are a matter of social cooperation, and science gives us the means to carry out better cooperative social projects than before. If social cooperation is what you want, the conjunction of the science and the common sense of your day is all you need. But if you want something else, then a religion that has been taken out of the epistemic arena, a religion which finds the question of theism versus atheism uninteresting, may be just what suits your solitude.

It may be, but it may not. There is still a big difference between people like myself and people like Vattimo. Considering that he was raised a Catholic and I was raised in no religion at all, this is not surprising. Only if one thinks that religious yearnings are somehow pre-cultural and "basic to human nature" will one be reluctant to leave the matter at that – reluctant to privatize religion completely by letting it swing free of the demand for universality.

But if one gives up the idea that either the quest for truth or the quest for God is hard-wired into all human organisms, and allows that both are matters of cultural formation, then such privatization will seem natural and proper. People like Vattimo will cease to think that my lack of religious feeling is a sign of vulgarity, and people like me will cease to think that his possession of such feelings is a sign of cowardice. Both of us can cite 1 Corinthians 13 in support of our refusal to engage in any such invidious explanations.

My differences with Vattimo come down to his ability to regard a past event as holy and my sense that holiness resides only in an ideal future. Vattimo thinks of God's decision to switch from being our master to being our friend as the decisive event upon which our present efforts are dependent. His sense of the holy is bound up with recollection of that event, and of the person who embodied it. My sense of the holy, insofar as I have one, is bound up with the hope that someday, any millennium now, my remote descendants will live in a global civilization in which love is pretty much the only law. In such a society, communication would be domination-free, class and caste would be unknown, hierarchy would be a matter of temporary pragmatic convenience, and power would be entirely at the disposal of the free agreement of a literate and well-educated electorate.

I have no idea how such a society could come about. It is, one might say, a mystery. That mystery, like that of the Incarnation, concerns the coming into existence of a love that is kind, patient, and endures all things; 1 Corinthians 13 is an equally useful text both for religious people like Vattimo, whose sense of what transcends our present condition is bound up with a feeling of dependence, and for non-religious people like myself, for whom this sense consists simply in hope for a better human future. The difference between these two sorts of people is that between unjustifiable gratitude and unjustifiable hope. This is not a matter of conflicting beliefs about what really exists and what does not.[12]

NOTES

1. Trans. Alan Bass (Chicago: University of Chicago Press, 1982).
2. (New Haven: Yale University Press, 2002).
3. Trans. John Macquarrie and Edward Robinson (New York: Harper & Row, 1962).
4. (Boston, Mass.: Beacon Press, 1948).
5. Trans. G. E. M. Anscombe (Oxford: Basil Blackwell, 1968).
6. I have argued this point in some detail in an essay on William James's "The Will to Believe": "Religious Faith, Intellectual Responsibility and Romance", included in my collection *Philosophy and Social Hope* (New York: Penguin, 1999), pp. 148–67. See also my "Pragmatism as Romantic Polytheism," in *The Revival of Pragmatism*, ed. Morris Dickstein (Durham, N.C.: Duke University Press, 1998), pp. 21–36.
7. Of course, we anti-clericalists who are also leftists in politics have a further reason for hoping that institutionalized religion will eventually disappear. We think other-worldliness dangerous because, as John Dewey put it, "Men have never fully used the powers they possess to advance the good in life, because they have waited upon some power external to themselves and to nature to do the work they are responsible for doing" ("A Common Faith," in *John Dewey: The Later Works, 1925–1953*, vol. IX, ed. Jo Ann Boydston [Carbondale: Southern Illinois University Press, 1993], p. 31).
8. (Garzanti Editore, 1996). This book has appeared in English as *Belief*, trans. Luka Disanto and David Webb (Stanford, Calif.: Stanford University Press, 1999). Page numbers in parentheses refer to that volume.
9. "The Trace of the Trace," in *Religion*, ed. Jacques Derrida and Gianni Vattimo (Stanford, Calif.: Stanford University Press, 1998), p. 84.
10. The question of whether this retreat is desirable is quite different from the Kant-style question "Is religious belief cognitive or non-cognitive?" My distinction between the epistemic arena and what lies outside is not drawn on the basis of a distinction between human faculties, or on the basis of a theory about the way in which the human mind is related to reality. It is a distinction between topics on which we are entitled to ask for universal agreement and other topics. Which topics these are – what should be in the epistemic arena and what should not – is a matter of cultural politics. Prior to what Jonathan Israel calls "the radical Enlightenment" it was assumed that religion was a topic of the former sort. Thanks to three hundred and fifty years of culture-political activity, this is no longer the case. For more on the relation between theology and cultural politics, see my essay "Cultural Politics and the Question of the Existence of God", in *Radical Interpretation in Religion*, ed. Nancy Frankenberry (New York: Cambridge University Press, 2002), pp. 53–77.

It is also a different question than the one about whether religious voices should be heard in the public square, where citizens deliberate on political questions. The latter question has been intensively discussed by Stephen Carter, Robert Audi, Nicholas Wolterstorff, and many others. I comment on this debate in my "Religion in the Public Square: A Reconsideration," *Journal of Religious Ethics* 31 (2003), pp. 141–9.

11. See Robert Brandom, *Making It Explicit* (Cambridge, Mass.: Harvard University Press, 1994).

12. This paper is a revised and expanded version of a talk given on the occasion of the award of the Meister-Eckhart Sachbuchpreis in December, 2001. The original version was published in German in *Süddeutsche Zeitung*.

CHAPTER 5

Closed world structures

Charles Taylor

I want to explore here the constitution in modernity of what I shall call "closed" or "horizontal" worlds. I mean by this shapes of our "world" in Heidegger's sense which leave no place for the "vertical" or "transcendent," but which in one way or another close these off, render them inaccessible, or even unthinkable.

This will be a way of making sense of a remarkable historical fact, which strikes us as soon as we take a certain distance, that, say five hundred years ago in our Western civilization, non-belief in God was close to unthinkable for the vast majority; whereas today this is not at all the case. One might be tempted to say that in certain milieux, the reverse has become the case, that belief is unthinkable. But this already concedes the lack of symmetry. It is truer to say that in our world, a whole gamut of positions, from the most militant atheism to the most orthodox traditional theisms, passing through every possible position on the way, is represented and defended somewhere in our society. Something like the unthinkability of some of these positions can be experienced in certain milieux, but what is ruled out will vary from context to context. An atheist in the Bible belt has trouble being understood, as often (in a rather different way) do believing Christians in certain reaches of the academy. But, of course, people in each of these contexts are aware that the others exist, and that the option they can't really credit is the default option elsewhere in the same society, whether they regard this with hostility or just perplexity. The existence of an alternative makes each context fragile, that is, makes its sense of the thinkable/unthinkable uncertain and wavering.

This making fragile is then increased by the fact that great numbers of people are not firmly embedded in any such context, but are puzzled, are cross-pressured, or have constituted by bricolage a sort of median position. The existence of these people raises sometimes even more acute doubts within the more assured milieux. The polar opposites can be written off as just mad or bad, as we see with the present American culture wars between "liberals" and "fundamentalists"; but the intermediate positions can sometimes not be as easily dismissed.

What I want to try is to articulate some of the worlds from within which the believing option seems strange and unjustifiable. But this articulation involves some degree of abstraction – indeed, three kinds of abstraction, with the corresponding dangers: (a) What I shall really be describing is not worlds in their entirety, but "world structures," aspects or features of the way experience and thought are shaped and cohere, but not the whole of which they are constituents; (b) I shall not be describing the world of any concrete human beings. A world is something which people inhabit. It gives the shape of what they experience, feel, opine, see, etc. The world of the cross-pressured is different from that of the assured. But what I'm doing is trying to articulate certain world-types ("ideal types" in a quasi-Weberian sense), which may not, will almost surely not, coincide with the totality of any real person's world; and (c) The articulation involves an intellectualization; one has to get at the connections in lived experience through ideas, and very often ideas which are not consciously available to the people concerned, unless they are forced to articulate them by themselves through challenge and argument.

Nevertheless, this effort, I believe, is very worth while, because it enables us to see the way in which we can be held within certain world structures without being aware that there are alternatives. A "picture" can "hold us captive," as Wittgenstein put it. And by the same token, we can gain insight into the way two people or groups can be arguing past each other, because their experience and thought are structured by two different pictures.

What I want to try to lay out is world structures which are closed to transcendence. All of these arise during the slow development in Latin Christendom and its sucessor civilization of a clear distinction between what came to be called the "natural" and the "supernatural," as two separate levels of reality. This kind of clear demarcation was foreign to any other civilization in history. There have always been distinctions between, for instance, the sacred and the profane, higher beings and worldly beings, and so forth, but in the "enchanted" worlds that humans inhabited in earlier times, these two kinds of reality were inextricably interwoven. The sacred was concentrated in certain times, places, acts, or persons. The natural/supernatural distinction implies a great sorting out, in which the "natural" becomes a level which can be described and understood on its own. This is the precondition for going the further step and declaring this the *only* reality. The "supernatural" can be denied only from a firm footing in the "natural" as an autonomous order.

So I want to look at some Closed world structures (CWSs), and try to draw from them some of the features of modern experience, or inability to experience the spiritual, the sacred, the transcendent. Of course, this term "transcendent" makes sense most clearly within a world in which natural and supernatural are distinguished; it is what "goes beyond" the natural. It would have been hard to explain this concept to a medieval peasant, or it would have slid quickly into other concepts (e.g., the realm of God, as against that of the saints). But we have to use some terms to discuss these issues, and they are bound to make sense in some epochs and not others. So I use one that does make sense to us.

Our time is full of struggle and cross-purposes on this issue of the transcendent. We are opposed, sometimes bitterly and strongly; but we are also often speaking past each other. I'm hoping that a study of some key CWSs will cast some light on the differences, and also the cross-purposes. I want to look ultimately at four, but with very unequal treatment. I shall give most of my attention to the third in the series (in the order of their introduction, not the order of their arising). That's because I think that it is in an important sense the most significant, and also the least explored or understood.

Here I want to introduce the structure of modern epistemology, which I am taking as more than a set of theories which have been widespread, but also at the level of a structure in my sense – that is, an underlying picture which is only partly consciously entertained, but which controls the way people think, argue, infer, and make sense of things.

At its most blatant, this structure operates with a picture of knowing agents as individuals, who build up their understanding of the world through combining and relating, in more and more comprehensive theories, the information which they take in, and which is couched in inner representations, be these conceived as mental pictures (in the earlier variants), or as something like sentences held true in the more contemporary versions.

Characteristic of this picture is a series of priority relations. Knowledge of the self and its states comes before knowledge of external reality and of others. The knowledge of reality as neutral fact comes before our attributing to it various "values" and relevances. And, of course, knowledge of the things of "this world," of the natural order, precedes any theoretical invocation of forces and realities transcendent to it.

The epistemological picture, combining as it does very often with some understanding of modern science, operates frequently as a CWS. The priority relations tell us not only what is learned before what, but also what can be inferred on the basis of what. There are foundational relations. I know the world through my representations. I must grasp the world as fact before I can posit values. I must accede to the transcendent, if at all, by inference from the natural. This can operate as a CWS, because it is obvious that the inference to the transcendent is at the extreme and most fragile end of a series of inferences; it is the most epistemically questionable. And indeed, granted the lack of consensus surrounding this move, as against earlier steps (e.g., to "other minds"), it is obviously highly problematic.

Now I introduce the epistemological picture in order to bring out some features of the way CWSs operate in our time, the way they are on the one hand contested, and on the other maintain themselves.

We are all aware of the contestation, because most of the authors in this volume have taken part in contesting epistemology. But referring to Heidegger and Merleau-Ponty as paradigm cases of the refutation of epistemology, we can see that this view has been comprehensibly turned on its head: (1) Our grasp of the world does not consist simply of our holding inner representations of outer reality. We do hold such representations, which are perhaps best understood in contemporary terms as sentences held true, but these only make the sense that they do for us because they are thrown up in the course of an ongoing activity of coping with the world by bodily, social, and cultural beings. This coping can never be accounted for in terms of representations, but provides the background against which our representations have the sense that they do; (2) As just implied, this coping activity, and the understanding which inhabits it, is not primarily that of each of us as individuals; rather, we are each inducted into the practices of coping as social "games" or activities; some of which do indeed, in the later stages of development, call upon us to assume a stance as individuals. But primordially, we are part of social action; (3) In this coping, the things which we deal with are not first and foremost objects, but what Heidegger calls "pragmata," things which are the focal points of our dealings, which therefore have relevance, meaning, significance for us, not as an add-on but from their first appearance in our world. Later, we learn to stand back, and consider things objectively, outside of the relevances of coping; and (4) In the later Heidegger, these significances include some which have a higher status, structuring our whole way of life, the ensemble of our significances. In the formulation of "das Geviert," there are four axes of our world in this more general sense: world and earth; human and divine.

Although all those who follow something like this deconstruction of epistemology do not go along with this fourth stage, it is clear that the general thrust of these arguments is to overturn utterly the priority relations of epistemology. Things which are considered as late inferences or additions are seen to be part of our primordial predicament. There is no getting behind them, and it makes no sense to place them in context. The "scandal of philosophy" is not the inability to attain to certainty of the external world, but rather that this should be considered a problem, says Heidegger in *Sein und Zeit*. We only have knowledge as agents coping with a world, which it makes no sense to doubt, since we are dealing with it. There is no priority of the neutral grasp of things over their value. There is no priority of the individual's sense of self over the society; our most primordial identity is as a new player being inducted into an old game. Even if we don't add the fourth stage, and consider something like the divine as part of the inescapable context of human action, the whole sense that it comes as a remote and most fragile inference or addition in a long chain is totally undercut by this overturning of epistemology. The new outlook can be built into a new CWS, but it doesn't offer itself as a CWS in the same direct and obvious way as the epistemological picture did.

We can learn something general about the way CWSs operate, suffer attack, and defend themselves, from this example. From within itself, the epistemological picture seems unproblematic. It comes across as an obvious discovery we make when we reflect on our perception and acquisition of knowledge. All the great foundational figures (Descartes, Locke, Hume) claimed to be just saying what was obvious once one examined experience itself reflectively.

Seen from the deconstruction, this is a most massive self-blindness. Rather what happened is that experience was carved into shape by a powerful theory which posited the primacy of the individual, the neutral, the intramental as the locus of certainty. What was driving this theory? Certain "values," virtues, excellences: those of the independent, disengaged subject, reflexively controlling his own thought processes, "self-responsibly," in Husserl's famous phrase. There is an ethic here, of independence, self-control, self-responsibility, of a disengagement which brings control; a stance which requires courage, the refusal of the easy comforts of conformity to authority, of the consolations of an enchanted world, of the surrender to the promptings of the senses. The entire picture, shot through with "values," which is meant to emerge out of the careful, objective, pre-suppositionless scrutiny, is now presented as having been there from the beginning, driving the whole process of "discovery."

Once you shift to the deconstructing point of view, the CWS can no longer operate as such. It seemed to offer a neutral point of view from which we could problematize certain values – e.g., "transcendent" ones – more than others. But now it appears that it is itself driven by its own set of values. Its "neutrality" appears bogus.

To put this another way, the CWS in a sense "naturalizes" a certain view on things. This is just the way things are, and once you look at experience, without preconceptions, this is what appears. "Natural" is opposed here to something like "socially constructed"; and from the deconstructing point of view, you have to tell a quite different story of the rise of this outlook. It isn't just that one day people looked without blinkers and discovered epistemology; rather this is the way things could be made to look from within a new historical formation of human identity, that of the disengaged, objectifying subject. The process involves a reinvention, a re-creation, of human identity, along with great changes in society and social practices. There is no simple stepping out of an earlier such identity into the pure light of bare nature.

It is a feature of our contemporary CWSs that they are understood by those who inhabit them in this naturalizing way. It also follows from this that those who inhabit them see no alternative, except the return to earlier myth or illusion. That's what gives them their strength. People within the redoubt fight as it were to the last, and feeblest, argument, because they cannot envisage surrender except as regression. The naturalizing emerges in a kind of narration they proffer of their genesis, which I want to call a "subtraction story."

But to develop this idea I should move to another, richer CWS, or constellation of CWSs. It is what people often gesture at with an expression like "the death of God." Of course, this expression is used in an uncountable range of ways; I can't be faithful to all of them, nor even will I be simply following the originator of the phrase (though I think that my version is not too far from his),[1] if I say that one essential idea which this phrase captures is that conditions have arisen in the modern world in which it is no longer possible, honestly, rationally, without confusions, fudging, or mental reservation, to believe in God. These conditions leave us nothing we can believe in beyond the human – human happiness, potentialities, or heroism.

What conditions? Essentially, they are of two orders: first, and most important, the deliverances of science; and then secondarily also, the shape of contemporary moral experience.

To take up the first, perhaps the most powerful CWS operating today, the central idea seems to be that the whole thrust of modern science has been to establish materialism. For people who cling to this idea, the second order of conditions, the contemporary moral predicament, is unnecessary or merely secondary. Science alone can explain why belief is no longer possible in the above sense. This is a view held by people on all levels; from the most sophisticated: "We exist as material beings in a material world, all of whose phenomena are the consequences of physical relations among material entities";[2] to the most direct and simple: Madonna's "material girl, living in a material world."

Religion or spirituality involves substituting wrong and mythical explanations, explaining by "demons."[3] At bottom it's just a matter of facing the obvious truth.

This doesn't mean that moral issues don't come into it. But they enter as accounts of why people run away from reality, why they want to go on believing illusion. They do so because it's comforting. The real world is utterly indifferent to us, and even to a certain degree dangerous, threatening. As children, we have to see ourselves as surrounded by love and concern, or we shrivel up. But in growing up, we have to learn to face the fact that this environment of concern can't extend beyond the human sphere, and mostly doesn't extend very far within it. But this transition is hard. So we project a world which is providential, created by a benign God. Or at least, we see the world as meaningful in terms of the ultimate human good. Not only is the providential world soothing, but it also takes the burden of evaluating things off our shoulders. The meanings of things are already given. So religion emanates from a childish lack of courage. We need to stand up like men, and face reality.

Now the traditional unbelieving attack on religion since the Enlightenment contains this accusation of childish pusillanimity, but also an attack on religion as calling for terrible self-mutilation, actuated by pride. Human desire has to be checked, mortified. And then this mortification is often imposed on others, so that religion is the source of a terrible infliction of suffering, and the visiting of severe punishment, on heretics and outsiders. This shows that the unbelieving critique of religion is more complex and many-tracked than I'm dealing with here; but on one very widespread version of this critique, the basic reason for resisting the truth is pusillanimity.

Unbelief has the opposite features. The unbeliever has the courage to take up an adult stance, and face reality. He knows that human beings are on their own. But this doesn't cause him just to cave in. On the contrary, he determines to affirm human worth, and the human good, and to work for it, without false illusion or consolation. So he is counter-mortification. Moreover, he has no reason to exclude anyone as a heretic; so his philanthropy is universal. Unbelief goes together with modern (exclusive) humanism.

So goes one story. The crucial idea is that the scientific-epistemic part of it is completely self-supporting. That's something the rational mind will believe independently of any moral convictions. The moral attributions to one side or the other come when you are trying to explain why some people accept and others resist these truths. The connection between materialist science and humanist affirmation comes because you have to be a mature, courageous being to face these facts. As to why mature courage embraces benevolence, which figures here in the portrait of this humanism, the answer can simply be that left to ourselves we do want to benefit our fellow humans; or that we have developed this way culturally, and we value it, and we can keep this going if we set ourselves to it.

From the believer's perspective, all this falls out rather differently. We start with an epistemic response: the argument from modern science to all-around materialism seems quite unconvincing. Whenever this is worked out in something closer to detail, it seems full of holes. The best example today might be evolution, socio-biology, and the like – Dawkins, Dennett, etc.

So the believer returns the compliment. He casts about for an explanation of why the materialist is so eager to believe very inconclusive arguments. Here the moral outlook just mentioned comes back in, but in a different role. Not that failure to rise to this outlook makes you unable to face the facts of materialism; but rather that its moral attraction and seeming plausibility given the facts of the human moral condition draw you to it, so that you readily grant the materialist argument from science its various leaps of faith. The whole package seems plausible, so we don't pick too closely at the details.

But how can this be? Surely, the whole package is meant to be plausible precisely because science has shown... etc. That's certainly the way the package of epistemic and moral views presents itself officially; that's the official story, as it were. But the supposition here is that the official story isn't the real one; that the real power that the package has to attract and convince lies in it as a definition of our moral predicament.

This means that this ideal of the courageous acknowledger of unpalatable truths, ready to eschew all easy comfort and consolation, and who by the same token becomes capable of grasping and controlling the world, sits well with us, draws us, that we feel tempted to make it our own. And/or it means that the counter-ideals of belief, devotion, piety can all too easily seem actuated by a still immature desire for consolation, meaning, and extra-human sustenance.

What seems to accredit the view of the package as epistemically driven is all the famous conversion stories, starting with post-Darwinian Victorians but continuing to our day, where people who had a strong faith early in life found that they had reluctantly, even with anguish of soul, to relinquish it, because "Darwin has refuted the Bible." Surely, we want to say, these people in a sense preferred the Christian outlook morally, but had to bow, with whatever degree of inner pain, to the facts.

But that's exactly what I'm resisting saying. What happened here was not that a moral outlook bowed to brute facts. Rather it gave way to another moral outlook; another model of what was higher triumphed. And much was going for this model: images of power, of untrammeled agency, of spiritual self-possession (the "buffered self"). On the other side, one's childhood faith had perhaps in many respects remained childish; it was all too easy to come to see it as essentially and constitutionally so.

Of course, the change was painful, because one could be deeply attached to this childhood faith, not just as part of one's past, but also to what it promised. But even this pain could work for the conversion. It has been noted how many of the crop of great Victorian agnostics came from Evangelical families. They transposed the model of the strenuous, manly, philanthropic concern into the new secular key. But the very core of that model, manly self-conquest, rising above the pain of loss, now told in favor of the apostasy.

So I am less than fully convinced by the major thrust of the "death of God" account of the rise of secularity; its account, in other words, of the modern conditions of belief. What makes belief problematical, often difficult and full of doubts, is not simply "science."

This is not to deny that science (and even more "science") has had an important place in the story; and that in a number of ways. For one thing, the universe which this science reveals is very different from the centered hierarchic cosmos which our civilization grew up within; it hardly suggests to us that humans have any kind of special place in its story; its temporal and spatial dimensions are mind-numbing. This, and the conception of natural law by which we understand it, makes it refractory to the interventions of Providence as these were envisaged in the framework of the earlier cosmos, and the connected understanding of the biblical story. Seen in this light, "Darwin" has indeed "refuted the Bible."

For another thing, the development of modern science has gone hand in hand with the rise of the ethic of austere, disengaged reason I invoked above. But all this still doesn't amount to an endorsement of the official story, that the present climate of unbelief in many milieux in contemporary society is a response to the strong case for materialism which science has drawn up during the last three centuries.

Of course, a good reason for my lack of conviction here is that I don't see the case for materialism as all that strong. To state just why would take me much too far afield, and lead me away from the inquiry I want to pursue. But I acknowledge that this is a loose end in my argument which I won't be able to tie up. I hope, however, that this untidiness in my case can be partly compensated for by the plausibility of the explanation I offer in place of the official account, and which sees the attraction of materialism arising not so much from the conclusions of science as from the ethic which is associated with it.

But, one might object, why shouldn't bad arguments have an important effect in history, as much as if not more than good arguments? In a sense, this objection is well taken; and in a sense, therefore, the official story is also true. Since lots of people believe that they are atheists and materialists because science has shown atheism and materialism to be irrefutable, there is a perfectly good sense in which we can say that this is their reason.

But an explanation in terms of a bad reason calls for supplementation. We need an account of why the bad reason nevertheless works. This is not necessarily so, of course, in individual cases. Individuals can just take some conclusion on authority from their milieu. Just as we laypeople take the latest report about the micro-constitution of the atom from the Sunday paper, so we may take it on authority from a Sagan or a Dawkins that Science has refuted God. But this leaves still unexplained how an authority of this kind gets constituted. What makes it the case that we laypeople, as also the scientific luminaries, get so easily sucked into invalid arguments? Why do we and they not more readily see the alternatives? My proffered account in terms of the attraction of an ethic vision is meant to answer this deeper question.

I am not arguing that an account of someone's action in terms of erroneous belief always needs supplementation. I may leave the house without an umbrella because I believe the radio forecast to be reliable, and it predicted fair weather. But the difference between this kind of case and the issue we're dealing with here is first, that the weather, beyond the inconvenience of getting wet today, doesn't matter to me in anything like the same way; and second, that I have no alternative access to this afternoon's weather than the forecast.

The latter is not simply true in the question of belief in God. Of course, as a layperson, I have to take on authority the findings of paleontology.

But I am not similarly without resources on the issue whether what science has shown about the material world denies the existence of God. This is because I can also have a religious life, a sense of God and how he impinges on my existence, against which I can check the supposed claims to refutation.

I want to draw the Desdemona analogy. What makes *Othello* a tragedy, and not just a tale of misfortune, is that we hold its protagonist culpable in his too-ready belief in the evidence fabricated by Iago. He had an alternative mode of access to her innocence in Desdemona herself, if he could only have opened his heart/mind to her love and devotion. The fatal flaw in the tragic hero Othello is his inability to do this, partly induced by his outsider's status and sudden promotion.

The reason why I can't accept the arguments that "science has refuted God," without any supplement, as an explanation of the rise of unbelief is that we are on this issue like Othello, rather than a person listening to the forecast as he hesitates before the umbrella stand. We can't just explain what we do on the basis of the information we received from external sources, without seeing what we made of the internal ones.

All this doesn't mean that a perfectly valid description of an individual's experience might not be that he felt forced to give up a faith he cherished, because the brute facts of the universe contradicted it. Once you go this way, once you accept unbelief, then you will probably also accept the ideology which accords primacy to the external sources, which depreciates the internal ones as incompetent here, indeed, as likely sources of childish illusion. That's how it now looks ex post facto – and how it looked to Othello. But we who have seen this happen need a further account of why Desdemona's testimony wasn't heard.

Thus, once one has taken the step into unbelief, there are overwhelming reasons why one will be induced to buy into the official, science-driven story. And because we very often make these choices under the influence of others, on whose authority we buy the official story, it is not surprising that lots of people have thought of their conversion as science-driven, even perhaps in the most dramatic form. Science seemed to show that we are nothing but a fleeting life form on a dying star; or that the universe is nothing but decaying matter, under ever-increasing entropy, that there is thus no place for spirit or God, miracles or salvation. Something like the vision which Dostoyevsky had, before a picture of the crucified Christ, of the absolute finality of death, which convinced him that there must be something more, might easily have the opposite effect, of dragging you down and forcing an abandonment of your faith.

But the question remains: If the arguments in fact aren't conclusive, why do they seem so convincing, where at other times and places God's existence just seems obvious? This is the question I'm trying to answer, and the "death of God" doesn't help me here; rather it blocks the way with a pseudo-solution.

So my contention is that the power of materialism today does not come from the scientific "facts," but has rather to be explained in terms of the power of a certain package uniting materialism with a moral outlook, the package we could call "atheist humanism," or exclusive humanism. But this doesn't bring me to the end of my search; rather, the further question arises: how in turn to explain something like the power of this package?

Here's where we might invoke the second level of the "death of God" account, the one which starts from our contemporary moral predicament. The conclusion here is the same as with the argument from science, that we can no longer rationally believe in God; but the starting point is now the ethical outlook of the modern age.

Now, it is true that a great deal of our political and moral life is focused on human ends: human welfare, human rights, human flourishing, equality between human beings. Indeed, our public life, in societies which are secular in a familiar modern sense, is exclusively concerned with human goods. And our age is certainly unique in human history in this respect. Some people see no place in this kind of world for belief in God. A faith of this kind would have to make one an outsider, an enemy of this world, in unrelenting combat with it. Thus one is either thoroughly in this world, living by its premises, and then one cannot really believe in God; or one believes, and is in some sense living like a resident alien in modernity. Since we find ourselves more and more inducted into it, belief becomes harder and harder; the horizon of faith steadily recedes.[4]

This adversarial picture of the relation of faith to modernity is not an invention of unbelievers. It is matched and encouraged by a strand of Christian hostility to the humanist world. We have only to think of Pius IX, fulminating in his Syllabus of 1864 against all the errors of the modern world, including human rights, democracy, equality, and just about everything our contemporary liberal state embodies. And there are other, more recent, examples, among Christians as well as believers in other religions.

But this convergence between fundamentalists and hard-line atheists doesn't make their common interpretation of the relation of faith to modernity the only possible one. And it is clear that there are many people of faith who have helped to build and are now sustaining this modern humanist world, and are strongly committed to the modes of human well-being and flourishing that it has made central. Once again, the "death of God" account leaps to a conclusion which is far from being warranted. It is possible to see modern humanism as the enemy of religion, just as it is possible to take science as having proved atheism. But since the conclusion is in neither case warranted, the question arises why so many people come to it. And that brings me back to the central issue I've been raising.

This moral version of the "death of God" account seems plausible to many people, because they make an assumption about the rise of modernity which helps to screen from them how complex and difficult this quest is. The assumption is what I have called "the view from Dover Beach": The transition to modernity comes about through the loss of traditional beliefs and allegiances. This may be seen as resulting from institutional changes: E.g., mobility and urbanization erode the beliefs and reference points of static rural society. Or the loss may be supposed to arise from the increasing operation of modern scientific reason. The change may be positively valued – or it may be judged a disaster by those for whom the traditional reference points were valuable, and scientific reason too narrow. But all these theories concur in describing the process: old views and loyalties are eroded. Old horizons are washed away, in Nietzsche's image. The sea of faith recedes, to follow Arnold. This stanza from his 'Dover Beach' captures this perspective:

> The Sea of Faith
> Was once, too, at the full, and round earth's shore
> Lay like the folds of a bright girdle furled.
> But now I only hear
> Its melancholy, long, withdrawing roar,
> Retreating, to the breath
> Of the night-wind, down the vast edges drear
> And naked shingles of the world.[5]

The tone here is one of regret and nostalgia. But the underlying image of eroded faith could serve just as well for an upbeat story of the progress of triumphant scientific reason. From one point of view, humanity has shed a lot of false and harmful myths. From another, it has lost touch with crucial spiritual realities. But in either case, the change is seen as a loss of belief.

What emerges comes about through this loss. The upbeat story cherishes the dominance of an empirical-scientific approach to knowledge claims, of individualism, negative freedom, instrumental rationality. But these come to the fore because they are what we humans "normally" value, once we are no longer impeded or blinded by false or superstitious beliefs and the stultifying modes of life which accompany them. Once myth and error are dissipated, these are the only games in town. The empirical approach is the only valid way of acquiring knowledge, and this becomes evident as soon as we free ourselves from the thraldom of a false metaphysics. Increasing recourse to instrumental rationality allows us to get more and more of what we want, and we were only ever deterred from this by unfounded injunctions to limit ourselves. Individualism is the normal fruit of human self-regard absent the illusory claims of God, the Chain of Being, or the sacred order of society.

In other words, we moderns behave as we do because we have "come to see" that certain claims were false – or on the negative reading, because we have lost from view certain perennial truths. What this view reads out of the picture is the possibility that Western modernity might be powered by its own positive visions of the good, that is, by one constellation of such visions among available others, rather than by the only viable set left after the old myths and legends have been exploded. It screens out whatever there might be of a specific moral direction to Western modernity, beyond what is dictated by the general form of human life itself, once old error is shown up (or old truth forgotten) – e.g., people behave as individuals, because that's what they "naturally" do when no longer held in by the old religions, metaphysics, and customs, though this may be seen as a glorious liberation, or a purblind enmiring in egoism, depending on our perspective. What it cannot be seen as is a novel form of moral self-understanding, not definable simply by the negation of what preceded it.

In terms of my discussion a few pages ago, all these accounts "naturalize" the features of the modern, liberal identity. They cannot see it as one, historically constructed understanding of human agency among others.

On this "subtraction" view of modernity, as what arises from the washing away of old horizons, modern humanism can only have arisen through the fading of earlier forms. It can only be conceived as coming to be through a "death of God." It just follows that you can't be fully into contemporary humanist concerns if you haven't sloughed off the old beliefs. You can't be fully with the modern age and still believe in God. Or alternatively, if you still believe, then you have reservations, you are at least partly, and perhaps covertly, some kind of adversary.

But of course, as I have argued at length elsewhere,[6] this is a quite inadequate account of modernity. What has got screened out is the possibility that Western modernity might be sustained by its own original spiritual vision, that is, not one generated simply and inescapably out of the transition. But this possibility is in fact the reality.

The logic of the subtraction story is something like this: Once we slough off our concern with serving God, or attending to any other transcendent reality, what we're left with is human good, and that is what modern societies are concerned with. But this radically under-describes what I'm calling modern humanism. That I am left with only human concerns doesn't tell me to take universal human welfare as my goal; nor does it tell me that freedom is important, or fulfillment, or equality. Just being confined to human goods could just as well find expression in my concerning myself exclusively with my own material welfare, or that of my family or immediate milieu. The, in fact, very exigent demands of universal justice and benevolence which characterize modern humanism can't be explained just by the subtraction of earlier goals and allegiances.

The subtraction story, inadequate though it is, is deeply embedded in modern humanist consciousness. It is by no means propounded only by the more simplistic theorists. Even such a penetrating and sophisticated thinker as Paul Bénichou subscribed to a version of it in his *Morales du grand siècle*: "L'humanité s'estime dès qu'elle se voit capable de faire reculer sa misère; elle tend à oublier, en même temps que sa détresse, l'humiliante morale par laquelle, faisant de nécessité vertu, elle condamnait la vie."[7] Modern humanism arises, in other words, because humans become capable of sloughing off the older, other-worldly ethics of asceticism.

Moreover, this story is grounded in a certain view of human motivation in general, and of the wellsprings of religious belief in particular. The latter is seen as the fruit of misery, and the accompanying self-renunciation is "making a virtue of necessity." Belief is a product of deprivation, humiliation, and a lack of hope. It is the obverse of the human desire for flourishing; where we are driven by our despair at the frustration of this desire.

Thus human flourishing is taken as our perennial goal, even though it is in eclipse in periods of misery and humiliation, and its content is taken as fairly unproblematic, once one begins to affirm it.

We see here the outlines of one version of an account of modern secularity, which in its general form is widely and deeply implanted in modern humanist culture. It tends to have four connected facets, of which the first three are (a) the "death of God" thesis that one can no longer honestly, lucidly, sincerely believe in God; (b) some "subtraction" story of the rise of modern humanism; and (c) a view on the original reasons for religious belief, and on their place in perennial human motivations, which grounds the subtraction story. These views vary all the way from nineteenth-century theories about primitives' fears of the unknown, or desire to control the elements, to speculations like Freud's, linking religion to neurosis. On many of these accounts, religion simply becomes unnecessary when technology gets to a certain level: we don't need God any more, because we know how to get it ourselves.[8] These theories are generally wildly and implausibly reductive.

These three facets issue in (d) a take on modern secularization as mainly a recession of religion in the face of science, technology, and rationality. As against the nineteenth century, when thinkers like Comte confidently predicted the supersession of religion by science, as did Renan: "il viendra un jour où l'humanité ne croira plus, mais où elle saura; un jour où elle saura le monde métaphysique et moral, comme elle sait déjà le monde physique,"[9] today everybody thinks that the illusion has some future; but on the vision I'm describing here it is in for some more shrinkage.

These four facets together give an idea of what modern secularization often looks like from within the humanist camp. Against this, I want to offer a rather different picture.

(If I can manage to tell this story properly, then we will see that there is some, phenomenal, truth to the "death of God" account. A humanism has come about which can be seen, and hence lived, as exclusive. And from within this, it can indeed seem plausible that science points us toward a materialist account of spirit. The "death of God" is not just an erroneous account of secularity on a theoretical level; it is also a way we may be tempted to interpret, and hence experience, the modern condition. It is not the explanans I am looking for, but it is a crucial part of the explanandum. In this role, I am very far from wanting to deny it.)

In order to develop this alternative picture, I want to explore another domain of CWSs, which I think is more fundamental. This is the domain in which the moral self-understanding of moderns has been forged. I would want to tell a longish story here. But in its main lines, my account centers on the development of an ascending series of attempts to establish a Christian order, of which the Reformation is a key phase. These attempts show a progressive impatience with older modes of post-Axial religion in which certain collective, ritualistic forms of earlier religions coexisted uneasily with the demands of individual devotion and ethical reform which came from the "higher" revelations. In Latin Christendom, the attempt was to recover and impose on everyone a more individually committed and Christocentric religion of devotion and action, and to repress or even abolish older, supposedly "magical," or "superstitious" forms of collective ritual practice.

Allied with a neo-Stoic outlook, this became the charter for a series of attempts to establish new forms of social order, drawing on new disciplines (Foucault enters the story here) which helped to reduce violence and disorder, and create populations of relatively pacific and productive artisans and peasants, who were more and more induced/forced into the new forms of devotional practice and moral behaviour, be this in Protestant England, Holland, or later the American colonies, counter-Reformation France, or the Germany of the "Polizeistaat."

My hypothesis is that this new creation of a civilized, "polite" order succeeded beyond what its first originators could have hoped for, and that this in turn led to a new reading of what a Christian order might be, one which was seen more and more in "immanent" terms (the polite, civilized order is the Christian order). This version of Christianity was shorn of much of its "transcendent" content, and was thus open to a new departure, in which the understanding of good order (what I call the "modern moral order") could be embraced outside of the original theological, providential framework, and in certain cases even against it (as with Voltaire, Gibbon, and in another way Hume).

Disbelief in God arises in close symbiosis with this belief in a moral order of rights-bearing individuals, who are destined (by God or Nature) to act for mutual benefit; an order which thus rejects the earlier honor ethic which exalted the warrior, as it also tends to occlude any transcendent horizon. We see one good formulation of this notion of order in Locke's *Second Treatise*.[10]

This ideal order was not thought to be a mere human invention. Rather it was designed by God, an order in which everything coheres according to God's purposes. Later in the eighteenth century, the same model is projected onto the cosmos, in a vision of the universe as a set of perfectly interlocking parts, in which the purposes of each kind of creature mesh with those of all the others.

This order sets the goal for our constructive activity, insofar as it lies within our power to upset it, or realize it. Of course, when we look at the whole, we see how much the order is already realized; but when we cast our eye on human affairs, we see how much we have deviated from it and upset it; it becomes the norm to which we should strive to return.

This order was thought to be evident in the nature of things. Of course, if we consult Revelation, we shall also find the demand formulated there that we abide by it. But reason alone can tell us God's purposes. Living things, including ourselves, strive to preserve themselves. This is God's doing.

God having made Man, and planted in him, as in all other Animals, a strong desire of Self-preservation, and furnished the World with things fit for Food and Rayment and other Necessaries of Life, Subservient to his design, that Man should live and abide for some time upon the Face of the Earth, and not that so curious and wonderful a piece of Workmanship by its own Negligence, or want of Necessaries, should perish again... God... spoke to him, [that is] directed him by his Senses and Reason... to the use of those things, which were serviceable for his Subsistence, and given him as the means of his Preservation... For the desire, strong desire, of Preserving his Life and Being having been Planted in him, as a Principle of Action by God himself, Reason, which was the voice of God in him, could not but teach him and assure him, that pursuing that natural Inclination he had to preserve his Being, he followed the Will of his Maker.[11]

Being endowed with reason, we see that not only our lives but those of all humans are to be preserved. And in addition, God made us sociable beings. So that "every one as he is bound to preserve himself, and not to quit his Station wilfully, so by the like reason when his own Preservation comes not in competition, ought he as much as he can to preserve the rest of Mankind."[12]

Similarly, Locke reasons that God gave us our powers of reason and discipline so that we could most effectively go about the business of preserving ourselves. It follows that we ought to be "Industrious and Rational."[13] The ethic of discipline and improvement is itself a requirement of the natural order that God has designed. The imposition of order by human will is itself called for by his scheme.

We can see in Locke's formulation how much he sees mutual service in terms of profitable exchange. "Economic" (that is, ordered, peaceful, productive) activity has become the model for human behavior, and the key for harmonious coexistence. In contrast to the theories of hierarchical complementarity, we meet in a zone of concord and mutual service, not to the extent that we transcend our ordinary goals and purposes, but on the contrary, in the process of carrying them out according to God's design.

This understanding of order has profoundly shaped the forms of social imagery which dominate in the modern West: the market economy, the public sphere, the sovereign "people."

This is the key entry point to modern secularity. Within this somewhat stripped-down notion of Providence and divinely sanctioned order, one which made ordinary human flourishing so central, it became more and more conceivable to slide toward forms of deism, and ultimately even atheistic humanism. Indeed, religion could be portrayed as a threat to this order. We see this in the critique offered by Gibbon and Hume, for instance. Key terms of opprobrium were: "superstition," by which was meant continuing belief in an enchanted world, the kind of thing which modern Reform Christianity had left behind it; "fanaticism," by which was meant the invocation of religion to justify violations of the modern moral order, be they persecutions or any other type of irrational, counterproductive behavior;

"enthusiasm," by which was meant the claim to some kind of special revelation, whereby one could once more challenge the norms of the modern
order. One might say that "superstition" was the speciality of Catholics,
and "enthusiasm" of extreme Protestant sects; but "fanaticism" was a sin of
which both were capable.

The rooting of the Enlightened critique in this modern idea of moral
order can be seen again if one looks at the two lists of virtues which Hume
lists in the *Enquiries*, those he considers properly virtues, and the "monkish"
ones for which he has no use.[14]

Here we have one of the most powerful CWSs in modern history. Religion was to be severely limited, even in some versions banned, because it
ran against the natural order itself. From within the acceptance of this order
as the end of history, nothing could seem more obvious and secure, even
if this could also accommodate milder positions which espoused deism, or
some carefully controlled and parsimoniously dosed religion.

But this was also the structure which inspired the most bitter contro-
versies, because this understanding of order was and is hotly contested;
and that from a host of directions. Some saw it as insufficiently inspiring
and uplifting; others as poisoned by forms of discipline which repress and
crush the spontaneous or the emotional in us; others as rejecting true human sympathy and generosity in condemning "enthusiasm." But others
again rejected it because it turned its back on violence, and hence heroism,
and hence greatness; because it leveled us all in a demeaning equality. We
find some of the latter kind of reaction in Tocqueville, for instance; but
most famously in Nietzsche.

As the second name reminds us, the remarkable thing about this wave
of protests, which begins in the latter half of the eighteenth century, is that
each can be taken in more than one direction. The sense of the moral order
as unliveable and reductive could either lead back to a more full-hearted
religion (e.g., Wesley, the Pietists) or lead beyond to modes of unbelieving romanticism. Similarly, the "tragic" dimension could be invoked for
a return to a real sense of human sin; or it could justify a rejection of
Christianity as the original historical source of modern morality, the trail
blazed by Nietzsche. Again, dissatisfactions with existing forms could lead
to more radical and utopian versions of order, as we see with Jacobinism,
later communism and Marx; or it could justify abandoning it, as with
the Catholic Reaction after 1815; or again, in a quite different way, with
Nietzsche.

So while the modern ideal of moral order can be the center of one of
the most influential CWSs of modern society, the attempts to criticize

it, to denounce its "self-naturalization," can also be a source of new and more profound CWSs. After all, the source whence the expression "death of God" flows into general circulation is *The Gay Science*. Modern culture is characterized by what we could call the "nova effect," the multiplication of more and more spiritual and anti-spiritual positions. This multiplicity further fragilizes any of the positions it contains. There is no longer any clear, unambiguous way of drawing the main issue.

But a crucial reference point in this swirling multiplicity is the modern idea of order, in the sense that our stance to that is an important defining characteristic of our position, as much as our stance, positive or negative, on transcendence. The dimension in which interesting new positions have arisen is that which combines severe criticism of the order with a rejection of the transcendent. This is where we find what we might call the "immanent Counter-Enlightenment," following Nietzsche,[15] as well as new ways of invoking paganism against Christianity. This is as old as the Enlightenment in one sense; Gibbon clearly had some sympathy for what he saw as the skeptical, very unfanatical ruling class of Rome, puzzled by the rush to martyrdom of this obscure sect of Christians; Mill spoke of "pagan self-assertion"; Peter Gay has even described the Enlightenment as a kind of "modern paganism."[16] But we find more recently attempts to rehabilitate precisely what was suppressed by monotheism. There is a discourse of "polytheism" (Calosso, Spinosa), which completely rejects the notion of a single, dominant moral code, an essential feature of the modern moral order. One can even hope to erect a novel CWS on this basis.

Among these new forms, Heidegger deserves a mention. I said above that he is one of those who have contributed to undoing the CWS of epistemology, but also that of scientism, and the belief that "science has shown" that there is no God. He even has a place for "the gods" in some sense in his notion of *das Geviert*. And yet there seems to be a rejection of the Christian God here; or at least some unwillingness to allow that the Christian God can ever escape the dead end of onto-theology: "auch der Gott ist, wenn er ist, ein Seiender."[17]

I have been trying to explore the modern landscape of belief/unbelief, in the main by laying out some of the principal world structures which occult or blank out the transcendent. The main intellectual struggle around belief and unbelief turns on the validity/invalidity of these CWSs. It is clear that modern society generates these, but not in any consistent fashion. Some of them can only define our horizon through our rejecting others. Many of them have already shown that they are grounded on a false and over-hasty naturalization. The crucial question at stake in the debate is, are they all similarly invalid? It may be beyond the reach of any single set of arguments to show this. And even if it were determined, it wouldn't by itself decide the question whether there is a God or not, whether there is transcendence. But it could open this issue for a more active and fruitful search.

NOTES

1. The "death of God" reference is from *The Gay Science*, para. 125. Later on, Nietzsche says: "Man sieht, *was* eigentlich über den christlichen Gott gesiegt hat: die christliche Moralität selbst, der immer strenger genommene Begriff der Wahrhaftigkeit, die Beichtväterfeinheit des christlichen Gewissens, übersetzt und sublimiert zum wissenschaftlichen Gewissen, zur intellektuellen Sauberkeit um jeden Preis. Die Natur ansehn, als ob sie ein Beweis für die Güte und Obhut eines Gottes sei; die Geschichte interpretieren zu Ehren einer göttlichen Vernunft, als beständiges Zeugnis einer sittlichen Weltordnung und sittlicher Schlussabsichten; die eignen Erlebnisse auslegen, wie sie fromme Menschen lange genug ausgelegt haben, wie als ob alles Fügung, alles Wink, alles dem Heil der Seele zuliebe ausgedacht und geschickt sei: Das ist numehr *vorbei*, das hat das Gewissen *gegen* sich, das gilt allen feineren Gewissen als unanständig, unehrlich, als Lügnerei, Feminismus, Schwachheit, Feigheit" – "One can see *what* it was that actually triumphed over the Christian god: Christian morality itself, the concept of truthfulness that was taken ever more rigorously; the father confessor's refinement of the Christian conscience, translated and sublimated into a scientific conscience, into intellectual cleanliness at any price. Looking at nature as if it were proof of the goodness and care of a god; interpreting history in honour of some divine reason, as a continual testimony of a moral world order and ultimate moral purposes; interpreting one's own experiences as pious people have long interpreted theirs, as if everything were providential, a hint, designed and ordained for the sake of salvation of the soul – that is *over* now; that has conscience *against* it; every refined conscience considers it to be indecent, dishonest, a form of mendacity, effeminacy, weakness, cowardice." *The Gay Science*, trans. Josefine Nauckhoff (Cambridge University Press, 2001), section 357. It will be clear later on where my interpretation agrees with Nietzsche's.
2. Richard C. Lewontin, "Billions and Billions of Demons," *New York Review*, January 9, 1997, p. 28.
3. *Ibid.*, quoting Carl Sagan.
4. Nietzsche, *The Gay Science*, para. 125, the famous passage about the madman who announces the death of God, also makes use of this horizon image.
5. Matthew Arnold, "Dover Beach," in *The Poems of Matthew Arnold*, ed. Kenneth Allott, 2nd edn, ed. Miriam Allott (New York: Longman, 1979), p. 256, lines 21–8.
6. *Sources of the Self* (Cambridge, Mass.: Harvard University Press, 1989).

7. *Morales du grand siècle* (Paris: Gallimard, 1948), p. 226. Translated as *Man and Ethics*, trans. Elizabeth Hughes (New York: Anchor Books, 1971), p. 251 ("Man appreciates his own worth from the time he sees that he is able to make inroads against poverty. He tends to forget, along with his material distress, the humiliating ethics by which he condemned life, making a virtue of necessity.")
8. There is a more sophisticated version of this in Steve Bruce, *Religion in Modern Britain* (Oxford University Press, 1995), pp. 131–3.
9. Quoted in Sylvette Denèfle, *Sociologie de la sécularisation* (Paris–Montreal: L'Harmattan, 1997), pp. 93–4.
10. See John Locke, *Two Treatises of Government* (London: Black Swan, 1698).
11. *Ibid.*, 1.86.
12. *Ibid.*, II.6; see also II.135; and *Some Thoughts Concerning Education*, ed. John W. and Jean S. Yolton (Oxford: Clarendon Press, 2000), para. 116.
13. *Two Treatises of Government*, II.34.
14. See David Hume, *An Enquiry Concerning the Principles of Morals*, ed. Tom L. Beauchamp (Oxford University Press, 1998).
15. See Charles Taylor, "The Immanent Counter-Enlightenment," in *Canadian Political Philosophy*, ed. Ronald Beiner and Wayne Norman (Oxford University Press, 2001), p. 397.
16. Peter Gay, *The Enlightenment: An Interpretation. Volume I: The Rise of Modern Paganism* (New York: Norton, 1977).
17. ("The god also is, when he is, a being.") Quoted in Jean-Luc Marion, *Dieu sans l'être* (Paris: Presses Universitaires de France, 1991), p. 105. I have found Marion's discussion of this issue extremely enlightening.

CHAPTER 6

Between the earth and the sky: Heidegger on life after the death of God

Mark A. Wrathall

In the last decades of his life, Heidegger was preoccupied with the dangers of technology, and tried to articulate a non-technological form of "poetical dwelling" that could save us from those dangers. On Heidegger's account, dwelling consists in achieving a nearness to the earth, the sky, mortals, and divinities.

Viewed with the kind of historical detachment exemplified in Charles Taylor's chapter in this volume, Heidegger's reaction against technology is just one ripple in the "wave of protests" that formed what Taylor calls the "nova effect" – that is, "the multiplication of more and more spiritual and anti-spiritual positions" (see p. 66 above). Such a multiplication, in turn, "further fragilizes any of the positions it contains" in the sense that it undermines the claim of each position to legitimacy. This is because the disagreements between positions are disagreements at the most fundamental levels. As a consequence, Taylor argues, "there is no longer any clear, unambiguous way of drawing the main issue" – the issue at hand being the nature and place of religion in a post-metaphysical, technological age.

Taylor's observations are valuable as a reminder that Heidegger's diagnosis of our age is itself couched in terms that are not only contestable from a number of sides, but perhaps almost unintelligible to other splinter positions in the overall fragmentation of modern culture. If, then, Heidegger's view of religious life after the death of God is to have an importance to anyone beyond the initiates in Heideggerese, it can only do so by helping to bring this overall pattern of fragmentation into some kind of focus. I would like to try making the case that it does. In particular, as I read the later Heidegger's work on the divinities and the fourfold, Heidegger is offering us a way of pulling into focus a problem that is scarcely articulable from a detached, historiographical perspective – namely, why is it that a *religious* life should remain an appealing possibility, that a *religious* life, in any incarnation – new age or traditional – should seem a plausible way to redress the failings of our technological and secular age?

To answer this question, one has to say something specific about the deficiencies of the technological age. One needs to articulate what crucial element of a worthwhile life is lost with the death of God, and why we should think that a religious life after the death of God can correct that loss. I would like to present Heidegger's reflections on the fourfold as responses to just these questions.

Because Heidegger's account of the technological age grew out of his reading of Nietzsche, the place to start is with Heidegger's interpretation of the "death of God." Although I will refer to a number of passages from Nietzsche, I am not concerned here either to argue that Heidegger interpreted Nietzsche correctly, or that Heidegger's critique of Nietzsche found its mark. Instead, I am interested in what Heidegger thought he learned from Nietzsche; this can stand or fall independently of questions about what Nietzsche really thought.

Heidegger interprets the death of God in ontological terms – that is, according to Heidegger's understanding of ontology, in terms of the "mode" in which "whatever is, as such, comes to appearance."[1] In particular, the death of God is understood as the process by which everything is turned into resource.

Thus, from Heidegger's perspective, it is a terrible misreading of Nietzsche's proclamation of the death of God to take it as a bald atheism, an undisguised declaration of the end of everything that is divine. As Heidegger points out, those who think that the proclamation could mean *this* must themselves be starting with an inadequate conception of God. To think that Nietzsche is a bald atheist, Heidegger claims, they would have to "deal with and treat their God the same way they deal with a pocketknife. If a pocketknife is lost, it is just gone. But to lose God means something other."[2] Heidegger's point is that the loss of a God, properly understood, is an apocalyptic event – one that cannot be treated with the same equanimity that we might treat the loss of some mundane object. To own up to the loss of God requires of us that we reach for a new kind of divinity – a divinity that can withstand the loss of the old God.

Heidegger sees this as apparent already in the very passages in which Nietzsche proclaims the death of God. These explicitly place the focus on discovering a sort of divinity which would render us able to endure a world from which the old God is gone. The madman in *Gay Science* §125, for instance, follows up the proclamation of God's death with a series of questions – questions that culminate in the following:

How shall we comfort ourselves, the murderers of all murderers? What was holiest and mightiest of all that the world has yet owned has bled to death under our knives: who will wipe this blood off us? What water is there for us to clean ourselves? What festivals of atonement, what sacred games shall we have to invent? Is not the greatness of this deed too great for us? Must we ourselves not become gods simply to appear worthy of it?[3]

Heidegger does not pass over such questions lightly. He closes the "Word of Nietzsche" essay with a reflection on the fact that the madman seeks God: "the madman ... is clearly, according to the first, and more clearly still according to the last, sentences of the passage, for him who can hear, the one who seeks God, since he cries out after God. Has a thinking man perhaps here really cried out *de profundis*?" (WN 112).

The proclamation of the death of God, then, means something other than a mere denial of the real existence of the Christian God. It is rather an attempt to really come to grips with the loss we suffer when religious practices become marginalized. The Christian God was important because our practices for devotion to him provided us with a source of meaning and intelligibility. We kill God, Nietzsche's madman declares, when we "drink up the sea," when we "wipe away the entire horizon," when we "unchain this earth from its sun." Heidegger reads the sea as Nietzsche's metaphor for the sensible world – a world in flux, constantly changing, malleable and flexible in the paths it permits us to take. God served as a land and horizon, giving the sensible world a fixed point of reference. The horizon is thus Nietzsche's metaphor for focal practices that gives us a place, determining what is important to us, and what counts as unimportant or trivial. Finally, the sun is the God in whose light everything appears *as* what it is. When we drink up the sea, we become responsible for the way the sensible world shows up – that is, we ourselves, rather than a fixed suprasensible God, encompass the world. When we wipe away the horizon, we destroy any fixed point of reference for valuing the world. When we unchain the earth from the sun, we deprive things of any fixed or stable essence (WN 107).

The history of Western culture prior to the advent of the technological age can be seen in terms of a transition through a long series of Gods, each of which has filled the position of giver of meaning, setter of norms, source of gravity and value. Heidegger, commenting on Nietzsche, observed that since the Reformation, the role of highest value has been played by "the authority of conscience," "the authority of reason," "historical progress," "the earthly happiness of the greatest number," "the creating of a culture or the spreading of civilization," and finally "the business enterprise." However, all these are "variations on the Christian-ecclesiastical and theological interpretation of the world" (WN 64). Thus the Christian God has long since ceased, at least for most in the West, to serve as horizon and sun. What is unique about this moment in history is that there is no candidate to step into the position of shared source of meaning and value. Our form of life has changed in such a way that we are no longer able to submit ourselves to such a God. The sea-drinking, horizon-wiping, earth-unchaining process is a process, not of filling in the position of God with yet another God in the same mold, but of overturning the whole onto-theological interpretation of the world which sets things under some suprasensory value.

This interpretation of the death of God ultimately underwrites Heidegger's reading of Nietzsche as the thinker of the technological epoch. According to Heidegger, every thinker, Nietzsche included, "has at any given time his fundamental philosophical position within metaphysics." But by this he does not refer to the thinker's explicit doctrine on metaphysical issues; rather he means that their work manifests a particular understanding about the nature "of what is as such in its entirety." Heidegger's interest in Nietzsche, then, is driven by a desire to gain insight into the most fundamental way in which our age understands what is: "The thinking through of Nietzsche's metaphysics becomes a reflection on the situation and place of contemporary man, whose destiny is still but little experienced with respect to its truth" (WN 54).

Heidegger's ultimate aim, then, was to use Nietzsche to get clear about the ontological structure of what is becoming the most prominent feature of the place of contemporary man – namely, the technologizing of everyday life. The technological world, Heidegger argues, is grounded in the fact that everything that is shows up as lacking in any inherent significance, use, or purpose. Heidegger's name for the way in which entities appear and are experienced in the technological world is "resource." Such entities are removed from their natural conditions and contexts, and reorganized in such a way as to be completely available, flexible, interchangeable, and ready to be employed in an indefinite variety of manners.[4] In the technological age, even people are reduced from modern subjects with fixed desires and a deep immanent truth to "functionaries of enframing."[5] In such a world, nothing is encountered as really mattering, that is, as having a worth that exceeds its purely instrumental value for satisfying transitory urges.

This is, by the way, the Heideggerian way of cashing out Nietzsche's claim that the death of God results in a lack of gravity. As Heidegger notes,[6] Nietzsche connects the death of the Christian God with the emptiness of a life in which "it will appear for a long time as if all weightiness were gone from things."[7]

By a loss of "weightiness," Nietzsche means that nothing really matters to us any more; that everything is equally value-less. I will refer to weightiness as "mattering" or "importance." With the death of the old God, we lose a sense that *our* understanding of things – including having a shared vision of the good, or a notion of the correct way to live a life, or an idea of justice, etc. – is grounded in something more than our willing it to be so. And without such a grounding, Heidegger worries, it is not just our lives, but also all the things with which we deal that will lose a weightiness or importance. All becomes equally trivial, equally lacking in goodness and rightness and worth. The decisive question for our age, then, is "whether we let every being weightlessly drive into nothingness or whether we want to give a weightiness to things again and especially to ourselves; whether we become master over ourselves, in order to find ourselves in essence, or whether we lose ourselves in and with the existing nothingness."[8]

What the old God gave us, in short, was a way of being attuned to objects as having a transcendental importance or weightiness. Heidegger believes that a living God attunes a whole culture to objects in a particular way, and as having a transcendent meaning. For example, when God was the Judeo-Christian creator God of the theologians, we were attuned to things as instantiations of the ideal forms created by God. We, in turn, were called by all of creation to a certain reverence for the handiwork of God, and we were provoked to the intellectual project of coming to understand the mind of God as manifest in the world. In other words, God's attunement required of us particular modes of comportment. Because things could show up as making demands on us, things mattered.

But now we as a culture find ourselves in the position of being unable to share a reverence for God – that is, for some such source of attunement. Without God to attune us to objects as having weight or importance for us, the danger is that nothing will matter, and consequently life will not be worth while. The search for a new source of divinity, then, becomes a question of finding a mood, a mode of attunement, which will allow things once more to show up as having weight or importance. By the same token, the inquiry into the death of God needs to be understood in affective terms – that is, as oriented around the question of the mood appropriate to the death of God.

In particular, as we get in tune with the mood of the technological age, things will begin to show up as lacking any set purpose, any determinate inherent value, but instead as ready and on call to be taken up in any way that we choose. The problem of this chapter can now be posed in the following way: Why does Heidegger believe that an experience of the divine is necessary in order to live a worthwhile life in the kind of world that shows up after the death of God?

MEANING AND MATTERING

Before turning directly to this question, I want to develop a framework for the ensuing account. I begin with a brief discussion of the idea of meaning. Things have meaning when they hold a place in what Heidegger calls a "referential context," by which he refers to the way each object is defined by a network of practices in which it is employed, the result toward which it is directed, and the other objects with which it is used. So a hammer has the meaning it has both because of the function it plays in human activities (like making houses) and because of the way it "refers" to things like nails and boards.

Although the world is meaningful or intelligible to me when I grasp the practical and equipmental contexts that embed all the things that populate the world, nothing in the world *matters* to me on the basis of this intelligibility alone. It is only when I am engaged in activities myself that any particular object comes to hold a special significance for me. As a result, in a world where I am not active, where I have no purposes and goals, where I am drawn into no involvements, no thing or person could matter to me. Everything would be spread out before me in an undifferentiated (albeit meaningful) irrelevance.

We can now, on the basis of this, distinguish what I call an *instrumental* importance from an *existential* importance. Things have an instrumental importance anytime we take up some of the purposes made available by the intelligible structure of the world. In a world where it makes sense to be a doctor, for instance, one can take up the objects that a doctor employs, and come into relation with the people a doctor relates to in her doctoring activities. These people and objects will matter to her, just as long as she continues to be a doctor. But outside of her doctoring activity, these devices and people need not make any claim on her.

Existential importance, by contrast, would consist in some practice or object or person having an importance for our self-realization. That is, the object or person or practice is something without which we would cease to be who we are. Such objects or persons or practices thus make a demand on us – require of us that we value them, respect them, respond to them on pain of losing ourselves.

As we noted, a defining trait of resources is precisely that they do not make any demands on us, but instead stand ready and available to be ordered as we demand, given our current aims. We can now get a clearer picture of *one* threat posed by the technological world: In the technological world, because everything presents itself as a mere resource, and thus has at best instrumental importance, nothing is capable of existential importance.

There is also another, closely related danger posed by our becoming attuned to the world through technology – the danger that we will lose a sense of having a place in the world. A life organized (however temporarily) around an end or goal, in addition to giving us instrumentally important objects, also acquires at least a thin "sense of place." To illustrate, suppose that I am engaged in being a teacher. Then everything else I do (reading a book, learning a new software program, sleeping in on Saturday) has its value as an activity in terms of how it contributes to or detracts from my realization of my vocation as a teacher. A purposive life is a coherent pattern of activity, and activities require things with which to be active. My activities give me a sense of place by ranging over particular objects – these students, this classroom, this campus, etc. These are the things I relate to in realizing who I am. Another way to say this is to say that my activities determine what is near to me and what is far from me. A thing is far from me if it plays no role in helping me be the person I am trying to be. (Of course, as Heidegger likes to point out, the "near" and "far" here are not primarily spatial – if something on the other side of the world were important to my work, I could be closer to it even while sitting in my office in Utah than someone else might be who happened to be just next door to it.)

But as technology begins to increase the range of our activities, it by the same token undermines nearness and farness in our world, thus threatening to undercut our belonging to a place and, by the same token, the sense that anything genuinely matters. Thanks to technological devices like the internet, I, in fact, *can* act at the greatest possible distances. The subsequent extension of reach, in turn, leads to a homogenization of objects, which need to be placed on call for exploitation in the widest imaginable set of contexts. The result we are driving toward is that no *particular* thing or location will matter at all to our ability to live our lives, because an indistinguishable alternative is readily available. The perfectly technological world will be one in which we can be completely indifferent to particular places, people, and things. Or, in other words, all that is left is resources, the "formless formations of technological production" in which pre-technological natures "can no longer pierce through ... to show their own."[9] In justifying these claims, Heidegger quotes approvingly the following passage from a letter by Rilke:

To our grandparents, a "house," a "well," a familiar steeple, even their own clothes, their cloak *still* meant infinitely more, were infinitely more intimate . . . Now there are intruding, from America, empty indifferent things, sham things, *dummies of life* . . . A house, as the Americans understand it, an American apple or a winestock from over there, have *nothing* in common with the house, the fruit, the grape into which the hope and thoughtfulness of our forefathers had entered.[10]

Before the advent of technology, even merely instrumentally important objects had a veneer of existential importance, given that a substitute was often not readily available. Before the advent of technology, instrumentally important objects could give us a sense of place (or at least an analogue of a genuine, existential sense of place) in virtue of the fact that objects tended to be shaped by local and regional factors. But these thin forms of existential importance and place are undermined as the globalization and the technologization of the economy has made for easy interchangeability, and has created pressure toward standardization. "Everything becomes equal and indifferent," Heidegger argues, "in consequence of the uniformly calculated availability of the whole earth."[11]

For Heidegger, a worthwhile life in the technological age demands that we rediscover existentially important objects and a sense of place. The divinities play a crucial role in his account of this rediscovery. But before turning directly to an account of Heidegger's divinities, I would like to focus the issue more clearly by exploring a non-religious solution to the problem. One response to the loss of importance and place would be to overcome our addiction to a life of existential importance, and instead find fulfillment in experiencing ourselves as disclosers of the technological world.[12] This possibility has recently been articulated by Dreyfus and Spinosa in the course of an exploration of the possibility of learning to affirm technology.[13] Dreyfus and Spinosa suggest that we could have a fulfilling life in a technological age if we could learn to enjoy the excitement of being able to respond flexibly to a situation, rather than being constrained by the inherent nature of the objects in the situation that confronts us. The reason I think that Heidegger does not pursue this option is that in affirming technology, we embrace a style of living that actively seeks to empty objects of the kind of worth that would allow them to make demands on us. In the process, we might recover at least one thing with more than merely instrumental importance – namely, it matters that there are numerous different possible ways to respond to each situation. But we disclose these multiple possibilities precisely to the extent that no particular possibility is inherently worth while, and no particular action or involvement makes a demand on us, because no particular object or action plays a unique role in realizing who we are. In short, in such a life, nothing and nobody can make a claim on us.

For Heidegger, such a life makes us "homesick" – that is, makes us long for the fulfillment found in inhabiting a place populated with objects, people, and activities which themselves have existential as opposed to merely instrumental importance. We can thus see that, from Heidegger's perspective, Dreyfus and Spinoza offer us at best a contingency plan for addressing the dangers of our age. They show us how it is possible to have a life which is significant in the sense of making sense, of being intelligible, and in which it is even possible to have one thing – the existential space of free possibilities – show up as more than simply instrumentally important. But Heidegger takes the incessant appetite for amusement and entertainment, as well as the excitement over open possibilities that Dreyfus and Spinoza focus on, as an effort to cover over the attunement of profound boredom which overtakes us in a world where nothing matters to us. This attempt at a cover up, for Heidegger, attests to a continued longing for home.[14] Thus, if it were possible to have more – to have objects and practices themselves show up as important – such a life would be preferable. To have this kind of life, however, requires a role for the divinities that no life of attunement to technological things permits.

On Heidegger's account, then, the appeal of a religious life after the death of God is rooted in the possibility of repopulating the world with things that have a deep importance – indeed, of perhaps genuinely relating to such things for the first time. To explain this, let me start by restating how Heidegger understands the way in which the technological age has destroyed the possibility of existentially important things. Heidegger's analysis, to frame it as succinctly as I can, is as follows: It is a relationship to things that have intrinsic importance that makes a life genuinely fulfilling. It is only our belonging in a particular place (existentially understood) that makes some things really matter. The technological age has undermined our ability to feel rooted in a particular place. Therefore, the technological age has made it difficult to live a worthwhile life.

I now want to say more carefully how a sense of place contributes to the existential importance of things. I note first that the thin sense of place discussed above – where my place is a function of the things I happen to be dealing with – seems inadequate to provide things with existential importance. A sense of place in the thin sense only decides over which particular objects our activities will range. It does not necessarily make those objects ultimately worth while. To return to my teacher example, one could ask, "Why be the teacher of *these* students? There's nothing really special

about them, and there are students all over the world who need a teacher."
If that is true, it seems that my life is only contingently worth while. Once
I have a sense of being the teacher of these particular students, my life gets
the order that it has. But there is nothing that ultimately grounds my being
their teacher as opposed to somebody else's, and so my life ultimately lacks
real significance. What we would really need is a deeply rooted belonging
to a place – a kind of belonging in which the things we deal with really
matter, that is, they make demands on us that we cannot ignore.

But how can anything really come to matter in this thick sense in a
world that is moving swiftly toward abolishing all sense of place? This sort
of mattering or importance is not something we can bestow upon things
by a free act of will. The only way to get it would be as a gift – a gift of place
or a gift of a thing of intrinsic worth. An attunement that allows things to
show up as having an intrinsic worth, however, is precisely what we lost
with the death of God. So, it seems that a worthwhile life after the death
of God requires some new endowment of divine grace, an endowment in
which we can once again be attuned to the sacred and divine. To finish
this thought, however, I need to say something more about the role the
divinities play for Heidegger in determining our place in the world.

BETWEEN THE EARTH AND THE SKY

Heidegger's discussion of the divinities is part of his attempt to uncover
the way that real *things*, as opposed to mere resources and technological
devices, show up. We have already outlined the role that a relationship to
the old God plays in allowing things and a world to "show up" (Heidegger
calls it "unconcealment"). The old God attuned us to the sacred in the sense
that he made objects have a significance independent of their usefulness to
our current projects. The divinities we strive to encounter in the fourfold
will likewise attune us to the sacred.

Heidegger tells us that for a real thing, a thing with existential importance, to show up, we must have practices for dealing with the earth and
the sky, the divinities and our own mortality. Real things themselves, in
turn, will embody the way earth, sky, mortals, and divinities condition
each other. Heidegger's name for the interrelation of earth, sky, mortals,
and divinities is "the fourfold."

Initially, Heidegger's claim that things and dwelling require the mutual
"appropriation" of earth and sky, "mortals and divinities," is anything but
clear. He tends to use each of the terms in an infuriatingly literal fashion –
and does so frequently enough that the passages cannot simply be ignored.

To cite a couple of my favorite examples, Heidegger tells us that the sky contributes to the essence of a jug as a jug-thing because the jug holds and pours out wine and thus gathers the sky. The holding and pouring of the wine gathers the sky, he explains, because the grapes from which the wine is made "receive the rain and dew of the sky."[15] As a second example, the Black Forest peasant's farmhouse gathers the earth, he says, because it is placed on a "mountain slope... among the meadows close to the spring."[16]

Philosophers are not used to such talk, so it is tempting either simply to ignore these passages or to impose a metaphorical reading which, given the densely poetical nature of Heidegger's musings, can only be loosely connected to the actual text.[17] The unappealing alternative is to repeat lamely his semi-poetic musings about the sky in the dew on the grapes (and so on). In terms of doing any philosophical work with Heidegger's notion of the fourfold, the metaphorical reading is certainly preferable to a mere repetition. But it seems, at the least, to do violence to the text.

I think, however, that such approaches are mistaken, and miss the whole point of Heidegger's discussion of the fourfold. The four are meant, by Heidegger, quite literally. The earth *is* the earth beneath our feet, the earth that spreads out all around us as mountains and in trees, in rivers and streams. The sky *is* the sky above our heads, the stars and constellations, the sun and the moon, the shifting weather that brings the changing seasons. We *are* the mortals – we and our companions – living our lives and dying our deaths. And the divinities – the most elusive members of the fourfold in this age – *are* divine beings, the "beckoning messengers of the Godhead." To justify such a literal, straightforward reading of the fourfold, I need to be able to say how a discussion of the earth, sky, mortals, and divinities shows us how to dwell and thereby recover a sense of place.

We can see this if we remember that what is at issue is the problem of discovering things with existential importance. Heidegger's insight is this: We do not have things that matter to us if all there is is isolated, self-contained, interchangeable entities – in other words, resources. Such entities cannot matter to us, cannot have existential importance for us, because none of them is essential to being who we are. Their flexibility and interchangeability make them efficient, but also prevent any of them from playing a unique role in our lives: "In enframing [i.e., the technological understanding that orders our world], everything is set up in the constant replaceability of the same through the same."[18] Real things, by contrast, are of a nature to make demands on us and, in the process, *condition* us.

We can clarify this idea of conditioning by noting that even instrumental importance is a result of a certain degree of conditioning of one object by another. It is only because our activities are conditioned or constrained by the objects with which we act that any particular object has instrumental importance. It is only because I want to build a house, for example, that a hammer matters more than a fountain pen. This is because the need to drive nails, and the nature of nails and boards, conditions the kind of tools I can use successfully. If objects make no demands on us or each other, and thus do not condition us or each other, then no object can be of any more weight than any other.

Therefore, for things to matter, there must be mutual conditioning. Heidegger's name for the process of mutual condition is *Ereignis*, probably best translated as "appropriation," where this is heard not as saying that we take over as our own something that does not belong to us, but rather as the mutual conditioning through which we and the things around us "come into our own" – i.e., become what each can be when conditioned by the other.[19]

The danger of the technological age is that we are turning everything (things, earth, sky, our own mortality, divinities) into entities which cannot condition, and thus cannot matter to us. The way to counteract the technological age, then, is to allow ourselves to be conditioned. Precisely here is where the fourfold becomes important – namely, as a source of conditioning in our lives.

Heidegger's name for living in such a way that we are conditioned or appropriated by the fourfold is "dwelling." What does it mean to "dwell" – that is, to be conditioned by the fourfold?

We are conditioned by the earth when we incorporate into our practices the particular features of the environment around us. "Mortals dwell in that they save the earth," Heidegger explains, where "saving the earth" consists in not exploiting it, not mastering it, and not subjugating it.[20] In Utah, for instance, one way to be conditioned by the earth would be to live in harmony with the desert, rather than pushing it aside by planting grass and lawns to replicate the gardens of the East. The technology of modern irrigation and sprinkler systems allow us to push our own earth aside, to master it and subjugate it, rather than being conditioned by it (as Borgmann has beautifully demonstrated).[21] Human beings "only experience the appropriation of the earth in the home-coming to their land,"[22] that is, when we come to be at home with our land in its *own* characteristics, not those enforced upon it.

We are conditioned by our sky when we incorporate into our practices the peculiar features of the temporal cycles of the heavens, the day and the night, the seasons and the weather. We push aside the sky when, for example, our eating habits demand food on call, out of season, or when our patterns of work, rest, and play make no allowance for the times of day and year, or recognize no holy days or festivals.

We are conditioned by our mortality when our practices acknowledge our temporal course on earth – both growth and suffering, health and disease. Heidegger illustrates this through the example of the Black Forest peasant hut, which was intimately conditioned by (and correspondingly conditioning of) mortality: "It did not forget the altar corner behind the community table; it made room in its chamber for the hallowed places of childbed and the 'tree of the dead' – for that is what they call a coffin there: the *Totenbaum* – and in this way it designed for the different generations under one roof the character of their journey through time."[23] We push our mortality aside when we seek immediate gratification without discipline, when we set aside our own local culture, when we try to engineer biologically and pharmacologically an end to all infirmity, including even death.

We are conditioned by the divinities when, for instance, we incorporate into our practices a recognition of holy times and holy precincts – perhaps manifested where one experiences the earth as God's creation, or feels a reverence for holy days or the sanctity of human life.[24] Hölderlin's Hyperion expresses such a sense for divinity in the world:

And often, when I lay there among the flowers, basking in the delicate spring light, and looked up into the serene blue that embraced the warm earth, when I sat under the elms and willows on the side of the mountain, after a refreshing rain, when the branches were yet astir from the touch of the sky and golden clouds moved over the dripping woods; or when the evening star, breathing the spirit of peace, rose with the age-old youths and the other heroes of the sky, and I saw how the life in them moved on through the ether in eternal, effortless order, and the peace of the world surrounded and rejoiced me, so that I was suddenly alert and listening, yet did not know what was befalling me – "Do you love me, dear Father in Heaven," I whispered, and felt his answer so certainly and so blissfully in my heart.[25]

As suggested by this quotation, earth, sky, mortals, and divinities do not just condition us, however; they also condition each other. Heidegger says that the fourfold mirror each other by ringing or wrestling with each other. Mirroring, Heidegger explains, consists in each member of the four becoming lighted, or intelligible, in the process of reflecting the others. I take this to mean, for instance, that the sky is only intelligible as the sky it *is* in terms of the interaction it has with the earth striving to spring forth as the earth it is (or in terms of the mortal activities it blesses or restricts) – for example, the weather the sky brings is only intelligible as inclement weather given the fruits the earth bears (or the activities of mortals), and the earth first comes into its essence as the earth it is when "blossoming in the grace of the sky."[26] More importantly for our purposes here, the divinities only are divinities to the extent that they mirror and, mirroring, light up the other regions of the four. The implication is that Heidegger's divinities have to be beings who can condition and be conditioned by the earth, the sky, and mortals. Conversely, the "default of the gods" that characterizes our age is understood in terms of the failure of any divine being to condition us and the things around us: "The default of God means that no god any longer gathers men and things unto himself, visibly and unequivocally, and by such gathering disposes the world's history and man's sojourn in it."[27]

With this in mind, let's turn now to the question how such conditioning can give us things that "near" – that have an importance which orients our whole life and not just the particular activities in which we are currently engaged. It is important to emphasize that we cannot have such things through a mere change of attitude – through merely deciding to treat resources as things. Things are not things in virtue of being represented or valued in some special way, but rather by being shaped in light of the receptivity that we have developed for our local earth, sky, mortals, and divinities. If the objects with which our world is populated have not been conditioned in that way (and resources are not), then they will not solicit the practices we have developed for living on the earth, beneath the sky, before the divinities. As Heidegger explains, "nothing that stands today as an object in the distanceless can ever be simply switched over into a thing."[28] By the same token, Heidegger cannot be advocating a nostalgic return to living in Black Forest peasant farmhouses. He notes that "things as things do not ever come about if we merely avoid [technological] objects and *recollect former objects* which perhaps were once on the way to becoming things and even to actually presencing as things."[29] To the extent that the former things gathered a receptivity to a particular sky, a particular earth, particular divinities, and particular mortal practices, they cannot thing *for us*, because our sky, earth, divinities, and mortals have a different configuration. They might once have been things, in other words, but they cannot thing in *our* fourfold.

Thus, if we are to live with things, we ourselves need to "bring the four-fold's essence into things."[30] In other words, on the basis of our reawakened receptivity to the four, we need to learn to make things and nurture things into being more than mere resource, hence to let them embody the essence of our place or home – *our* earth, *our* sky, *our* mortality, and *our* divinities. Heidegger's name for the activity of constructing and cultivating things in such a way that they contain or gather the fourfold is "building." The idea is that, in building, things secure the fourfold because, in the way they draw us into action, they draw upon just the kind of responsiveness that we have acquired by dwelling before our local divinities, earth, sky, and mortal practices. As Heidegger puts it, "building takes its standard over from the fourfold."[31] When our practices incorporate the fourfold, such things will have importance beyond their instrumental use in our current activities because they and only they are geared to our way of inhabiting the world. As a result they, and only they, can be used to be who we are. We will thus finally be at home in our places, because our practices are oriented to our places alone.

We might now wonder, however, why a relation to divinities is important if things with existential importance are secured by a sense of place. It seems that if we could foster practices for our earth, our sky, and our mortality, we could have a receptivity to the world that could only be satisfied by particular things, not generic resources. Those things would then, at least if the argument I have outlined is correct, have existential importance without any mention of divinities. Thus, the divinities seem superfluous.

I think that there are two answers to this problem. First, there is the tactical observation that given the seductiveness of resources and technological devices, it would take an experience of the divine to awaken us to the flaws in the technological age. The God, Heidegger says, "deranges us" – in the sense that he calls us beyond the existing configuration of objects to see things that shine forth with a kind of holiness (i.e., a dignity and worth that exceeds our will). Heidegger understands receptivity to the sacred as the experience of being beheld – of recognizing that there is a kind of intelligibility to the world that we do not ourselves produce. If God is part of the fourfold, then he wrestles with each region of the four, and brings it into a sacred own-ness. If we, in turn, are receptive to God, our practices will embody a recognition that the technological reduction of objects to resources is an act of presumption, for it proceeds on the assumption that we are free to employ anything we encounter in any way whatsoever. Once attuned by the divinities, technology will no longer be able to seduce us into an endless and empty "switching about ever anew," because we will see certain things around us as invested with holiness – with an intelligibility inherent to them, which shines forth out of them. So attuned, we may be able to establish what Heidegger calls a "free relation" to technology – a relation in which we are able to use technological devices to support our dwelling with things. But because the draw of technology is so strong, it is only a God who can save us, as Heidegger once asserted.[32]

Second, there is something substantive that being conditioned by a God adds to our sense of place – namely, it shows us our place as necessary for us. In fact, the old theological interpretation of God and the world was never able to do the job of giving us existential importance (we only had it in spite of the theological interpretation). The God of the philosophers was a God removed from time and us personally. His primary role was the establishment of meaning. But unless he could somehow be present to us, manifest himself in conditioning particular things in this world, be embodied, so to speak, so that we could become dependent on the intelligibility he helps light up, God could do no more than guarantee the intelligibility of the world (and the thin instrumental mattering that comes with that intelligibility).

I alluded above to the idea that, for Heidegger, the death of the onto-theological god actually might allow for a richer, more fulfilling sense of the divine. I can at this point start to redeem this claim. The onto-theological god gave things an importance that we were not free to change. As the source of all intelligibility, that God decided what things *really* were. But because he was beyond any being that we have experience of, there was no way he could attune us directly, i.e., no way he could help give us a place in the whole cosmos that he had made intelligible, and thus no guarantee that we would live in such a way that the objects as God knew them were existentially important to us.[33] An openness to divinities that themselves attune us, however, makes it possible to experience things in the world as sacred, and as making demands on us, which in turn allows them to have existential importance for us.

The death of the metaphysical God thus presents us with a great danger but also a unique opportunity to find a relationship to the divine that can endow our lives with deep importance. To be conditioned by the divinities is to discover God embodied – to find him present in our world. The death of the theologian's God offers us at least the possibility of a recovery of an immediate experience of the divine that has only rarely been achieved – that is, an experience of a living God with a presence in our world. Such a God would have an importance incommensurate with any object. As the source of our attunement, God would matter to us not just in the sense that our practices require his presence for their fulfillment. He would also matter as the being which calls us into the kind of engagement with the world that we would embody. He would, in short, be a God before whom we could pray, to whom we could sacrifice, in front of whom we could fall to our knees in awe.[34]

It should be obvious that the hope of finding this sort of divinity is something we cannot bring about ourselves. All we can do is try to keep alive the practices that will attune us in such a way that we can experience the divine in the world. The only means we have available to this end are the religious practices we have inherited. Those who are conditioned by the divine, Heidegger explains, "await the divinities as divinities. In hope they hold up to the divinities what is unhoped for. They wait for intimations of their coming and do not mistake the signs of their absence. They do not make their gods for themselves and do not worship idols. In the very depth of misfortune they wait for the weal that has been withdrawn."[35]

Despite the obviously Christian overtones of this and other such passages, it is important to see that Heidegger is not a nostalgic and sentimental thinker. His claim here is not that lapse into an accustomed mode of religious life is an end in itself. To the contrary, we can only be conditioned by the divine if we find our own authentic relationship to divinities. The problem is that, barring a new revelation, the only practices we have left for getting in tune with the divine are the remnants of past religious practices. These, Heidegger thinks, must therefore be nurtured in order to preserve a sense for the holy, because God can only appear as a god in the dimension of the holy. This, I take it, is the point of the somewhat enigmatic comments Heidegger made about religion in the course of his "Conversations with a Buddhist Monk": "I consider only one thing to be decisive: to follow the words of the founder. That alone – and neither the systems nor the doctrines and dogmas are important. *Religion is succession*... Without the sacred we remain out of contact with the divinities. Without being touched by the divinities, the experience of God fails to come."[36] But even remaining true to the practices we inherit from the founders of religion provides no guarantee of an advent of God. All we can do, Heidegger argued, is prepare ourselves for the advent in the hope that, through a gift of grace, we can receive our own revelation. "I see the only possibility of a salvation in preparing a readiness, in thinking and poetizing, for the appearance of the God or for the absence of God in the case of decline; that we not, to put it coarsely, 'come to a wretched end,' but rather if we decline, we decline in the face of the absent God."[37]

NOTES

1. "The Word of Nietzsche: 'God is Dead'" (WN), in *The Question Concerning Technology and Other Essays*, trans. William Lovitt (New York: Harper & Row, 1977), p. 101, translation modified.

2. *Gesamtausgabe*, vol. 39: *Hölderlins Hymnen "Germanien" und "Der Rhein"* (Frankfurt-on-Main: Klostermann, 1999), p. 95.

3. Trans. Walter Kaufmann (New York: Vintage, 1974).

4. See "The Question Concerning Technology," in *The Question Concerning Technology and Other Essays*.

5. *Gesamtausgabe*, vol. 79: *Bremer und Freiburger Vorträge* (*GA* 79) (Frankfurt-on-Main: Klostermann, 1994), p. 30.

6. *Gesamtausgabe*, vol. 44: *Nietzsches metaphysische Grundstellung im abendländischen Denken: Die ewige Wiederkehr des Gleichen* (*GA* 44) (Frankfurt-on-Main: Klostermann, 1986), pp. 192–3.

7. *Sämtliche Werke: Kritische Studienausgabe*, vol. 11: *Nachgelassene Fragmente 1884–1885*, ed. Giorgio Colli and Mazzino Montinari (Berlin and New York: Walter de Gruyter, 1980), p. 424.

8. *GA* 44, pp. 193–4.

9. "What are Poets For?," in *Poetry, Language, Thought*, trans. Albert Hofstadter (New York: Harper & Row, 1971), p. 113.

10. "Letter to Muzot," quoted *ibid*.

11. "The Nature of Language," in *On the Way to Language*, trans. Peter D. Hertz (New York: Harper & Row, 1971), p. 105.

12. Nietzsche seems to think that this is the kind of experience that will properly attune us to the world as it appears after the death of God. After the death of God, he wrote in an unpublished note, all that is left is the issue "whether to abolish our reverences or us ourselves. The latter is nihilism." The former course – that of abolishing our reverences – is the course which will open us up to enjoying the thrill of responding freely to the world as technology offers it. Nietzsche's primary metaphor for the world after the death of God – a world in which there are no fixed points of reference, and in which no object has a real gravity or weight – is a sea with infinite horizons: "At long last the horizon appears free to us again, even if it should not be bright; at long last our ships may venture out again, venture out to face any danger; all the daring of the lover of knowledge is permitted again; the sea, *our* sea, lies open again; perhaps there has never yet been such an 'open sea'" (*Gay Science*, sec. 343).

13. Hubert L. Dreyfus and Charles Spinosa, "Highway Bridges and Feasts: Heidegger and Borgmann on how to Affirm Technology," *Man and World* 30 (1997).

14. "700 Jahre Messkirch," in *Gesamtausgabe*, vol. 16: *Reden und andere Zeugnisse eines Lebensweges 1910–1976* (*GA* 16) (Frankfurt-on-Main: Klostermann, 2000), pp. 578ff.

15. "The Thing," in *Poetry, Language, Thought*, p. 172.

16. "Building, Dwelling, Thinking" (BDT), in *Poetry, Language, Thought*, p. 160.

17. Dreyfus and Spinosa, for instance, explain earth, sky, mortals, and divinities without a single quotation from, or citation of, Heidegger's discussion of the fourfold. For interpretations which approach the literalness with which I think Heidegger should be read, see James C. Edwards, *The Plain Sense of Things: The Fate of Religion in an Age of Normal Nihilism* (University Park,

Pa.: Pennsylvania State University Press, 1997); Julian Young, *Heidegger's Later Philosophy* (Cambridge University Press, 2002); and Charles Taylor, "Heidegger, Language, and Ecology," in *Heidegger: A Critical Reader*, ed. Hubert L. Dreyfus and Harrison Hall (Oxford: Blackwell, 1992), pp. 247–69.

18. *GA* 79, p. 44.
19. See, for example, "Seminar in Le Thor," in *Gesamtausgabe*, vol. 15: *Seminare* (Frankfurt-on-Main: Klostermann, 1986), p. 363: "es ist das Ereignis des Seins als Bedingung der Ankunft des Seienden: das Sein läßt das Seiende anwesen."
20. BDT, p. 150.
21. *Technology and the Character of Contemporary Life* (University of Chicago Press, 1987).
22. *Besinnung auf unser Wesen* (Messkirch: Martin-Heidegger-Gesellschaft, 1994).
23. BDT, p. 160.
24. See "Origin of the Work of Art," in *Basic Writings*, ed. David Farrell Krell (New York: Harper & Row, 1993), p. 167.
25. Friedrich Hölderlin, "Hyperion," in *Hyperion and Selected Poems*, ed. Eric L. Santner (New York: Continuum, 1990), pp. 5–6.
26. *Besinnung auf unser Wesen* ("die Erde als Erde wesen läßt; das ist: Erblühen in der Huld des Himmels").
27. "What are Poets For?," p. 91.
28. "The Thing," p. 182. This passage, by the way, shows that the earlier reference to highway bridges gathering must have been sloppiness on Heidegger's part. If gathering is a term of art for what things do – as Heidegger sometimes indeed uses it – then highway bridges cannot thing because they do not gather the divinities; they push them aside. Cf. Dreyfus and Spinosa, "Highway Bridges and Feasts."
29. "The Thing," p. 182, translation modified, my italics.
30. BDT, p. 151, translation modified.
31. "Bauen Wohnen Denken," in *GA* 7, p. 161.
32. "'Only a God Can Save Us': *Der Spiegel*'s Interview with Martin Heidegger," in *The Heidegger Controversy: A Critical Reader*, ed. Richard Wolin (Cambridge, Mass.: MIT Press, 1992), pp. 91–116.
33. Kierkegaard makes just this point in *Fear and Trembling*, when he notes that if God "is understood in an altogether abstract sense . . . God becomes an invisible, vanishing point, an impotent thought." *Fear and Trembling*, trans. Alastair Hannay (London: Penguin Books, 1985), p. 96.
34. See "The Onto-Theo-Logical Constitution of Metaphysics," in *Identity and Difference*, trans. Joan Stambaugh (University of Chicago Press, 1969), p. 72.
35. BDT, p. 150.
36. *GA* 16, p. 590.
37. *Ibid.*, p. 671.

CHAPTER 7

Christianity without onto-theology: Kierkegaard's account of the self's movement from despair to bliss

Hubert L. Dreyfus

Kierkegaard belongs right after Mark Wrathall's eloquent explanation and defense of the later Heidegger's account of the fourfold: the local earth, the seasons, our mortality, and the remnants of the pagan gods. Wrathall presented the fourfold as an attempt to answer the question: Why do we need the divine and the sacred in our lives and how should we preserve and promote them?

If he had read Martin Heidegger, Kierkegaard would have answered that any attempt to preserve the local is doomed; that technicity, the drive toward optimization and efficiency, will sooner or later wipe out traditional practices, just as it has already wiped out the last stage of onto-theology, the metaphysics of the subject, and is turning us all into resources.

Heidegger was all too aware of this possibility, which he expresses in his lament that "the wasteland grows," that what is so dangerous about technology is that it is a drive toward the total efficient ordering of *everything*. The wilderness is turning into a resource – the Alaskan resource, human beings are no longer personnel, but rather material for the Human Resources Departments, and a recent advertisement proclaimed that children "are our most precious resource." What Robert Pippin called "farmer metaphysics" is on the way out. Heidegger sadly notes the television antennas on the peasants' huts and feels that we are already failing to dwell, and that our culture is rushing into the "longest night." For Heidegger, all we can do is carry out a holding action trying to preserve the endangered species of practices while awaiting a new God.

What Heidegger does not consider is that losing our appreciation of the jug of local wine, the seasons, our mortal vulnerability, and our local religious traditions might be a good thing; that these pagan practices might be standing in the way of a more intensely rewarding religious life.

This is where Kierkegaard comes in. He had a similar despairing analysis of the present age as nihilistic, and saw all meaningful differences being leveled by what he called "reflection." That was his name for the fact that more and more people in his time were becoming spectators and critics and fewer and fewer were willing to take the risk of making a serious commitment. He claimed that thanks to the media, this spectator attitude and the leveling it produces would get worse and worse, until, like a bonfire, it would "consume everything."[1] That is, it would level all meaningful differences between the trivial and the important.

But Kierkegaard, the radical Christian, has an entirely different response than Heidegger, the conservative pagan. Kierkegaard thinks that clearing away the local rootedness and the local gods is a good thing; when the bonfire has consumed everything local, we shall be left only with the choice between the meaningless distractions of the present age and what Kierkegaard calls the "decision in existence." If we heed the call, he says, we shall be able to leap over "the sharp scythe of the leveler... into the arms of God."[2] That would be to discover a new and better way of finding meaning, and mattering in our lives. As he puts it in the culminating exhortation of *The Present Age*:

There is no more action or decision in our day than there is perilous delight in swimming in shallow waters. But just as a grown-up, struggling delightedly in the waves, calls to those younger than himself: "Come on, jump in quickly" – the decision in existence...calls out... Come on, leap cheerfully, even if it means a lighthearted leap, so long as it is decisive. If you are capable of being a man, then danger and the harsh judgment of existence on your thoughtlessness will help you become one.[3]

The leap into the deep water refers to a series of total commitments, first to the enjoyment of possibility (the aesthetic), then to the universal ethical, and then to the mystical life of self-annihilation before God. Each opens what Kierkegaard calls a sphere of existence. But Kierkegaard also claims that if one lives passionately in each sphere, each sphere will break down and land one back in the leveling of the present age. In *Sickness unto Death*, Kierkegaard describes these breakdowns and presents the only sphere of existence that he claims will work. He does so by giving an account of the structure of the self that explains the breakdowns and also what is required for a meaningful life. He then shows how only Christianity, the religion of the God-man, meets this requirement.

I   WHAT IS A SELF?

According to Kierkegaard, a human being is a combination of two sets of factors:

The human being is spirit. But what is spirit? Spirit is the self. But what is the self? The self is a relation which relates to itself, or that in the relation which is its relating to itself. The self is not the relation but the relation's relating to itself. A human being is a synthesis of the infinite and the finite, of the eternal and the temporal, of possibility and necessity . . . A synthesis is a relation between two factors. Looked at in this way a human being is not yet a self.[4]

How can Kierkegaard argue for such an essentialist view? How can he say more than what Charles Taylor and Richard Rorty agree on, that anyone can have any relation to God or to the sacred that he or she feels called upon to have, as long as he or she does not seek to impose it on others? How can Kierkegaard claim, in this fractured world, to know the essential structure of the self, and consequently that one kind of religion is what every human being is called to have, whether he or she knows it or not?

We must try to understand what kind of claim this is. I used to think that it was a modest claim concerning how the self has come to be constituted in the Judeo-Christian tradition; that Christianity created the disease for which it is the cure. But, if that were so, I would have to agree with Rorty that it's high time we chose a new vocabulary. But now I think it's clear that Kierkegaard thinks that Christianity *discovered* the essential truth about the self – that it was sick unto death, not that Christianity produced this sick self.

But how can Kierkegaard claim to know the essential nature of the self? He doesn't claim a Husserlian *Wesenschau*, nor is he simply appealing to revelation. I think that his argument has the form introduced by Heidegger in *Being and Time* and worked out by Saul Kripke in *Naming and Necessity*.[5] Heidegger calls it "formal indication"; Kripke calls it "rigid designation." People also call it "black box essentialism."

The idea is that whether there are essences is an experimental question, and so cannot be decided a priori. The way natural science is practiced, we assume provisionally that there are natural kinds like water and gold with essential properties; we then designate such supposed kinds by some property and investigate, in the appropriate way, whether we have picked out a kind and found its essential property. So, to take a few Kripkean examples, we designate gold as that yellow stuff and then it finally turns out that yellowness is not essential but that gold has the atomic number 79. Or we designate heat as what feels warm to the touch and then discover that it is essentially molecular motion. We think that we've got it right, i.e., that we have found the essential property, when we can use it to explain all the other properties and account for all the anomalies that seem to contradict our essentialist account.

Heidegger had a similar idea. Taking his clue from Kierkegaard, he said in *Being and Time* that he would provisionally formally indicate[6] human beings as *Dasein*, i.e., as essentially beings that have to take a stand on their own being. He then did a lot of appropriate investigation, in this case hermeneutic and phenomenological investigation, and it turned out that this account of the self enabled him to understand a lot about human beings, and this confirmed his provisional designation, which of course could still run into problems later on and turn out to be wrong.[7]

Kierkegaard wants to discover the essential structure of the self. He is not the first to try. The self was designated by Plato and many others as some sort of combination of body and soul. Kierkegaard thinks that this approach fails to explain the possibility of despair, an important aspect of human life. He provisionally suggests that the self's essential property is that it is a relation that relates itself to itself, and that such a relation has a complex structure which he calls a "synthesis" of two sets of factors. Of course, whether this self is a kind, and whether this is its essential structure, indeed, whether there are any kinds with essences at all, will have to be answered by a description of human experience. The appropriate test is how much of human experience Kierkegaard can order and understand, and how he can account for anomalies that seem to contradict alternative accounts.

The Greeks called the two sets of factors you see in Figure 1 (p. 92) the soul and the body respectively. According to the ancients, the self begins with these factors in conflict, but once one realizes that *only one set of factors is essential* – that one is an eternal soul, and not a temporal body, or vice versa – the conflict and instability are overcome. Life is a voyage from confusion to clarity and from conflict to harmony. Since the self is potentially whole and harmonious, all one has to do is realize its true nature, find and satisfy its true needs rather than its superficial desires, and one can experience peace and fulfillment.

On the Greek account, if both sets of factors were equally essential the self would be in hopeless self-contradiction. It could not fully express all its bodily, finite, temporal needs and capacities while at the same time fully expressing all its intellectual, infinite, eternal needs and capacities. It seems, in fact, that the more you express one set of factors, the less you are able to express the other set. So it would seem that the factors were merely *combined*, and only one set of factors could be essential.

Starting with Pascal, however, Christian thinkers realized that according to Christianity, both sets of factors *were* essential and the self was, indeed, a contradiction. As Pascal put it: "What a chimera then is man! What a novelty! What a monster, what a chaos, what a contradiction!"[8]

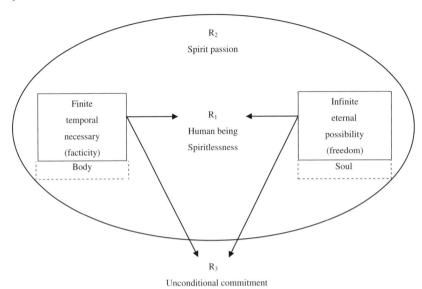

Figure 1 Kiergekaard's definition of the self

According to Pascal, a person's highest achievement was not to deny or overcome this contradiction – by getting rid of half the self – but to live in such a way as to express the tension of the contradiction fully. "We do not display greatness by going to one extreme, but in touching both extremes at once, and filling all the intervening space."[9]

Kierkegaard agrees that, according to the Judeo-Christian tradition, the self is a contradictory *synthesis* between two sets of factors and that *each set is essential* and requires the other. He calls this a dialectical relation. That means that both sets of factors are aspects of one whole. You can't satisfy one set of factors without satisfying the other.

Let us now look at this claim in more detail. (See Figure 1.)

2 WAYS OF ATTEMPTING TO BE A SELF

R_1 – This is what Kierkegaard calls spiritlessness. One has a sense that the self is a contradiction that has to be faced, but one lives in what Pascal called distraction so that one never has to take a stand in thought or action as to how to get the factors together. Pascal gives as examples of distraction playing tennis and sitting alone in one's room solving hard philosophical problems. (No doubt he had Descartes in mind.) Kierkegaard thought that the most important distraction in his time was the public sphere, where one could discuss events and people anonymously without ever having to take responsibility for one's views. One could debate, on the basis of principles, how the world should be run, without running the risk of testing these principles in action. This form of distraction is now perfected in chat rooms and news groups on the internet, but, of course, there are many other ways to avoid facing the contradictory nature of the self besides surfing the net.

R_2 – If a human being acts only as a combination of factors, he or she is not yet a self. To be a self, the relation must relate itself to itself, by taking a stand on both sets of factors through its actions. It must manifest that something about the self is essential by making something in its life absolute. This can take a negative and a positive form.

Negative R_2 – "In a relation between two things the relation is the third term in the form of a negative unity, and the two relate to the relation, and in the relation to that relation; this is what it is from the point of view of soul for soul and body to be in relation."[10]

When the relation is a negative unity, the relation relates to itself in the Greek way; denying one of the sets of factors and acting as if only the other aspect of the self were the essential one. One can, for example, take the soul to be eternal at the expense of the body as Plato did, or do the opposite, as Lucretius did.

Positive R_2 – Such selves try, by themselves, to express fully both sets of factors in thought and action, but this turns out to be impossible. For example, if one makes possibility absolute and lives for constant change, constantly open to new possibilities, one is in the aesthetic sphere – Kierkegaard's anticipation of Nietzsche and the post-moderns – but that gives no expression to the necessary and the eternal. Or, if one tries to make the infinite and the eternal absolute, one loses the finite and the temporal. As Kierkegaard puts it, such mystical types can't bring their God-relationship together with a decision whether or not to take a walk in the park.

Once he has worked through all the first three spheres of existence in this way, Kierkegaard claims to have shown that "the self cannot by itself arrive at or remain in equilibrium and rest."[11] His Christian view is that the self is unable to solve its own problem. It does not have the truth in it, that is, it does not have in itself the resources to live a stable and meaningful life.

3 DESPAIR: THE SICKNESS UNTO DEATH

In *Sickness unto Death*, Kierkegaard tries to show that every possible attempt to combine the factors by essentializing one or the other of each pair of factors leads to despair, as does every way of trying to do justice to both. And, according to Kierkegaard, everyone who has not managed to perform the impossible task of getting his or her self together in a stable, meaningful life is in despair.

You might well think that this is all ridiculous, since you, at least, are not in despair. You may feel that you are having a great time enjoying all your possibilities, or living a fulfilling life taking care of your family, or that your life is worth living because you are working to eliminate suffering, and so forth. In general, that you are fulfilling your capacities and everything is working out fine.

Kierkegaard would say that you might think you are living a life worth living, but in fact you are in despair. What right does he have to say this? His answer is in *Sickness unto Death*:

> Despair differs dialectically from what one usually calls sickness, because it is a sickness of the spirit. And this dialectical aspect, properly understood, brings further thousands under the category of despair. If at any time a physician is convinced that so and so is in good health, and then later that person becomes ill, then the physician may well be right about his *having been* well at the time but now being sick. Not so with despair. Once despair appears, what is apparent is that the person was in despair. In fact, it's never possible at any time to decide anything about a person who is not saved through having been in despair. For when whatever causes a person to despair occurs, it is immediately evident that he has been in despair his whole life.[12]

Kierkegaard is pointing out that despair is not like sadness, regret, disappointment, depression, etc. Rather, unlike these downers, despair exhibits what Kierkegaard calls "the dialectic of eternity." If you are sad, you know that it is temporary. Even if something so terrible happens to you that you feel that you were happy once but that whatever has happened makes it impossible for you ever to be happy again, that is certainly misery, but it is not despair. Despair is the feeling that life isn't working for you and, given the kind of person you are, it is impossible for things to work for you; that a life worth living is, in your case, literally impossible.

That means that once a person experiences despair – "it will be evident that his [previous] success was an illusion"[13] – i.e., all that person's past joys *must have been* self-deceptions. That in turn means that, if you ever experience despair, you realize that you have always been in despair and you always will be. So Kierkegaard concludes that, since the self is a contradiction, even though you now feel that things are going well for you, you must right now be in despair and not know it. Only if you have faced your despair – the sickness unto death – and been cured can you be sure that you are not now in despair. So, given the contradictory nature of the self, all of us, with the exception of those who have faced despair and been healed, must right now be in despair.

The ultimate despair, Kierkegaard contends, is denying that one is in despair by denying the demand that we express the two sets of factors in our lives in a way that enables them to reinforce each other. This is not the distraction of the present age where one represses the call to be a self. Rather, someone in this ultimate form of despair sees that in our religious tradition the self has, indeed, been constituted as having two sets of essential but incompatible factors, but claims that this is merely a traditional, essentialist view that we should opt out of. Since the traditional Judeo-Christian understanding of the self leads people to despair, we should simply give it up and adopt a vocabulary and practices that are healthier and more useful to us now.

How can we decide who is right here, Kierkegaard or the pragmatist? I think that this is a question we can only approach experimentally. In *Sickness unto Death*, Kierkegaard tries to show that the Christian claim that the self is a contradiction is confirmed by a purportedly exhaustive categorization of all the ways of being a self available to us and how each fails.

4 HOW THE FACTORS REINFORCE EACH OTHER IN AN UNCONDITIONAL COMMITMENT

If Kierkegaard is right, not being in despair must mean having been somehow cured of it for good. He says:

The possibility of this sickness is man's advantage over the beast; to be aware of this sickness is the Christian's advantage over natural man; to be cured of this sickness is the Christian's blessedness.[14]

Consequently, Kierkegaard proposed to preface *Sickness unto Death* with a prayer to Jesus as Savior:

O Lord Jesus Christ, who didst come to earth to heal them that suffer from this sickness... help Thou us in this sickness to hold fast to Thee, to the end that we may be healed of it.[15]

According to Kierkegaard, Jesus is "God in time as [an] individual man."[16] But how that enables him to cure us of despair is rather a long story. To begin with, Kierkegaard tells us that the self can only succeed in relating itself to itself by relating to another. Only when the self "in relating to itself relates to something else,"[17] Kierkegaard contends, can it get the two sets of factors into equilibrium. Only then is each factor defined in such a way as to support rather than be in conflict with the others. But how is this possible?

Whether you can get the factors together or whether they form a contradiction depends on how you define them. Or, to put it another way, the Greeks found that, if you define the factors from the point of view of detachment, you can't get them together. Kierkegaard tries to show that only if you define the factors in terms of a total involvement that gives you your identity do you get a positive synthesis.

This is the claim illustrated in *Fear and Trembling*. The story starts with Abraham the Father of the faith, who "believed he would . . . [be] blessed in his kin, eternally remembered in Isaac."[18] Isaac was obviously essential to Abraham's identity. To illustrate what is at stake in having an identity, Kierkegaard draws on the chivalric romances. The example on which he says "everything turns" is the case of "A young lad [who] falls in love with a princess, [so that] the content of his whole life lies in this love."[19] Kierkegaard adds in a footnote that "any other interest whatever in which an individual concentrates the whole of life's reality"[20] would do as well.

The lad who loves the princess relates himself to himself by way of this relation. Thanks to it, he knows who he is and what is relevant and important in his world. Any such unconditional commitment to some specific individual, cause, or vocation whereby a person gets an identity and a sense of reality would do to make the point Kierkegaard is trying to make. In such a case the person becomes an individual defined by his or her relation to the object of his or her unconditional commitment. The lad is the lover of the princess, Martin Luther King Jr. is the one who will bring justice to the American blacks, Steve Jobs identifies himself with Apple Computer, etc.

Kierkegaard's model for such a commitment is the knight whose life gets its meaning by his devotion to his lady. This is not a compulsion, an infatuation, or an obsession. That would not be an expression of freedom. Kierkegaard says that the knight is free to "forget the whole thing," but in so doing the knight would "contradict himself," since it is "a contradiction to forget the whole of one's life's content and still be the same."[21]

According to Kierkegaard, if and only if you let yourself be drawn into a defining commitment can you achieve that which, while you were in despair, looked impossible, i.e., that the two sets of factors reinforce each other, so that the more you manifest one the more you manifest the other. By responding to the call of such an unconditional commitment and thereby getting an identity, a person becomes what Kierkegaard, following the Bible, calls "a new creation."[22] Thus, Jesus gave those who were saved from despair by being unconditionally committed to him new names, and they called him their Savior.

But just how does this work?

The temporal and the eternal

For one to live fully in time, some moment must be absolutely important and make other moments significant relative to it. The moment when one is reborn is obviously such a moment. Kierkegaard, drawing on the biblical saying that we shall be changed in the twinkling of an eye, calls this moment the *Augenblick*. Moreover, after the transformation, other moments become significant since one's unconditional commitment must be expressed in one's day-to-day activity.

But the eternal is also absolutely important in one's life. Not the disinterested, abstract eternity of Plato, but the passionately involved eternity that Kierkegaard calls "eternity in time." Normally, the significance of events in one's life is subject to retroactive reinterpretation,[23] but, in an unconditional commitment that defines the self, one's identity is as eternal as a definition. The lad will henceforth always be the lover of the princess:

He first makes sure that this really is the content of his life, and his soul is too healthy and proud to squander the least thing on an infatuation. He is not cowardly, he is not afraid to let his love steal in upon his most secret, most hidden thoughts, to let it twine itself in countless coils around every ligament of his consciousness – if the love becomes unhappy he will never be able to wrench himself out of it.[24]

Further events will be interpreted in the light of the content given the self in the *Augenblick*, not vice versa. The way a commitment can produce a privileged moment is not something disinterested thought can understand. Kierkegaard says: "A concrete eternity within the existing individual is the maximum degree of his passion", and "the proposition inaccessible to thought is that one can become eternal although one was not such."[25]

In sum, if you define eternity in an involved way as that which remains constant throughout your life, then what is eternal is your identity. That is, if you are unconditionally committed to a particular person or cause, that will be your identity forever (for every moment of your life). This is a kind of involved eternity that must, in order to exist, be temporal. The paradoxical fact is that "only in existing do I become eternal."[26] But this does not make me any less temporal. "The existing individual *in time...* comes into relation with the eternal *in time*."[27]

The finite and the infinite

Kierkegaard calls an unconditional commitment an infinite passion for something finite. But just what makes an infinite passion count as infinite? It can't be just a very strong feeling; rather, it must in some sense transcend the finite. For Kierkegaard, an infinite passion can legitimately be called infinite because it opens up a world. Not only *what actually exists* gets its meaning from its connection with my defining passion; anything that could possibly come into existence would get its meaning for me from my defining commitment. As we saw earlier, according to Kierkegaard, one's commitment defines *reality*.

Of course, the object of my infinite passion is something *finite*. We are interested in the smallest particularities of our beloved. But any such finite being is vulnerable, and yet the meaning of my life depends on it. This makes a defining commitment very risky. It would certainly be safer to define one's life in some sort of theoretical quest or in terms of some abstract idea – say the eventual triumph of the proletariat – but that is not concrete enough to satisfy the need to make the finite absolutely significant. So it follows, as Kierkegaard says, that "without risk there is no faith."[28]

I can't go into details here, but suffice it to say that Kierkegaard holds that, given the risk, to let yourself be more and more involved with something finite, you need to live in a kind of absurdity:

Every moment to see the sword hanging over the loved one's head and yet find, not repose in the pain of resignation, but joy on the strength of the absurd – that is wonderful. The one who does that, he is great, the only great one.[29]

In the context of the Abraham story, Isaac will certainly be sacrificed, the sword will fall, and yet Abraham acts as if he will always have Isaac. The Knight of Faith can do this because he lives in the assurance that "God is the fact that everything is possible, or that everything is possible is God."[30]

In sum, when you have a defining commitment, the finite object of your commitment is infinitely important, i.e., the object of your passion is both something particular and also world-defining. Indeed, it is the condition for anything showing up as meaningful. It thus opens up a horizontal transcendence.

The necessary and the possible

We have seen that, when you have a defining commitment, you get an identity. That is what you are, and it is *necessary* that you be it. But, although your identity is fixed, it does not dictate an inflexible way of acting as if it were a compulsion. In anything less than total loss and subsequent world-collapse, one has to be able to adapt to even the most radical changes in the defining object. All such adaptive changes will, of course, be changes *in* the world but not changes *of* the world. Kierkegaard calls this freedom because, even though the central concern in one's life is fixed, one is free to adapt it to all sorts of possible situations in all sorts of ways.

There is, however, an even more radical kind of freedom: The freedom to change my world, i.e., to change my identity. To be born again *and again*. Although Kierkegaard does not say so in so many words, once we see that eternity can be in time, we can see that, not only can eternity *begin* at a moment of time (the *Augenblick*), but eternity can *change* in time. In Kierkegaard's terms, Abraham has faith that if he sacrifices Isaac "God could give him a new Isaac."[31] This can happen because God is "that everything is possible,"[32] and that means that even the inconceivable is possible.

Here we are touching on the paradox of mourning. This is a topic too complicated to go into here, but this much is clear. On Kierkegaard's view, one can only change worlds by being totally involved in one, deepening one's commitment, and taking all the risks involved, until it breaks down and becomes impossible. As in Thomas Kuhn's *Structure of Scientific Revolutions*, revolutions depend on prior unconditional commitment to a paradigm. One can't be a Christian in Kierkegaard's sense and agree with Nietzsche that "convictions are prisons."[33]

Thus, according to Kierkegaard, the radically impossible only makes sense if one is unconditionally committed to the current world. Otherwise, we have such flexibility that everything is possible, and although some events are highly improbable, they are not inconceivable. For the truly impossible to be possible, we must be able to open radically new worlds which we can't even make sense of until we are in them. Thus, John Caputo's understanding of religion as dealing with "the impossible" only makes sense if there are worlds, that is, if there are what Rorty once called final vocabularies. Only if one relates steadfastly rather than flexibly to the world established by one's defining commitment can one experience a gestalt switch in which one's sense of reality is transformed.

Kierkegaard concludes from his examination of all types of despairing ways to try to relate the factors that the only sphere of existence that can give equal weight to both sets of factors is a religion based on an infinite passion for something finite. Kierkegaard calls such a paradoxical religion Religiousness B. He is clear that "in Religiousness B the edifying is something outside the individual . . . The paradoxical edification [of Christianity] corresponds therefore to the determination of God in time as the individual man; for if such be the case, the individual is related to something outside himself."[34]

But, given the logic of Kierkegaard's position, it follows that the object of defining relation does not have to be the God-man. Indeed, in the *Postscript* Kierkegaard says, "Subjectively, reflection is directed to the question whether the individual is related to a something *in such a manner* that his relationship is in truth a God relationship."[35] And even more clearly that "it is the passion of the infinite that is the decisive factor and not its content, for its content is precisely itself."[36]

5   CONCLUSION

So now we can see why Kierkegaard claims that, unless the self relates itself to something else with an unconditional commitment, it is in despair; that only if it has an unconditional commitment will the self be able to get the two sets of factors together in such a way that they reinforce each other, and so be in bliss. Kierkegaard says rather obscurely:

This then is the formula that describes the state of the self when despair is completely eradicated: in relating to itself and in wanting to be itself, the self is grounded transparently in the power that established it.[37]

Grounded transparently means acting in such a way that what gives you your identity comes through in everything you do. But what is the power (lower case) that established the self? I used to think that it was whatever finite and temporal object of infinite passion created you as a new being by giving you your identity. But that would only be the power that established your identity, not the power that established the three sets of contradictory factors to which your identity is the solution. What, then, is the power that established the whole relation?

The power doesn't seem to be an onto-theological God since it is lower case and Kierkegaard doesn't say that the power *created* the relation. But Kierkegaard does say that one could not despair "unless the synthesis were originally in the right relationship from the hand of God."[38] How are we to cash out this metaphor, especially if we remember that "God is that everything is possible" – not an entity at all?

I think we have to say that "the fact that everything is possible" makes possible the contradictory God-man who then says, "he who has seen me has seen the Father." He is the paradoxical Paradigm who saves from despair all sinners – those who have tried to take a stand on themselves by themselves, either by relating only to themselves or by relating to an infinite, absolute, and eternal God. The God-man saves them by calling them to make an unconditional commitment to him – "God in time as an individual man."

Therefore, I think that the claim that God established the factors has to mean that by making it possible for people to have a defining commitment – in the first instance to him – and so be reborn, Jesus revealed that the two sets of factors are equally essential and can (and must) be brought into equilibrium. This is the truth about the essential nature of the self that went undiscovered until Jesus revealed it. In this way he established the Christian understanding of the self in which we now live. He is the call that demands "a decision in existence" which we cannot reject without despair.

So, on this reading, "to be grounded transparently in the power that established it" would mean that saved Christians (1) relate themselves to themselves by manifesting in all aspects of their lives that both sets of factors are essential; by, that is, relating to someone or something finite with an infinite passion and so becoming eternal in time. Whatever constituted the self as the individual self it is, healing it of despair by giving it its identity and, thereby, making it a new being – that "something" would be its Savior; and (2) all such lives are grounded in Jesus, the God-man, who first makes such radical transformation of the person and of the world possible.

In this way Kierkegaard has succeeded in saving Christianity from onto-theology by replacing the creator God, who is metaphysically infinite and eternal, with the God-man who is finite and temporal, yet who is the source of the infinity and eternity required by finite beings like us if we are to be saved from despair. In so doing, Kierkegaard has also shown how leveling and technicity can be positive forces in forcing us to leave behind both metaphysics and paganism's sense of the sacred for a more intense and rewarding form of religion.

NOTES

1. Søren Kierkegaard, *The Present Age*, trans. Alexander Dru (London: Collins, 1962), p. 56.
2. *Ibid.*, p. 82.
3. *Ibid.*, pp. 36–7.
4. Søren Kierkegaard, *The Sickness unto Death*, trans. Alastair Hannay (London: Penguin Books, 1989), p. 43.
   I have made several changes in the text in order to clarify what I believe to be its meaning. First, I have substituted Walter Lowrie's term "factors" for Hannay's "terms" in the definition of the self, because it provides a convenient shorthand for describing the constituents of the synthesis. Second, I have changed the word "freedom" to "possibility." In other passages in *The Sickness*

unto Death, and in *The Concept of Anxiety*, Kierkegaard uses the word "free-dom" to refer to the self-defining nature of human beings. He uses the word "possibility" to refer to one factor of the synthesis that a human being defines. Though Kierkegaard is inconsistent in his use of terminology, the distinction between the two concepts is clear. Thus, I have changed the terminology in order to preserve the clear distinction between the two concepts. Finally, I have reversed the order of the possibility/necessity and eternal/temporal factors, since Kierkegaard discusses them in this order in the remainder of *The Sickness unto Death*, and I have changed the order temporal/eternal to eternal/temporal to make it symmetrical with Kierkegaard's presentation of the other sets of factors.

5. Saul A. Kripke, *Naming and Necessity* (Cambridge, Mass.: Harvard University Press, 1972).

6. See Martin Heidegger, *Being and Time*, trans. John Macquarrie and Edward Robinson (New York: HarperCollins, 1962), pp. 152, 274.

7. Surprisingly, it seems that black box essentialism works for human beings but not for natural kinds such as gold. As Rorty points out, the determination of an essence involves a judgment as to which properties are important, e.g., that the color and ductility of gold are important and need to be explained, but not where it was mined or that it shines with divine radiance. Such judgments depend on one's culture. Thus, the essence that explains the important properties of a natural kind is relative to a background understanding of being. That the atomic number of gold is 79 is, indeed, true everywhere and for all times, but in other cultures, and other epochs in our culture, that might not be understood to be *the* essential property.

   But, as we shall see, Kierkegaard points to all human beings' susceptibility to despair, namely, that anyone in any culture might someday feel despair, as an important cross-cultural characteristic of the self, and argues that only his account of the self can explain this fact. So it seems that rigid designation might allow us to discover the essential structure of the self, even if it does not justify modern science's claim to be able to determine the unique essence of each natural kind.

8. *Pascal's Pensées*, trans. W. F. Trotter (New York: Dutton, 1958), number 434.

9. *Ibid.*, number 353.

10. *The Sickness unto Death*, p. 43.

11. *Ibid.*, p. 44.

12. *Ibid.*, p. 54.

13. *Ibid.*, p. 51.

14. *Ibid.*, p. 45.

15. *Sickness unto Death*, trans. Walter Lowrie (Princeton University Press, 1941), p. 134.

16. Søren Kierkegaard, *Concluding Unscientific Postscript*, 2nd edn, trans. David F. Swenson and Walter Lowrie (Princeton University Press, 1971), p. 498.

17. *Sickness unto Death*, trans. Hannay, p. 43.

18. Søren Kierkegaard, *Fear and Trembling*, trans. Alastair Hannay (London: Penguin Books, 1985), p. 54.
19. *Ibid.*, p. 70.
20. *Ibid.*, p. 71.
21. *Ibid.*, p. 72.
22. *Ibid.*, p. 70.
23. Sartre gives the example of a person who has an emotional crisis as an adolescent; he interprets it as a religious calling and acts on it by becoming a monk. Then later, he comes to interpret the experience as just a psychological upset during adolescence, and leaves the monastery to become a businessman. But on his deathbed, he feels that it was a religious calling after all, and repents. Sartre's point is that our past is constantly up for reinterpretation, and the final interpretation is an accidental result of what we happen to think as we die.
24. *Fear and Trembling*, p. 71, translation modified.
25. *Concluding Unscientific Postscript*, pp. 277, 508.
26. *Ibid.*, p. 508.
27. *Ibid.*
28. *Ibid.*, p. 188.
29. *Fear and Trembling*, p. 79.
30. *Sickness unto Death*, p. 71.
31. *Fear and Trembling*, p. 65.
32. *Sickness unto Death*, p. 71.
33. Friedrich Nietzsche, *The Anti-Christ*, number 54, in *Twilight of the Idols/The Anti-Christ*, trans. R. J. Hollingdale (New York: Penguin Books, 1990).

    Of course, individual world-change needs to be distinguished from cultural or what Heidegger calls epochal change, and also from Kuhn's scientific revolutions, but it is, nonetheless, important to note that all these thinkers share the view that, for there to be genuine world disclosure, there must be total involvement in one's current world.
34. *Concluding Unscientific Postscript*, p. 498.
35. *Ibid.*, p. 178.
36. *Ibid.*, p. 181.
37. *Sickness unto Death*, p. 44.
38. *Ibid.*, p. 46.

CHAPTER 8

Religion after onto-theology?

Adriaan Peperzak

"Religion after onto-theology" was the title of a conference held in July 2001. It summarizes the conviction found among "continental" philosophers that onto-theology is outdated, while religion still (or again) has enough meaning to be considered in philosophy. Of the questions such a title triggers, one has puzzled me more than others: To what extent can we declare that ontotheology (or onto-theology or onto-theo-logy)[1] belongs to our past, either in the sense of a definitively closed period, or as a heritage that is still alive and for which there might still be a future? It is the polysemic word "after" that bothers me most, but if we want to discuss it, we should first try to agree on the meaning of "onto-theo-logy."

Perhaps I am naïve in asking, "What should we mean by onto-theology?" Anyone who has followed the American development of "continental philosophy" should know the group language of its adherents, and not doubt their basic conquests. If this is the right answer to my question, I am afraid that "onto-theology" has become one of those code words that characterize a regional language through which one version of continental philosophy fences off the ignorant – i.e., those who do not agree with the basic tenets proclaimed by the recognized stars. That similar fences are inevitable in all learned discussions might be true (although some philosophers are widely understandable, even to non-professional philosophers); but should we not be alerted when the fence is made of a whole range of key words which by themselves are not clear enough to convey an insight into the news they summarize? All of us know examples of such words. Most of them have at least two meanings according to the context in which they are used. As elements of the everyday language, they are perfectly understandable by anyone who is familiar with idiomatic English, but as elements of the regional language in which "onto-theo-logy" is used to characterize the past, they restrict their meaning to a particular interpretation of their use in characteristic contexts of a particular philosophy. Such double meanings are found, for example, in "presence," "subject" ("after the subject"), "foundation," "violence," "transgression," and "impossible," while examples of *philosophical* words whose meanings have become different from their *historical* meanings are "cause," "ground," "idea," "metaphysics" and "metaphysics of presence," "ethics" (cf. "against ethics"), "modern" (cf. "post-modern"), "Plato," "Platonism," and "Neoplatonism."

The difference between the peculiar meanings that many words have within the language of a certain school and their meaning in "ordinary" or historical use has struck me most when studying such classical authors as Plato, Plotinus, Aquinas, or Hegel. Often I did not recognize their work in interpretations whose orthodoxy is not contested by most members of that school.[2] Their "reading" might be interesting in itself and point at hidden promises of the interpreted texts, but do they facilitate our discovery of the latter's meaning? This question becomes even more critical when certain "post-modernists" try to justify their anti-onto-(theo)-logical position by biased or false interpretations of the best metaphysical texts. When such interpretations are accepted by those who skip a personal fight with the classics, their access to the past is blocked – but then also their access to the present, insofar as this lives on the capital of its heritage.

If certain concepts, such as "presence," "metaphysics," "grounding," and "founding," are used to summarize and outdo entire œuvres, they prevent or distort direct study; and if a new orthodoxy wins over personal confrontation with those œuvres, philosophy has become a scholastic enterprise. Appeals to hermeneutic authorities, repetition, simplification and hardening, arrogance, and trivialization then imprison thought. Scholasticism not only blocks originality, however; it also blocks the possibility of transforming the past into a future. By condemning, for example, 2,600 years of "metaphysics" and "ontotheology," we waste a heritage that could have been promising, if we had not been insensitive to its wealth. By thinking of ourselves as "after metaphysics," or "after ontotheology," we might have already lost one of the most promising promises.

ONTO-THEO-LOGY

If the word "onto-theo-logy" is used to characterize a certain past as closed and no longer inspiring, what exactly then lies behind us? It cannot be the logical element in ontotheology that irritates us if we want to continue using some sort of logic in our meditations. Does the *theos* or the *theion* bother us? But why then is there still "religion" after all? Or does religion not imply some reference to the divine, the godly, "the God or the gods"?[3]

We will come back to the latter question, but let's focus first on the "*on*" (beings) in "onto-theo-logy."

By way of preparation it may be necessary to consider the particular interpretation of the word "onto-theo-logy" that has become a shibboleth for those who use it to distinguish their own thought from an allegedly obsolete past: the interpretation given by Heidegger in "The Onto-theological Constitution of Metaphysics."[4] Since there is no room for a close reading of this intricate text here, I will limit myself to a succinct summary of the passages that are immediately relevant for our purpose, from which I will then draw a few conclusions.

(1) Heidegger criticizes the entire onto-theo-logical tradition as irreligious insofar as it is "perhaps" (*vielleicht*) further removed from the godly God than "the god-less thinking that must give up the God of philosophy, the God as *causa sui*" (*ID*, p. 71). I take the word "perhaps" in the quoted phrase as a rhetorical formula of politeness, because the next sentence firmly declares: "This means here only: It [scil. the god-less thinking] is freer for the godly God than onto-theo-logic likes to acknowledge" (*ID*, p. 71).

(2) The phenomenological criterion Heidegger offers for the recognition of a godly God is that humans can "pray and sacrifice to him," "in awe fall on their knees," and "make music and dance for this God" (*ID*, p. 70). This criterion fits many religions, especially the Greek one (think, for instance, of Homer's description of the funeral rites for Patroclus). Applying it to the philosophical tradition, which has always been an onto-theo-logical tradition, Heidegger concludes that those religious activities are not possible with regard to the God of philosophy. I interpret this to mean that the latter does not invite or inspire music making, dancing, sacrifices, and prayers as appropriate answers to his emergence from the philosophical tradition.

(3) Heidegger declares that the quintessence of the ontotheological God lies in his being a "cause of himself" (*causa sui*). Without analysis or presentation of the relevant texts, he refers here to a name of God that is found in modern, mainly Cartesian and Spinozistic, texts.[5]

(4) Heidegger comes to this result of his survey of Western onto-theology by insisting on the "grounding" (*gründen*), "founding" (*begründen*), and "finding out" or "fathoming" (*ergründen*) that, according to him, has obsessed the tradition. He apparently thinks that the philosophers could not stop their quest for grounds once they arrived at God, whom some of them called the first or ultimate "cause" (*archē*, *aitia*, *causa*) (*ID*, pp. 54–7). Without paying attention to the historical polysemy of the word "cause" (including the meanings of *eidos*, *idea*, *morphē*, *forma*, *ousia*, *telos*, *hylē*,

materia, esse, existere, and *essentia*), Heidegger declares that "the most originary *Sache*" itself has been thought to be not only the ground of the being
of all beings, but also the ground or *cause* of *itself*. This, he writes, is the
appropriate or pertinent (*sachgerechte*) name of God within philosophy
(insofar as it has been a *founding* discipline). He thus states, but without
proof, that the philosophical tradition has been blind to the question of a
groundless beginning or origin.[6]

In response to Heidegger's text, I can only summarize, in the form of
counterpoints, what I see as theses guaranteed by the best historical scholarship, most of which I have checked within the limits of my own struggle
with classical texts of the philosophical tradition.

For a fair assessment of (4) Heidegger's diagnosis, and especially of his
view that the ontological framework of Western philosophy is permeated
by the logic of a grounding thought, a full retrieval of all the great classics
would be necessary. That would demand (a) a full rehabilitation of those
thinkers who are excluded from Heidegger's history of philosophy, namely
all post-Aristotelian "Greeks" (i.e., all thinkers from 300 BC to AD 600),
most Christian thinkers from Justin and Clement (± AD 200) to Cusanus
(± AD 1500), all Jewish and Muslim thinkers, all English and American
thinkers, all French thinkers except Descartes, and some other geniuses
such as Spinoza, Jacobi, Marx, Freud, Blondel, and Bergson. From my
perspective, Heidegger's circumvention of the entire period of what the
Enlightenment's ignorance called the "dark ages" is particularly ominous. If
we want to know how philosophy of religion might be possible, shouldn't
we learn from those who were highly skilled professionals not only in
philosophy, but also in religion? (b) Such rehabilitation would also demand
the recognition that the classics have not submitted God to the question:
What is the ground of God? On the contrary, all of them – and most
clearly the Neoplatonists – have insisted on the abyss that separates *all*
caused causes and connections, as integral parts of the universe or the *Nous*
(spirit), from God as the One who cannot be caught by any categorical or
conceptual grasp.

With regard to the third point, concerning God as *causa sui*, I claim
that a close reading of the passages in which Descartes, Spinoza, and Hegel
call God *causa sui* shows that this name, in conjunction with the other
names they use ("the infinite," *substantia*, *Geist*) does not justify Heidegger's
interpretation. Heidegger ignores or hides the stubborn resistance of most
thinkers from Antiquity to the end of the Middle Ages to the theological
use of the expression "*causa sui*." No great philosopher has ever maintained
that God is the cause or ground of his own being, and even Spinoza and

Descartes did not and could not think that, because it is unthinkable, a pure contradiction.[7]

As for (2) Heidegger's appeal to his own criterion for a godly God, it is remarkable that, for example, Bonaventura, whose profound involvement with religion cannot be doubted, did not have any problem with an ontological approach to God. In the fifth chapter of his *Journey of the Mind to God*, Bonaventura refers to God as *esse ipsum* in a specific, infinite (and therefore utterly obscure, but supremely meaningful) sense, but he subordinates this rather Aristotelian onto-theo-logy to a more Platonic and Dionysian evocation, while integrating both traditions in his theological version of God as revealed in the life of a crucified man.[8]

As for (1) Heidegger's suggestion that a godless thinker or a godless time might be closer to the authentic God than "the philosophers" (and thus very close to authentic mystics), this question cannot be decided by a general statement or an individual testimony. I gladly agree that certain atheists can be more religious than certain Christians or Jews, and that certain experiences and expressions of the practical and theoretical atheism of our time might have mystical aspects, if indeed we take religion on its deepest level; but I do not see why the ontological program as such would be an obstacle to approaching God, and I am sure that Heidegger has not proved that it would be. Whether it is the *best* way for a thinker to reflect about religion as a communitarian and individual dimension of life remains to be seen, however. Besides, is onto-logy not a correct translation into Greek of Heidegger's own *Denken des Seins*? And if we take Heidegger's Hölderlinian religion seriously, may we not characterize his meditation on the gods of that religion as an onto-theo-logy (or perhaps rather an onto-theio-logy)?

If the onto-theo-logical project that has fascinated the great minds from Parmenides to Hegel (i.e., during 2,400 years of the 2,600 philosophy has lived) is not destroyed by Heidegger's critique, and if no pre- or post-Heideggerian thinker has given a more convincing refutation, we must ask whether that long tradition can still be retrieved in a way that allows for the recognition of a godly God. The question itself implies that we know what "godly" means, but is that not precisely what we want to discover? As a criterion that might guide our search, I choose only one word from Heidegger's description of authentic religion: *prayer*, though I am not sure whether we understand it in the same way.

What religion is and how it can be lived in authentic and inauthentic ways cannot be stipulated by philosophers independently; it is lived religion itself that decides about this. Just as art cannot be constructed by philosophy, religion has its own criteria for authenticity. True, some or even many requirements of philosophy coincide with the requirements of religion, but religion has its own origin and orientation, and its attitude differs from the philosophical attitude.

It is obvious that nobody is able to talk in the name of religion as such, because religion, just like art, exists only in concrete varieties, and no one represents all of them in an authentic way. What we can do, however, is to state clearly what, after having lived and experienced a particular religion, we believe has been discovered as a core without which no religion would be possible, though each religion has its own version of that core. The unfolding of that core and its self-critical evaluation might need or invite philosophical skills; it might thus generate philosophical and/or theological discourses and texts, but no religion would recognize itself – and certainly not its most authentic version – in a "religion" that is independently construed, deduced, or imagined by philosophy. My own experience of Christian life has led me to the conviction that religion in its full, corporeal, communitarian, historical, individual, and spiritual (i.e., charitable and contemplative) sense can be summarized as trust or faith in God, if we include in this expression gratitude and hope, grace and peace. All these words simultaneously veil and reveal one unique "relation," which can also be expressed in the word "prayer," if this is understood in its deepest and simplest sense – scil. as the most originary and all-permeating responsivity of an existence in devotion to the creative, all-permeating, and healing God.

It seems to me that "prayer," of which I venture here a clumsy description, can be recognized as a summary of religion by the faithful adherents of all religions, though, of course, its unfolding into communal traditions, practices, liturgies, laws, and beliefs shows many apparently irreconcilable differences. Whether philosophers can recognize their own philosophical faith (for philosophers, too, have a faith) in "prayer" depends on many factors, but that at least some form of prayer is central to all religions can hardly be denied. If my statement may be accepted not only as a "subjective" impression but as a (hypo)thesis that deserves to be considered, we can simplify our problem by asking how the onto-theo-logical project can be related to the possibility and actuality of prayer. As I hope to show, this question is fundamentally a question about the relation between two basically different attitudes. But before we come to that, we must ask ourselves why the God to whom Abraham, Isaac, Jacob, Moses, David, and Jesus prayed seems to be forgotten or even contradicted by "the God of the philosophers." According to an answer this question has often received, the God of the philosophers is not interested in human history or nature;

he is not an inspiring, protecting, compassionate, creative and recreative, saving, and consoling presence. Is he even a person?

I allude here to the view of those who oppose the philosophical God to the God of their faith as an impersonal to a personal God. However, can they explain what it means to conceive of God as a person? What we know about persons concerns a multitude of individual and finite human beings, but God is neither finite nor an individual. Can we, by thinking, purify the concept of a person of its individual and finite constrictions? Can we think an infinite person? If we can, this will not be enough to approach God, because God is not only the infinite Other; he/she/it is also that in which "we live and move and have our being" (Acts 17:28). But let us reserve the latter thought for a later moment of our investigation.

Though I am not wholly convinced that the God of philosophy (e.g., Plato's Good, and Plotinus' or Bonaventura's One) is necessarily cold and impersonal, I do agree that *modern*, and to a certain extent *all*, concrete attempts at ontology and ontotheology have (at least partially) failed because they were not capable of clarifying what and how *persons* are. If you permit me a sweeping generalization for the sake of clarity, I would like to say that Western philosophy, since its beginning, has remained a reflection about things, *res*, *realia*, reality, the cosmos, *physis*, nature, the world; entities that can be objectified, posited, put in place, set, caught in theses and antitheses, thematized, treated as pieces, parts, or moments of a cosmos; an overseeable totality, a panoramic whole. The paradigm in light of which philosophers have considered being was not beings (*to on*, *onta*) as such, but *thematizable*, and in this sense *objectifiable*, beings. In this light, human beings were treated as special sorts of things (*res*). Their *essentia* was treated as a *realitas* different from, but wholly connected with, other parts of the world.

The clearest example of such treatment we find in social philosophy. From Hobbes to Hegel, human beings were thought of as moments of a system, parts and participants of a world whose structure could be reconstructed *ordine* and *more geometrico*. The thinker was an engineer who not only analyzed the existing community as a complex system but also ventured to construct a better system, called utopia, while puzzled by the fact that the existing social systems did not work so well as the system of nature.

An obvious objection to the thesis that even modern philosophy did not develop a philosophy of the person is found in the overarching importance of the *ego* that thinks, the birth and growth of psychology in all its varieties, the thorough analyses of self-consciousness, and so on. However, twentieth-century behaviorism shows how little humanity can be found in a discipline that focuses on human existence. Phenomenology has reminded us that material objects do not guarantee an appropriate perspective for their "formal" treatment. As I will argue further on, modern philosophy was not able to discover the quintessence of human personality for two reasons: (1) it has not developed a theory of intersubjectivity as distinct from sociality, and (2) its attitude and method do not allow us to encounter and fully perceive what is proper to persons.

Other objections to my (hypo)thesis can be made through commentaries on Kant's and Hegel's theories of subjectivity and intersubjectivity. As for Hegel, I must refer to my studies on Hegel's practical philosophy,[9] but with regard to Kant, I recognize that the basis of his ethics shows a sense for the extraordinariness of human personality, insofar as the basic *fact* to which he appeals (the "fact of reason") includes a dignity that is irreducible to any impersonal value or economy and thus differs radically from all thinghood or *res*-like "*reality*."[10] However, his explication of this fact (humanity in myself and others is not a means, but an "object" or "end in itself"), though fitting well in his framework, does little justice to the phenomenon that he tries to describe.

A third response to my (hypo)thesis could be that Heidegger has given us something like or something better than a philosophy of the person in his phenomenology of *Dasein* as temporal and historical being-in-the-world-with-others. Again, a long discussion would be necessary to come to an agreement about this claim. My strategy in such a discussion would be to stress the following points:

(1) Heidegger's *Sein und Zeit* can be read as a partial fulfillment of the ontological project. Initiated by Aristotle, this project emerges from the impossibility of thinking "being" in a univocal way. While maintaining that "being" is all-encompassing, it recognizes various modes and dimensions of being, which cannot be conceived of as species of one genus. Heidegger has followed the injunction implicit in Aristotle's *legetai pollachōs*, insofar as, against those who reduce all being to *Vorhandenes* and *Vorgestelltes*, he shows that *Zuhandenheit*, worldliness, and *Dasein* – including its *Existenzialia* such as *Jemeinigkeit, Geworfenheit, Mitsein*, and *Zeitlichkeit* – are different or otherwise than the being of things and objects. But, however groundbreaking and splendid his descriptions are, the horizon of his enterprise remains within the orbit of the modern egology, according to which all beings are there (or given) to and for a center whose awareness encompasses all of them within the total but finite horizon of its universe. This explains why Heidegger's philosophy of intersubjectivity is reduced

to a very general indication of *Mitsein* and a few wise, but unsystematic, remarks about *Fürsorge*.[11] The other is one of the beings that belong to the wider world in which *Dasein* is involved; he or she can leave the scene as soon as the massive importance of such collective phenomena as *das Man*, *das Volk*, or the *schicksalhafte Gemeinschaft* is discovered.

(2) At this point, the lessons of Emmanuel Levinas interrupt the Heideggerian phenomenology of *Dasein*'s "being-in" (*Insein*). To a certain extent, the phenomenology deployed in *Totality and Infinity*[12] can also be interpreted as a partial fulfillment of the ontological project, but in its realization something dramatic happens that makes a rethinking of that project necessary. In his first *opus magnum*, Levinas's wavering between an ontological and a meontological language is remarkable.[13] The reason for this wavering lies in a certain indecisiveness with regard to the question of whether "being" should be accepted as the absolutely all-embracing word or rather reserved for all beings except God. In an ontological language, one could express the abyss between the totality and God as the difference between the universe of finite beings and the only one infinite being; but it is obvious that "being" then cannot be understood as generically encompassing both. The difference between the finite and the infinite is itself infinite; God is not *a* being and therefore not a highest being, either. And why should we use the same word for two "realities" that are infinitely different?

The only alternative seems to lie in finding another word for God, while continuing to use "being" for all finite beings. The word "infinite" could be tried out to name God, as Scotus and other thinkers have done, but Levinas uses this word (for reasons we will see) also for the description of the human other, which makes that word ambivalent. Already in *Totality and Infinity* Levinas appeals to Plato's difference between *ousia* (being or essence/*essance*) and *to agathon* (the Good) as names for the world of beings and God, respectively. The Good, or God, is neither a being, nor an essence, nor being (*ousia* or *einai*) as such. However, with regard to religion, Levinas's main thesis holds that the relation to God (which I have named "prayer") coincides with the relation to the other human person. In order to retrieve Levinas's thinking about religion, we must therefore pass through his phenomenology of the human other. His approach to God and his philosophy of prayer cannot be separated from his analysis of interhuman proximity, but for the sake of clarity, we can provisionally focus on the latter aspect.

(3) Presupposing your acquaintance with *Totality and Infinity*, I here resume some of its main points insofar as they are relevant for a possible retrieval of the onto-theo-logical project. In doing so, I will use the

language of phenomenology, although Levinas has progressively replaced this language with another language that tries to avoid such expressions as "phenomenon," "appearance," "manifestation," "experience," "being," and even "consciousness."

Someone who looks at me or speaks to me cannot be seen or understood as a part or moment of the world. In a face-to-face relation, you do not belong to me, who am settled in the world. Levinas does not claim that Heidegger is wrong in showing that we are involved and always already engaged in the world – on the contrary, in both *Totality and Infinity* and *Otherwise than Being*[14] he gives his own phenomenology of our worldly or "economic" mode of being – but he denies that this worldly involvement, as still dominated by the centrality of me, ego, is the absolute or ultimate horizon of life and thought. The appearance of a human other disrupts this horizon; he or she is "a hole" in the world's being, an exception and contestation of the economic universe ruled by laws of interest and exchange. As a code name for our being-with(-one-another), *Mitsein* resumes our sharing one world within which *we*, as much as everything else, are exchangeable. The social context in which we are involved by birth and enculturation is basic for a hermeneutical perspective on our being-there. Levinas recognizes and stresses its importance for our hedonic, interested, civil and political dwelling, working, and thinking. However, the Other who speaks to me or looks at me urges and obliges me to respect and esteem her existence – not by what she says or does, but by the fact of her meeting me. Presentation imposes obligation. The Other's face or speech or gesture cannot be treated or conceived of as one of the exchangeable things or events that populate and compose the "world"; they do not fit the economy of values and equivalences, as Kant already firmly stated. Another human neither is nor has a value. While Kant states that a person has dignity (*Würde*), not a value (*Wert*),[15] Levinas affirms that the Other has "height" (*hauteur*). In comparison to all the interchangeable elements of "the world," this height is absolute and "*infinite*."

The reason why the word "height" is chosen by Levinas to describe what phenomenologically distinguishes the emergence of the Other "in" and "from" the world is twofold. The first reason lies in the *fact* that the Other's existence before me is experienced as simultaneously and indivisibly being a command: the Other's existence, as present before me (or rather turned toward me), obligates me. The scission between is and ought is not pertinent in this "case." Theory and practice, violently separated by Descartes and his followers,[16] are bound together in the Other's face and my appropriate perception of its demanding factuality. That I experience the Other as commanding me does not have anything to do with a difference in social (or other worldly) *roles*, such as those of master and valet or husband and wife. As a radical and "quasi-transcendental" (or, as Levinas says, "pre-original" and "an-archic") "fact," the Other imports a pre-social and pre-political, pre-scientific, and pre-theoretical perspective into my being-in-and-belonging-to-the-world. Thus it becomes clear that Levinas responds to the modern question of how we can understand intersubjectivity: the presuppositions that the Other is *primarily* an *alter ego* and that ethics must be grounded on non-normative and value-free facts are false. A freer and more adequate description shows otherwise. The second reason for using the words "high" and "infinite" for a characterization of the Other lies in Levinas's thesis about the coincidence of ethics and religion. The only possible contact with God, "the Most High,"[17] who cannot be seen or felt, lies in a fully appropriate response to the presence of human Others. Religion is charity. The two main commandments are one. Those who recognize here a long biblical tradition and accuse Levinas of translating his faith into philosophy seem to suggest that one cannot be a serious philosopher if one shows phenomenologically that certain convictions can *also* be understood – at least in part or approximately – from the standpoint of philosophy.

If Levinas is right, many implications can be made explicit that shock the foundations of modern and post-modern philosophy, probably even of the entire philosophical tradition of the West. I would like to dwell a while on one of these implications.

If Levinas recognizes that, on the one hand, we are in the world,[18] while, on the other hand, the Other disrupts my worldly life, it is obvious that he must look for a synthesis of both perspectives by subordinating the world (or the totality) and our economic, social, political, and scholarly involvement in it to the moral dimension opened by the Other's facing and speaking. I, the subject whom the Other obligates, am steeped in the economy of a world that we share, the world of our *Mitsein*, but the face-to-face shows that you – but also I, as facing and speaking to you – are rooted in another dimension than the worldly one. The world and *Mitsein* do not form the ultimate and absolute horizon; the moral perspective disrupts and pierces that horizon and shows its relativity. The infinite refutes the pretensions of the totality to be the ultimate. But if the totality, and therewith the horizon and context of the universe of beings, is not the ultimate, is philosophy itself then not dethroned? Not if philosophy itself can recognize, produce, or accept the infinite difference between the totality and the infinite. That is, if the Platonic difference between the being of all (finite) beings and the Good can still be retrieved.

(4) At this point, I would like to make a metaphenomenological remark with regard to all Levinas's statements about the human other as a hole in being, as coming from on high, as disruption of the world and interruption of the economy, and so forth. Such statements can be justified only if the life of the speaker or writer himself is involved in the relation expressed by those statements. In other words, the perception of the Other is possible and true only if it is achieved in the first person – me.

This is the condition of all basic experiences in ethics and religion, and ignorance of it has caused many false and superfluous problems. That all philosophy must ultimately be founded on the *immediacy* of surprising phenomena has been known since Aristotle's epistemology, and phenomenology has elaborated this insight in its descriptions of the intuitive elements of all acquaintance and understanding. Less attention has been paid, however, to the extent to which the first-person perspective of an involved speaker is a necessary component of many statements whose truth cannot be "seen" by outsiders.

If, for example, "the Other" is nothing else than person B who is seen by person A (while I, the speaker, am the Cogito who reflects about the universal genus "persons"), it seems foolish to say that B is not equal but higher and commanding in relation to A. The main speaker is here the outsider who, from the height of a panoramic overview, perceives A and B as instances of a universal genus "persons" or "the person" (or "the essence of a person").

Everything changes, however, if I, the thinker, ask myself how you, whom I meet as a phenomenon that surprises and confronts me, appear and what you are. When you face me, you not only surprise and amaze me; your facing provokes me to a response, which I cannot refuse (turning away or keeping silent is also an answer). My unavoidable response involves me in a specific relation with you, but this relation is preceded and triggered by your being-there. The question "Who and what are you?" is now an element of an existential involvement. As part of my life's involvement with you ("the Other"), philosophy itself, including the basic perceptions to which it must appeal, becomes (again) an existential enterprise.

What I formulate here in terms of a first-person perspective plays a constitutive role in Levinas's distinctions between (a) "the Other" and "the Same," (b) the Other and the third (*le tiers*, all others), and (c) the Saying (*le Dire*) and the Said (*le Dit*). Without entering into the difficult discussions of the many complicated problems these distinctions carry with them, I will try to investigate in my own terms to what extent a phenomenological epistemology should be concerned about the difference between an involved speaking and the speaking of an "uninvolved onlooker" (Husserl's *unbeteiligter Zuschauer*), who was the hero of modern philosophy and early phenomenology. If later phenomenologists have replaced Husserl's transcendentalism with a hermeneutical involvement, only Levinas, I think, has given the personal involvement of the speaker and listener (or of the face that looks and the face that responds) in discourse and the face-to-face of conversation its full significance.

(5) If we acknowledge Descartes's *Discours de la méthode*[19] as paradigmatic for the basic position or stance of the modern philosopher, the following features are obvious. One of the first decisions to be made consists of the separation between the practice of life, especially in its utilitarian, interhuman, poetic, moral, and religious aspects, on the one hand, and the intuitions, principles, and scientifically permitted moves of pure theory, on the other. This decision immediately assigns a particular position to the philosopher: It places him outside all involvement in corporeal, worldly, and historical affairs, reducing his thinking to the most uninvolved movement of intellectual elements. Since the task of this purely theoretical movement lies in a metaphysically and scientifically justified (and possibly rectified) reconstruction of the real world in which all of us (including the philosopher) live, the philosopher has a superior standpoint from which he must recreate the world, including the praxis in which he has always already been involved. The philosopher thus studies the natural and human universe from a distance. In order to be complete, he must have a panoramic standpoint, which he finds in the Cogito itself. Since his only access to the Cogito lies in his self-consciousness, he himself is, or participates in, the highest possible viewpoint from which the totality of all things (*ta panta*) becomes visible.

We know how Descartes failed to accomplish the task, whose phases he designed in his metaphor of the tree.[20] Only Spinoza and Hegel, and to some extent Leibniz, succeeded in fulfilling the great program. Most modern philosophers followed Descartes's advice to adopt a purely theoretical – neutral, panoramic, and universalistic – perspective in order to justify the principles of the existing universe, but almost all modern works show weakness in those passages where the original union of theory and praxis and their promised reunion become a problem. Thought has left life behind and, despite a few existentialistic revolts, ethics and religion continue to lead a marginal and unjustified subsistence. For the question of you and me this means that, in this kind of philosophy, you and I can be perceived and treated only as instances of "the I" in general (well known by, but not quite identical with, the philosopher who studies it) or as hardly different varieties of human subjectivity. The human subject has been studied by idealists and empiricists under the species of "the mind," "consciousness" and "self-consciousness," or "the I," but *you* have disappeared from the scene. It did not seem necessary to focus on you in philosophy, since you, as another I, were equal to me in all essential aspects. A good illustration of this viewpoint and the attitude that is expressed in it is found not only in the literature about "other minds" but also in the basic postulates of Fichte's, Hegel's, Husserl's, and Scheler's attempts to deduce a multiplicity of (self-)consciousnesses, subjects, and *egos* from the *ego's* mind.

As for the stance of post-modern philosophy, several of its basic presuppositions notably differ from the axioms of modernity, but with regard to the Cartesian position sketched above, it wavers. Though it is conscious of the erotic, social, cultural, linguistic, and unconscious forces and contexts that co-determine our thinking, the view from the outside and above and the superiority of autonomous judgments are maintained, while the possibility of universal validity – at least in theory – is given up. In practice, however, post-modern scholasticism, sketched above, combines peremptory judgments about impossibilities and necessities with numerous appeals to the opinions and authority of its own stars and traditions.

Everything that can be seen and said from the standpoint of the modern *Ego Cogito* becomes necessarily a part of the panoramic universe that the philosopher tries to systematize. "The Said" (*le Dit*) indicates the economy of this *Ego's* world. Then, your provocative speaking and my response can no longer be heard differently than exchanges within the universal context of a world-constituting economy. From this perspective, my, the surveying philosopher's, involvement in our conversation is only one of the many exchanges between the innumerable, essentially indifferent, persons who make up the various groups, communities, peoples, nations, continents, and so on. Sociology and social philosophy in the modern style take over, whereas interpersonality and individuality vanish from the scene. The old dicta *De individuo non est scientia* and *Individuum est ineffabile* are then confirmed again. The divorce between philosophy and *real* – i.e., not only individual but unique – *lives* is then "justified."

However, if philosophy is nothing else than life's own stylized and refined reflection upon the surprising universe in which it has long been involved, the Cartesian approach cannot be justified. The theoretical neutralization of life, including its affective and practical determinations, cannot be more than an abstractive experiment in unbiased searching for elements that can be recognized by many, perhaps all, other people who remain engaged in life while thinking about it. If reflection remains as close as possible to the experiences of life that can be shared by many, it cannot deny its dependence on the "first-person perspective" from which the most important adventures are perceived and digested. Before I can oversee and analyze the phenomena that amaze me, they have already provoked, affected, and engaged me. One of the most originary affections I have always undergone is the encounter with some "you's," who have prevented my death by greeting me at birth and educating me, listening to me, befriending me, accepting me as a colleague, and so on. "The Other" in Levinas's emphatic sense is a philosophical pseudonym for some neighbors with whom I have become personally acquainted, and, by extension, for all others whom I should look at and listen to in light of such closeness as befits the other who, by existing, demands my esteem. The secret of the stance that allows for Levinas's language about the other as revealed in his or her speaking lies in the willingness of the philosopher *not* to separate his observations from his commitment to the other who appears. Speaking is in the first place speaking *to* another – *in response* to the other's appearance; speaking "*about*" another can be done only afterwards. Responsivity, involvement, commitment, and devotion *to you* precede all that can be said *about* you. To reduce you to an object, a theme, or a problem is the beginning of murder.

(6) Let us now return to the question of whether Levinas's phenomenology of the Other might be accepted as a contribution to the project of a transformed onto-theo-logy. I have said that the onto-theo-logical project can perhaps be renewed if we are able finally to produce a complete analysis of the different but related and mutually referential dimensions of being. The last step we have sketched involves us in a debate on the essence of another human being in its twofold appearance: (1) the Other, as facing and obligating me (you, the neighbor or *proximus*) and (2) the Other as sharing with me the world (i.e., the "third," each other, all people, including myself). If we can finish this debate, we might come close to answering the question asked above of how a *person* or *persons* appear "in general." However, a phenomenology of the Other is only a first step in the direction of a philosophy of the person. While and after discovering how other humans, as *you, he, she, we, they*, and *all of them*, should be respected within philosophy, we should also rethink the essence of *me*. Levinas has attempted to renew the philosophy of the I in *Otherwise than Being*, but perhaps his

emphasis on certain aspects of the relation between the other(s) and me has obscured other aspects that should not be forgotten in a retrieval of the tradition about the ego.[21]

(7) Only a phenomenology of the person in its multiple versions as you, me, we, all of you, he, she, and they can give us an idea of personality, but such an idea is *neither adequate nor sufficient* for an understanding of prayer, religion, and God. Though it brings us closer to the "being" or "essence" of God, it also blocks the ascent by imposing an inherent finitude on any mind that tries to think of God as "a person." We do not have a concept of non-finite personality – the predicate "infinite" that Levinas uses to describe the extraordinary essence of the Other cannot mean that the Other does not have limits – and we cannot conquer such a concept by trying to extend the limits or take them away, because of the *infinite* distance between the finite and the infinite. After exploring the possibilities contained in the concept of a person to direct our mind to God, a phase of negative theology is thus necessary to overcome the finitude of this concept. However, in this essay, I shall leave the necessary negations implicit; instead I shall briefly point to another aspect of our referring to God, which presupposes God's not-being-a-person.

To approach God *in philosophy* we need more or better than a philosophy of personality. We need at least two transitions: (1) one from the "reality" of things to the personality of persons – God as a person to whom one can look up and pray is already better than a cold Object, but not sufficient for true religion; and (2) a second transition from God's being "like" a person or quasi-person to being that "in" which we live as in a "context" and "horizon" which contains in some infinite way all that is given in the finite totality of beings and their different dimensions. Especially in the texts of mystics and very good theologians we find many expressions in both directions: God is not only the Face to whom we direct our prayers; God's presence is also the horizon and the *all* (*omnia* – *esse ipsum*?) in which we move and participate, the fire of which we are sparks, the spirit to whom we owe our breath. All my statements here are extremely sketchy, but they can be made more concrete by the religious and theological literature produced in the last three thousand years of civilization. Their unfolding demands difficult discussions about the intricacies of analogical and apophatic thinking about God, and especially about the theological texts in which learned mystics, like Gregory of Nyssa, Bonaventura, and Nicholas of Cusa, tried to approach conceptually the quintessence of the religion to which they were devoted. At stake here is the question of creation: If God can be approached through the metaphorics around persons and personality, on the one hand, while God's infinity invites us to appeal to an analogically transformed "being-in" and "participation," the entire network of categories related to efficient causality crumbles. Medieval philosophers have always known that the full meaning of "grounding" cannot be reduced to *poiēsis*, and even less to the causality of modern science, but neither of their causes fitted the relation between God and the universe either. Some of them have tried to think of God as a "quasi-form" (*causa quasi-formalis*) of the created totality, but not only is this expression obscure (like all predicates that are attributed to God), but it must also be defended against accusations of pantheism.

(8) If onto-theo-logy still has a chance, and if the sketch presented here makes some sense, the realization of such a project demands much thorough thinking, perhaps too much. The most extensive and subtle discussions about the questions I have briefly indicated can be found in the Muslim, Jewish, and Christian philosophies of the Middle Ages. Authors who were committed and devoted to God through the affective, imaginative, practical, liturgical, institutional, and intellectual possibilities that their religion offered them wrote most of them. Their reflection was supported and animated by a religious experience for which the mystery that caused their (onto-theo-)logical problems did not appear as impossible. In their prayers, the otherness of God and their unity with the embracing quasi-totality of God's presence – i.e., the identity of the infinite difference with the quasi-identity that separated them from *and* unified them with God – was experienced as quite appropriate to the only non-idolic God, although a formulation of this contradictory unity on the level of logic remained clumsy and inadequate. What became obvious in lived devotion broke through the limits of their reflection, because their devotion reached farther than reflection. The latter is tempted by exaggeration and reduction: deism sticks to God's otherness and separation, whereas pantheism exaggerates the identity without being bothered by the abyss. Both have a partial conception of presence, while atheism prefers to stay within the walls of the finite totality.[22]

NOTES

1. If we read "ontotheology" as an "ontology" in which *to theion* or *Deus* inevitably emerges, we can use it to characterize the philosophies of Plato and Aristotle and most metaphysicians, Hegel and Heidegger included. As a *logia* that studies the relations between beings and God, it could be named "onto-theo-logy." An "onto-theology" seems to stress a theological perspective on the being (*to einai, das Sein*) of all beings (*to on*).

2. Some of them, for instance, follow the Platonic interpretations of Nietzsche and Heidegger, but do not always display familiarity with the primary texts. For an analysis of the transformation Plato's *Politeia* undergoes in Heidegger's interpretation, for example, see my *Platonic Transformations* (Lanham: Rowman and Littlefield, 1997), pp. 57–111.

3. As Heidegger so often writes. Whether this expression by itself already includes the thought that the word "god" in "God" and "the gods" has the same or a radically different meaning, and whether its use excludes the possibility of an infinite God, has to be shown by further analysis.

4. *Identität und Differenz* (*ID*) (Pfullingen: Neske, 1957), pp. 35–73.

5. See *Historisches Wörterbuch der Philosophie*, ed. Joachim Ritter, Karlfried Gründer, and Gottfried Gabriel (Basle: Schwabe, 1971), vol. I, cols. 976–7.

6. Cf., however, Aristotle's *anangkē stēnai*.

7. Careful reading of, e.g., Plotinus, *Enneads* VI, in *Opera*, vol. III, ed. Paul Henry and Hans-Rudolf Schwyzer (Oxford: Clarendon Press, 1964), VI.8.13.55 and 8.18.49 (where *aition heautou* is used metaphorically to point at the One's originality and freedom); Aquinas, *Summa Contra Gentiles* (Notre Dame: University of Notre Dame Press, 1975), 1.22 (where Thomas rejects the expression); Descartes's responses to the first and fourth objections to his *Meditationes de Prima Philosophia*, translated as *Meditations on First Philosophy*, rev. edn, trans. John Cottingham (Cambridge: Cambridge University Press, 1996), and Spinoza's *Ethica* (which Heidegger may have read although he never showed any acquaintance with it), translated as *Ethics*, trans. G. H. R. Parkinson (Oxford: Oxford University Press, 2000) suffices to justify the conclusion that Heidegger's claim rests on shaky ground.

8. *Itinerarium Mentis in Deum*, translated as *The Journey of the Mind to God*, trans. Philotheus Boehner (Indianapolis: Hackett, 1993), chapters 5–7.

9. *Modern Freedom: Hegel's Legal, Moral, and Political Philosophy* (Boston: Kluwer, 2001); *Hegels praktische Philosophie* (Stuttgart-Bad Cannstatt: Frommann-Holzboog, 1991); and *Selbsterkenntnis des Absoluten* (Stuttgart-Bad Cannstatt: Frommann-Holzboog, 1987).

10. *Kants gesammelte Schriften: Grundlegung zur Metaphysik der Sitten*, vol. IV (Berlin: Georg Reimer, 1911), pp. 429–37.

11. *Gesamtausgabe*, vol. II: *Sein und Zeit* (Frankfurt-on-Main: Klostermann, 1977), §26, pp. 157–68.

12. Emmanuel Levinas, *Totality and Infinity*, trans. Alphonso Lingis (Pittsburgh: Duquesne University Press, 1969).

13. See my *To the Other* (Lafayette: Purdue University Press, 1992), pp. 202–8, and *Beyond: The Philosophy of Emmanuel Levinas* (Evanston: Northwestern University Press, 1997), pp. 82–6.

14. Emmanuel Levinas, *Otherwise Than Being or Beyond Essence*, trans. Alphonso Lingis (The Hague: Martinus Nijhoff, 1981).

15. See n. 10 above.

16. See *Œuvres de Descartes: discours de la méthode*, Troisième Partie, vol. VI, ed. Charles Adam and Paul Tannery (Paris: L. Cerf, 1902), pp. 22–8, and my

commentary in "Life, Science and Wisdom According to Descartes," *History of Philosophy Quarterly* 12 (1995), pp. 133–53.

17. *Totalité et infini*, 4th edn (The Hague: Martinus Nijhoff, 1971), pp. 4–5.

18. *Ibid.*, p. 3.

19. Translated as *Discourse on the Method*, ed. David Weissman (New Haven: Yale University Press, 1996).

20. See the last pages of the *Lettre-préface* to the French edition of Descartes's *Principia*, e.g., in *Œuvres philosophiques*, vol. III, ed. F. Alquié (Paris: Garnier, 1973), pp. 779–82. Descartes achieved only his metaphysics and a part of his physics, while he hardly touched *médecine*, *mécanique*, and (the scientifically proven) *morale*.

21. See especially chapter 5 of *Otherwise Than Being*. For one of my reservations, see *Beyond*, pp. 176–7 and 226–7.

22. I am grateful for the assistance of Jason Barrett and Ryan Madison.

CHAPTER 9

The experience of God and the axiology of the impossible

John D. Caputo

Who would not want to have an experience of God? But if no one has seen God and lived, who would want to risk it? Would this experience be some very extraordinary and death-defying event, like landing on the moon or being abducted by aliens? Or would it rather be a much calmer, cooler, and more calculated affair, like trying to read extremely complex computer data from the Galileo telescope that only a few highly trained experts can understand? What would "experience" mean if one had an experience of God and, for that matter, what would "God" mean if God could be experienced?

Rather than engage in any speculative adventure, I will keep close to the phenomenological ground, for phenomenology, which is nothing but the cartography of experience, is what for me comes "after onto-theology."[1] Although I will speak of a certain leap, what I offer here is a careful explication of what is going on here below, in experience. On that basis, then, let me pose a risky hypothesis: I will venture the idea that the very idea of "experience" drives us to the idea of God – which may sound at first a little bit like the dream of an "absolute empiricism" that Derrida discusses at the end of "Violence and Metaphysics" – and in a strictly parallel way that the very idea of "God" is of something that (or of someone who) sustains and sharpens what we mean by experience, with the result that the "experience of God" requires a "God of experience." On this hypothesis, then, "God" and "experience" are intersecting, pre-fitted notions that fit together hand in glove. This is all possible, I will hypothesize, only in virtue of the impossible, of what I call, after Derrida, "*the* impossible." The impossible will be the bridge, the crucial middle term in my logic, that links "God" and "experience." I will pursue the hypothesis that the experience of the impossible makes the experience of God possible, or, to put it slightly differently, that we love God because we cannot help but love the impossible. But by "the impossible," I hasten to add, I do not mean a simple contradiction, the simple *logical* negation of the possible, like (p and $\sim p$), which is a cornerstone of the old onto-theology,[2] but something *phenomenological*, namely, that which shatters the horizon of expectation and foreseeability. For if every experience occurs within a horizon of possibility, the experience of the impossible is the experience of the shattering of this horizon. I am resisting all *a priori* logical and onto-theological constraints about the possible and the impossible in order to work my way back into the texture of the phenomenological structure of experience.

THE IMPOSSIBLE

Let us assume as an axiom that *only the impossible will do*, that anything less will produce what the noted Danish phenomenologist Johannes Climacus calls a "mediocre fellow." Climacus is speaking about the phenomenon of the paradox:

> But one must not think ill of the paradox, for the paradox is the passion of thought, and the thinker without the paradox is like the lover without passion: a mediocre fellow. But the ultimate potentiation of every passion is to will its own downfall, and so it is also the ultimate passion of the understanding to will the collision, although in one way or another, the collision must become its downfall. This then is the ultimate paradox of thought: to want to discover something that thought itself cannot think.[3]

On Climacus's hypothesis, the highest passion of thought is to think something that cannot be thought. To think something less, to confine oneself to thinking within the horizon of what it is possible to think, is to fail to extend thinking beyond itself or push it beyond its normal range. Thinking within the horizon of the possible has all the makings of mediocrity, of that measured, moderate middle ground that wants to minimize risk and maintain present boundaries. Mediocrity confines itself to practicing the art of the possible. What Climacus here calls the ultimate "potentiation" of a passion, which means raising it to its highest pitch, means at the same time reaching a point of impotency and impossibility (which are at root the same word, *adynaton*) in a kind of phenomenological *coincidentia oppositorum*. The full intensity of experience, the fullest passion, is attained only *in extremis*, only when a power – which here is "thinking" – is pushed to its limits, indeed beyond its limits, to the breaking point, to the point where it breaks open by colliding against what is beyond its power.

Clearly we can extend Climacus's hypothesis to other passions and other powers and formulate a kind of general theory of impossibility, turning on a certain axiom of impossibility, which might represent a kind of Aristotelianism – a theory of potencies and powers – gone mad but with a divine madness. Thus the ultimate potentiation of desire would be to discover something that exceeds desire, that desire cannot desire, in a desire beyond desire; to desire something that it is impossible to desire because it is beyond desire's reach. Desire is thus fully extended and reaches its apex only when desire wills or desires its own downfall. When we confine our desire within the horizon of the possible, of the realistically attainable, will that not always result in something less than we truly desire? What can arouse desire more than to be told that we cannot have the object of our desire, that it is forbidden or unattainable? Rather than extinguishing desire, does not the very impossibility fire and provoke the desire all the more? Desire is really desire when we desire beyond desire, when the desire of desire is in collision with itself.

The highest potentiation of a passion and a power is reached when that power is brought face to face with its own impotency. The impotency and the impossibility provide the condition of possibility of the potentiation. The very condition that blocks the expenditure is what intensifies it. Anything less than the impossible just will not do; anything less will leave the power intact, still standing within the horizon of the same, and will not push it beyond itself or force it to another register. So to put our axiom very precisely we can say that for any x, where x is a power, like thinking or desiring, x reaches its highest potentiation only when it is impossible for x to act. Thus a power is most intensely itself only when it is brought to a standstill, brought to the point that it breaks up or breaks open and is forced beyond itself; it reaches its highest potentiation only when by a kind of discontinuous leap it moves, or is moved, to another sphere or register, beyond its own proper potency.

EXPERIENCE

The axiom of impossibility, the law of the highest potentiation, goes to the heart of what I mean by *experience*, by the passion and intensity of experience, for an experience must have passion to be worthy of the name. To have an experience is to have a taste for adventure, for venturing and risk, which is the meaning of the root *peira*. Thus to be a real "empiricist" means not to sniff along the ground of experience like a hound dog but to search for op*por*tunities, even *peril*ous ones, like *pi*racy (all of which have the same etymology).[4] So experience in the positive and maximal sense, experience that is really worth its salt – and salt is my criterion of experience – is not for mediocre fellows. The easy hum-drum drift of everydayness is experience only in the minimal and negative sense that we are not stone dead, fast asleep, dead drunk, or completely unconscious, although sometimes, it seems, we might just as well be. Experience is really experience when we venture where we cannot or should not go; experience happens only if we take a chance, only if we risk going where we cannot go, only if we have the nerve to step where angels fear to tread, precisely where taking another step farther is impossible. (Since the condition of its possibility is its impossibility.)

Having, or rather venturing, an experience involves a double operation: *first* we understand full well that it is impossible to go, that we are blocked from moving ahead, that we cannot take another step, that we have reached the limit: *then* we go. We venture out and take the risk, perilous as it may be. First, immobilization, then movement. The movement is mobilized by the immobilization. We take the Kierkegaardian leap into the rush of existence, come what may. First we are frozen with fear and immobility; then we leap. When we go where we cannot go, then we are really moving and something is really happening, over and above the routinized flow of tick-tock time that runs on automatic pilot. The immobilization belongs more to the cognitive domain: we *know* that this can't be done; we have been instructed by the understanding about the limits of what is possible. But then we go. Thus the movement is carried out by a shift to the sphere of praxis and the pragmatic order (which is also related to *peira*), to a certain non-cognitive leap which overcomes the hesitations of the understanding; that is what Augustine calls *doing* the truth, *facere veritatem*. We know better but we do it anyway against our knowledge, or – to give this a sharper edge – we do it for just that reason. Experience is for leapers and risk takers, for venturers and adventurers, while mediocre fellows would rather stay home and let the clock run out on life, preferring the safety and security of their living rooms to the leap. The impossible is what gives experience its bite, its kick, and draws us out of the circle of sameness, safety, ease, and familiarity.

Seen from a modernist and Kantian point of view, the position I adopt is perverse and quite contrarian. According to my axiom of impossibility, whatever conforms to what Kant calls the "conditions of possibility of experience" is precisely not what I mean by experience, while the mark of experience in the highest sense, *sensu eminentiore*, is the impossible, which defies and exceeds Kant's conditions. Experience has to do precisely with what is not possible, with what violates or breaches the conditions of possibility that have been set forth by the understanding. Seen from a

Lyotardian point of view, experience does not mean merely to make a new move in an old game, but to invent a new game altogether. An experience does not move about safely within fixed limits, abiding within prescribed conditions of possibility, playing the game by the existing rules; rather, it ventures forth and crosses the borders, transgressing and trespassing the limits laid down by the understanding, the limits of the possible, of the safe and sane and the "same."

GOD

By "God," I mean the possibility of the impossible, a sense that is both Scriptural and phenomenological. I am not speculating about this name in the manner of an onto-theology, but consulting one of its oldest and most venerable uses in the biblical tradition.[5] When the angel Gabriel visits the Virgin Mary and gives her the startling news, Mary first remarks upon the great unlikelihood that the angel is right, to which Gabriel replies with angelic imperturbability not to fear "for nothing will be impossible with God" (Luke 1:37). When Jesus heals the epileptic boy, the disciples wonder why they could not do the same, and Jesus tells them that it is because they have too little faith. "For truly I tell you, if you have faith the size of a mustard seed, you will say to this mountain, 'Move from here to there,' and it will move; and nothing will be impossible for you" (Matt. 17:20–1). Nothing is impossible for God, or for those who being faced squarely with the impossible put their faith in God and let God do the heavy lifting. When Jesus tells the rich man to sell everything he has and give it to the poor, and then adds that it will be harder for a rich man to gain entrance to the kingdom of God than for a camel to pass through the eye of a needle, the disciples are thrown into despair, for who then be saved? They have reached the point of the impossible; they see that there is no way to take a single step forward. Then, when they have been driven to that point, Jesus says, "For human beings it is impossible, but for God all things are possible" (Matt. 19:26) – including the impossible. What is impossible for us (*para anthropois*) is God's business, for with God (*para theo*) nothing is impossible. That is why Nicholas of Cusa says, and this is another axiom to add to our axiology of the impossible, "since nothing is impossible for God, we should look for Him (in whom impossibility is necessity) in those things which are impossible in this world."[6] Wherever the impossible happens, there is God. The impossible (*adynaton*), then, is a sign of God, like a marker in the road that points us toward God, *à Dieu*, where the road swings off, occasioning a shift from our powers and our possibilities to the powers and possibilities of God, where we pass from the sphere of human rule to the sphere where God rules, which is what the Scriptures call the kingdom of God (*basileia tou theou*). The mark of God's kingdom is that there *impossibile* becomes *possibile*, *adynaton* becomes *dynaton*. The impossible draws us out of the sphere of the sane and the same, of the "human," into another sphere, where a divine madness rules, which is the rule of God.

It follows that the "experience of God" is closely tied to the "God of experience" and that the love of God is tied to our love of the impossible. "Experience" is the sort of thing that calls for God, and the name of "God" is the sort of thing that raises experience to its highest pitch. Anything that falls short of God will not have the bite of experience. By the same token, anything that eludes or has nothing to do with charging experience to the utmost will not be God. In the experience of God, "experience" and "God" are keyed to each other in such an intimate way that experience enters into what we *mean* by God. To which I should hasten to add, what *we* mean by God and what *we* mean by experience, for by tracking experience phenomenologists are always tracking *someone's* experience, not some transcendental, transhistorical "essence" in the manner of classical Husserlian phenomenology; in that sense, phenomenology is ineluctably hermeneutical, probing the structure of a historical experience.[7] So I am trying to get a sense of what we westerners mean, we who have a specific Scriptural and historical tradition behind us, where there is a taste for time and history, for freedom and decision, in a word, for "experience," for what we mean by experience. *The* experience of God always comes down to *our* experience, and our experience is of a God of *experience*, a God who lends himself to experience.

THE EXPERTS OF THE POSSIBLE

We can put a sharper point on what we mean by this experience of the impossible by contrasting it with what I will call here the experts of the possible, the master practitioners of the art of the possible. The experts of the possible practice what was called by the medieval theologians the "cardinal" virtues, which would be precisely those virtues that are possible "for humans" (*para anthropois*), as Matthew has Jesus say, namely, those virtues that remain within the horizon of the powers of human beings. The cardinal virtues are, as the image goes, the "hinges" (*cardines*) upon which a hale and whole human life swings, if we have a door hinge in mind. But since there are in fact four cardinal virtues – practical wisdom, justice, courage, and moderation – the metaphor seems to suggest the hinges by which the four legs of a table are attached to the table top, and hence the hinges upon which our moral life is stabilized and firmly planted on the floor. Either way, the cardinal virtues, which go back to Plato and Aristotle, have to do with the life of *arete*, of human excellence. They turn on the figure of what Aristotle called the *phronimos*, the man of "practical wisdom," or "prudent" man (*phronesis* was translated as *prudentia* in the Middle Ages). Aristotle was the master of those who know what is what about the possible and the actual, the master theoretician of potencies and possibilities, and he thought that you could explain anything in those terms, so long as you saw that the actual moved about within the horizon fixed by the potential and stayed as far away as possible from the impossible. That is the central thesis of onto-theo-logy, which tended to keep a metaphysical lid on experience in a way that I am resisting. The *phronimos* is a well-bred, well-educated, well-trained, and in general well-hinged fellow who knows how to conduct the business of life amidst its shifting circumstances. He is a man of good habits and insight, the noble, aristocratic sort of fellow who shows up all the time in the novels of Jane Austen and Anthony Trollope. We need not strain to use gender-neutral language here because Aristotle was only talking about men; it did not occur to him that women (or slaves) could hit the mark of *arete* just as regularly as men do (which was not true of Austen and Trollope).

The *phronimos* does the good so regularly that it comes to be a kind of second nature for him, a stratum of virtuous conduct layered over his basic human nature so thickly that doing the right thing comes almost as naturally as breathing. The facility in virtuous conduct comes to him by dint of practice, and the practice breeds the "habit," the *hexis*, the natural possession, of hitting the mark, like the skill acquired by an archer who practices every day for many hours. All this practice sharpens his eye so that he can easily sight the mark and hit it. The exact mark is the middle of the target, neither too high nor too low, neither too much nor too little. The mark is the median point of moderation, the well-measured middle mark, right in the center. This moderation does not produce mediocrity but excellence (*arete*), because finding the right mark is rare and hard to do and most people miss it, which is where mediocrity would lie for Aristotle. For example, the *phronimos* knows that "courage" does not consist in being stupid, in putting one's body in front of a six-axle truck that is roaring down a street out of control in order to stop it from plowing into a crowd. He also knows that courage does not mean being cowardly under the cover of caution, avoiding a situation we should confront, failing to speak up when a word is required of us. Now this can be very hard to determine and sometimes requires exquisite judgment. When Pius XII held his tongue about Nazi atrocities during the Second World War, his defenders said that he was being prudent and his critics said that he was being cowardly. The *phronimos* avoids excess (*hyperbole*), overshooting the mark, and defect (*elleipsis*), undershooting the mark. He regularly sees and does what is just right. But this is not a fixed but a moving target, a floating mark that bobs up and down in the flux of changing circumstances, and it takes a practiced eye to spot it, which what defines the *phronimos*.

Now when the *phronimos* runs into trouble, that is, when he hits an idiosyncratic and anomalous situation, then far from falling apart, far from willing his own downfall, far from breaking up from the force of the collision, this well-hinged fellow hits full stride and comes into his own precisely as the prudent man that he is. For the *phronimos* has so sharp and practiced an eye, an eye that so regularly sizes up what is to be done and what is not to be done in most situations, that when he hits an irregular and incommensurable circumstance, he has the insight to make a good judgment, to adjudicate just what is demanded here and now by this particular situation, in just these singular circumstances. He is not bowled over by the oddity of the situation but gets on top of it and reaches a judicious and equitable judgment about just what is demanded, about just what justice requires, or courage. The oddity of the situation does not knock him off his hinges, but he stands firm like a table with all four feet firmly fixed on the ground.

From our point of view, the *phronimos* is a self-possessed fellow who does not lose it, whose highest potentiation is to maintain the calm possession of his powers. He is smart enough to know not to tamper with what lies outside the domain of his own possibilities. He wisely remains within the realm of things over which he retains the powers of disposition, over which he rules with a seasoned eye and practiced self-control. He is, in a word, a master of his powers, an expert of the possible. He undertakes the risky business of the hitting the mark in unforeseen circumstances, which is why we admire his expertise, but he does not dare venture out into that abyss where he does not rule. The latter is the place where there are no experts, where, according to the Scriptures, God rules, with whom all things are possible, including the impossible, where the experts of the possible are forced to yield to the experience of the impossible.

FAITH AND THE UNBELIEVABLE

The *expert* of the possible is a well-hinged fellow, and who can fail to admire such excellence? He knows what is what and remains in control. But the requirement of a genuine *experience* involves taking a greater risk than that, venturing into the domain where our powers of self-possession slip away and we are exposed to risk on every side. So in contra-distinction to the four virtues of the well-hinged, let us offer the three "virtues" of the unhinged – if that phallocentrism is a word we still want to use at this point (virtues suggest something virile). In the interest of coming up with something that comes after onto-theology, let us propose three cases of the frame of mind of those who will the ultimate potentiation of their powers right on up to the point of the impossible, where the highest potentiation of one's powers lies in willing their downfall.

The *phronimos* is a prudent man and he does not do foolish things. He knows what his chances are and he carefully deliberates about when a risk is worth taking. This is the sort of fellow one wants as an investment counselor. So when he believes something we can be assured that he has good reasons for believing it, that it is eminently believable. What he believes is credible, and his willingness to believe is warranted. His idea is the *moderation*, not the *ultimate potentiation*, of belief, not to believe too much too easily or to believe too little with too much resistance. For he believes in things just insofar as they are warranted and reasonable. But that is to believe something just so far as he can see that it is likely to be so, just where the evidence is the greatest and the amount of actual faith required is the least. Inasmuch as his beliefs are organized around the principle of the possible, which is here the probable or likely, he always prefers the situation that requires the *least* faith and the most evidence possible. Once the scale of probabilities tips against him, he will abandon his belief and put his confidence elsewhere. So it is not faith that has won the heart of the *phronimos* but evidence, seeing, where faith is a kind of tentative supplement or prosthesis that he employs while waiting for all the evidence to arrive to support his primary thetic act. But clearly this is a fellow with only a moderate faith in faith, with only a moderate heart for the ultimate potentiation of belief, for is not faith most required when things start to look a little unbelievable? Is not faith really faith just insofar as it tends to be impossible to believe? We need faith precisely when the odds are against us, when everyone else thinks it mad to go on, when it starts to look incredible. Faith is faith not in the reasonable and likely, which is less a matter of faith and more a calculus of probabilities; faith is faith in the incredible. That's when we need faith to go on – just in order to keep on going.

Let us take the case of an innocent man who has been unjustly accused of wrongdoing. At first his friends believe in his innocence and rally around him in support, especially early on, when they do not know the whole story and the facts are on his side. But as the tide of evidence shifts against the fellow, the more faint hearted among his friends fade away and the crowd of his supporters thins. For they, alas, are disciples of the principle of the possible, and they shy away from the axiom of the impossible. They believe things only insofar as they are believable, that is, reasonable, which is to believe something only insofar as it requires a minimum of belief. That is what Johannes Climacus would call the faith of a mediocre fellow who tries to stick to the golden middle where all the evidence is clustered. But this poor fellow under unjust accusation needs friends precisely at the extreme point, which requires a maximum of belief, where all the evidence is against him, in that darkest midnight hour in which he is condemned as a guilty man by all the world. To go on believing in this fellow then, when in all likelihood he is a guilty man, at that point when it seems unbelievable, *that* is faith, the ultimate potentiation of the faith one has in a friend, a faith tried and tested in the fire of the impossible. The rest is just happy-hour companionship, the vacillating support of a hail fellow well met who heads for the door at the first sound of trouble.

Faith does not come down to believing things just insofar as they are believable, but believing in what has become unbelievable, when it has become impossible to believe. Only the impossible will do to fire the steel of faith. At that most extreme point, at that darkest hour, when we have run up against the impossibility of believing and going on, just then, we believe. Before that, it was just a poker game and we were playing the odds. At that point, we reach one of the edges of our experience, a boundary or limit case where our own powers and potentialities reach a breaking point and we realize that we have entered a domain where we have no control, where we do not rule, and we put our faith in God – or something, God knows what, since it is out of our hands. That is one of the ways that the name of "God" enters out "experience." For God to gain admission, for the name of God to come into play, the walls of the possible must be razed and the experts of the possible must have fled the scene. For God is given in the experience of the impossible, when we have reached our limits and conceded that we do not know what to do.

"I believe you, I believe *in* you, I will stand by you no matter what, even if for all the world you are condemned as guilty. I will believe the unbelievable, right on up to the end. And I commend you to God. I will pray for you and ask God to watch over you. For with God all things are possible, even the impossible." For us, for our limited powers, it is impossible, but it is possible for God. For God makes the crooked straight and makes the lamb to lie down with the lion. God watches over the little ones and sets his heart not on the ninety-nine who are in the fold but on the one who is lost, the odd one out. The name of God is the name of one who can make this possible, even if it is impossible. For God is the giver of all good gifts, above all if they are impossible. That is what we *mean* by God, what the *name* of God means, and it is this sort of limit-experience – a term that is in a certain sense redundant – that gives the name of God meaning, what we might call its phenomenological content, which is in the truest sense of the word *experiential*. For to have an experience is to take a risk, to brave the stormy seas of the impossible, to venture out where common sense tells us to stick close to the land and keep the shoreline in sight, to expose ourselves where the odds are against us. We look for God, as Cusa says, where the impossible happens. The experience of God is to "see" the hand of God in the course that things take, to take the course of experience as guided by God, to find a loving hand, a providential care where others see chance, so that when things happen they happen as a gift, not fortuitously but gratuitously. But the gift is not a gift of chance, a bit of fortuitousness, but a gratuity that is marked by a divine graciousness.

Of course, we must concede that this will always include the possibility that the outcome will be a disaster, that God will have permitted a disaster, God knows why. As Qoheleth points out, God also makes his sun to shine upon the wicked and the just so we none of us know how this will turn out. The disaster may strengthen the hand of those who say that our lives are not held in the palm of God's hand but exposed to chance and the play of forces. That is true, but only on the basis of the logic or onto-logic of the possible. For the disaster also strengthens the hand of those who believe in God, because faith is faith in the face of the impossible, in the midnight hour where night is its element and it has become impossible to believe, according not to the logic of the possible but to the axiom of the impossible. I will come back to this complication about chance below.

HOPING AGAINST HOPE

The experts of the possible have reasonable hopes. Their hope is well founded on the facts so that they can have every reasonable expectation that things will turn out well. The physician says that the disease has been caught in its earliest stages and he expects a full recovery. He has treated many such cases before and the outcome is almost always favorable. The future has all the weight of the past behind it; the course of events seems almost inevitable. That is hope with a minimum of hope and a maximum of reasonable expectation. That is hope in a "future-present," a future I can almost see and taste on the basis of the present, a future that is so strongly

predictable that it has practically happened already. I have done everything
that is possible, everything that is in my power, to make the future happen
just as I planned. One is reminded of the "future" for stockbrokers who bid
up the price of stocks on the basis of the expectation of good news – like
the expectation that the Federal Reserve Board will lower interest rates –
so that when the expected action by the Board in fact takes place, nothing
happens to the stocks; the future event was already built into the price.

But in the experience of the impossible, all such reasonable calculation
breaks down and things look hopeless: the disease has spread too far and
has not been caught in time and there is no hope for the patient. But are
not those bleak and hopeless times just when hope is required? Is not hope
really hope only when things begin to look hopeless and it is mad to hope?
Is that not when we need to brave the stormy waters of hope, undertake the
risk of hope, which is, we recall, what having an experience means? That
at least is the opinion not of the stockbrokers or of Aristotle but of the
Apostle Paul, whose favorite example is not the *phronimos* but Abraham,
the father of us all. Abraham is remembered not as the father of the stock
market or of the *phronimoi* but as the father of faith and hope. Abraham
trusted in the promise of the Lord that he would be the father of many
generations just when it was hopeless, when his body was as good as dead,
and he was nearly a hundred years old, and Sarah's body was barren. Being
fully convinced that it was impossible, Abraham continued to hope, even
to the point of what Paul calls "hoping against hope" (Rom. 4:18), which
is, it seems to me, an exquisite formulation of the axiom of impossibility.
Hope is hope only when one hopes against hope, only when the situation
is hopeless. Hope has the full force of hope only when we have first been
led to the point where it is impossible to hope – and then we hope against
hope, even as faith is faith in the face of the incredible. Hope is hope when I
all I can do is to try to keep hope alive even though there is no hope. There
is no hope, I know that and I am convinced of that, but still I hope. Only
the impossible will do for the highest potentiation of faith and hope. The
experts of the possible will have long since slipped out the back door.

But why did Abraham continue to hope even when it was hopeless?
Because "God was able to do what he had promised" (Rom. 4:21). For the
name of God is the name of the possibility of the impossible. We invoke
the name of God in order to "keep hope alive," as Jesse Jackson says – the
name of God is the name of hope for Jackson and for Martin Luther King,
for Ghandi and Dietrich Bonhoeffer, for Nelson Mandela and Archbishop
Tutu – to keep the future open, even when every door has been closed. We
need hope when we see no way out, no way to go, when we are blocked

on every side in an *aporia* more complete and encompassing than Aristotle ever imagined. The name of God is the name of our hope, the power that steps in our weakness and hopelessness. For "if God is for us, who is against us?" (Rom. 8:31). Nothing at all – "neither death nor life, nor angels, nor rulers, nor things present, nor things to come, nor powers, nor height nor depth, nor anything else in all creation" – will be able to stand between us and our hope (Rom. 8:38–9).

Paul says that "hope that is seen is not hope. For who hopes for what is seen? But if we hope for what we do not see, we wait in patience" (Rom. 8:24–5). If hope has to do precisely with the unseen, then, in its highest potentiation, it is concerned not with the unseen but foreseeable, but with the absolutely unforeseeable, which constitutes a more radical and "absolute" future than the "future-present" of the stockbrokers. When the future is more or less planned and foreseeable, time becomes a certain approximation process which gradually edges closer and closer to the hoped-for point in the future, making asymptotic progress toward the goal. Then we are filled with rising expectations. But hope that has pushed to its highest potentiation is blinder than that, more open-ended than that, and cannot see its way. Hope cannot imagine what the future holds, or how things will turn around, and when the unexpected happens we are left wondering how that was possible, given that it was impossible. So insofar as the name of God is linked to the experience of the impossible, it also opens up another experience of time and a certain phenomenology of an absolute future.

The name of God is the name of a horizon of absolute expectation, of unconditional hope. More precisely, the name of God is not the horizon but rather the hope that lies beyond the horizon when there is no hope in sight, no hope on the horizon. The name of God opens closed horizons, interrupts the predictability of the future. When we are surrounded on every side by an encompassing horizon that encloses us within hopelessness, when we see nowhere to turn, then we turn to God. When every possibility has been dashed, then the way has been made clear for God, for with God everything is possible, including the impossible. When we reach the limits of our power to hope, then the power of God steps in to lift us out of despair.

That, I am suggesting on purely phenomenological grounds, is an important part of what we *mean* by God and hope, what *we* mean, as I have said, we in the West, where there is a taste for time and history, in a word, for "experience." Our experience of God is very much tied to a God of *experience* where experience has the sense of venture and adventure, of risk and exposure to the future. I do not deny that this experience of God is *our* experience, and *our* idea of God, whoever we are, we who are an ambiguous mix of Greek and Jew, who live in the difference between the two.

LOVE IS WITHOUT WHY

Let there be no mistake, the *phronimos* has friends and is an advocate of *philia*. He thinks that when it comes to friendship the best should stick with the best and that true *philia* is possible only among those of equal station, where it can be properly reciprocated, so that men may love women, slaves, and animals only in an increasingly weak and proportionate extension of the term. You need friends to be happy because no mere mortal can make it alone. You need a talent for friendship and you need the good fortune not to be born mean, repulsive, and curmudgeonly so that you drive people away from you. Having a closed circle of friends, of people who mutually will the good of one another and support each other when times are tough, belongs to the circle of good that one draws around oneself in order to be happy. A good wine, a good job, a good investment counselor, and good friends are all part of the good life.

Now of all the "virtues" that least lend themselves to the *phronimos*'s idea of measured moderation, love leads the list, for the only measure of love is love without measure. The fellow who says that he loves something – be it a woman or a cause or even his cat – just so far but not too far, neither too little nor too much, all within the limits of reason and moderation, since one never wants to go overboard – is a lover without passion, the very idea of what Climacus means by a mediocre fellow. If upon being pressed whether he loves his spouse or fiancée, this fellow says, after a certain amount of deliberation, "yes, in certain respects, and up to a certain point, very definitely – but you always have to watch out for number one," then whatever it is the poor fellow feels, it is not love. For love is measured by its measureless expenditure, its unconditionality, its no holds barred, until death us do part commitment and giving. Love does not calculate the return for its expenditure; it is perfectly true that one loves and desires the return of love for love, but the return is not the condition or precondition of the expenditure. Love is a gift that is given unconditionally.

Love, too, perhaps love above all, is governed by this axiom of the impossible, is potentiated or raised to its highest potentiation by the impossible. For, after all, what is easier than to love those who love us, who sing our praises, who stick by us, who think well of us, and return our love with love? Is that not even a common practice among the Mafia, an organization not widely known for love? Loving those who are lovable and who return our love with love – is that not possible, all too entirely possible? Does it not rank high among the achievements of the experts of the possible?

But does not love begin to reach its higher registers only when it starts to become a little more mad, a little more impossible, which would mean when what we love is not so lovable and tends not to return our love? Like loving an aged parent who no longer even knows our name or recognizes us? Or loving an ungrateful child who has no appreciation of the genuine bond that unites children with their parents? Or an ungrateful friend who only shows up when he needs a handout and never shows the least bit of gratitude for all we do for him? We are beginning to move into a space where love is tested and fired by the increasing heat of – what else? – the impossible. We start to hit a point where it is not possible to love these people, where the understanding says, "these people do not deserve our love," which is, of course, an eminently reasonable thing to say. But then again, must love be deserved – or is love a gift? If love must be deserved or earned, then it is something we owe to the one who earned it, and then it is more like wages for labor than a gift we give without condition. Is love given unconditionally or do you have to meet certain conditions in order to earn it? Does love always have to have be reasonable, to have a logos, a why, a reason – or is love without why?

But let us raise the stakes still higher, and push love to its highest potentiation. Consider the following hymn to the impossible:

> But I say to you that listen, love your enemies, do good to those who hate you, bless those who curse you, pray for those who abuse you.
> If you love those who love you, what credit is it to you? For even sinners love those who love them. If you do good to those who do good to you, what credit is that to you? For even sinners do the same. If you lend to those from whom you hope to receive, what credit is that to you? Even sinners lend to sinners, to receive as much again. But love your enemies, do good, and lend, expecting nothing in return. Your reward will be great and you will be children of the Most High; for he is kind to the ungrateful and the wicked. Be merciful, just as your Father is merciful. (Luke 6:27–8, 32–6)

These sayings are predicated directly on the axiom of impossibility, turning on the idea that nothing short of the impossible will do, that the impossible makes for the highest potentiation of love, for here we are asked to love the completely unlovable, and to love those who return love with hate.

But that is impossible. To be sure. It is mad; yes, indeed. That is why this love is what it is and why we love this love so much, or at least recognize in it love's highest potentiation, even if we keep a safe distance from it ourselves and would not blame someone who avoided it. Just as thought desires to think what cannot be thought, and faith is asked to believe what is most unbelievable, and hope is called for when it is hopeless, so love is love when love is faced with the most loveless and unlovable hate, when it is mad to love. When your love is like that, then this text from 1 John says that you are the children of love, or of God, for God is love:

Beloved, let us love one another, because love is from God; everyone who loves is born of God and knows God. Whoever does not love does not know God, for God is love…God is love and those who abide in love abide in God and God abides in them. (1 John 4:7–8, 16)

There is no name more closely associated in the Christian Scriptures with "God" than love.[8] That is what God is, and this comes as close as the New Testament comes to a "definition" of God, as opposed to defining God onto-theo-logically in terms of possibility and actuality, essence and existence. Even so, it would be at best a quasi-definition because in saying that God is love one is not de-fining God in the sense of setting forth God's limits and boundaries, but saying that God is unbounded and unlimited and unconditional excess, for love is love only in excess and overflow, not in moderation.

So the experience of God is given in the experience of love. But love is perfect not when love is drawn around a closed circle of friends and intimates, which makes perfect sense and is perfectly possible, but precisely when love is stretched to the breaking point of loving when love is mad and impossible. The God of love and the God of the impossible seem like a nice fit, a kind of pre-fit.

THANKING OUR LUCKY STARS

Thus to the well-hinged experts of the possible, sane and moderate fellows that they are, whose acts are always well ordered within the horizon of the possible and properly proportioned to their potencies, we oppose the experience of the impossible, which is a kind of divine madness that is intoxicated with excess and the impossible, that does not get going unless it is provoked by the impossible, which is when or where God rules.

God – or perhaps just chance? Now we come back to a point I intimated earlier. With the experience of the impossible, we cannot avoid feeling a little like June bugs with which children play of a summer's night, or like fish caught in a cosmic net, twisting and flipping about until the air gives out. Here, at this limit point, *in extremis*, when we are or when someone we love is struck by a potentially fatal disease, a qualitative shift takes place in our experience and we enter another domain where things slip out of our control. To speak in strictly phenomenological terms, the things that are not under our control, where we have run up against the limits of our powers, are the raw materials of religion, the stuff of which it is made, the occasion upon which the name of God makes its entry.

We would do well to make it clear that in this confrontation with the impossible we are not praying for a magical divine intervention in the course of nature. For a God who, upon being pressed by our prayers, alters natural processes is every bit as onto-theological as the *causa sui* of metaphysical theology, constituting a kind of divine super-cause who produces effects that are beyond our human powers. For even *after* the event, after the death of the beloved, when history or nature has taken its deadly course and God has not intervened to stop the disaster or the disease in its tracks, we are still praying. For our prayer is a way to affirm that there is meaning in our lives, that behind the meaninglessness and tragic course that is taken by our lives, both personal and collective, there is a mysterious love, not blind chance, that our lives have meaning for God in the midst of this tragedy. The impossible is not that, against all the odds, there will be a miraculous intervention from on high, but that there is a meaning here, in this impossible situation, that a meaning is possible where it is impossible that this death or illness, this tragedy or misfortune, could have any meaning, for with God all things are possible.

The prayer of Jesus in Gethsemane is paradigmatic in this regard. Fore-seeing the sufferings that lay ahead, he "threw himself on the ground and prayed, that if it were possible (*dynaton estin*), the hour might pass." Then he said, "Abba, Father, for you all things are possible (*panta dynata soi*); remove this cup from me; yet, not what I want, but what you want" (Mark 14:35–6). First we pray for a specific outcome, for what I want, for with God, all things are possible. Then, in a second motion, we amend that prayer and pray for what God wants, that we will have the strength to believe and hope and love that, come what may, God's mysterious love is unfolding in our lives. We do not pray that God rethink the matter and alter his present plans, but that what is happening in our lives, which it is impossible to comprehend, is sustained by incomprehensible love.

Still, the question persists, do these limit-situations necessarily present us with "God" – or with what we sometimes call "the gods," by which we just mean chance? At these limit points in our experience have we come face to face with the gift of God's grace? *Or* with a fortuitous turn of events? Might the impossible be a mark not of the "kingdom of God" but of the domain of fortune and chance, not of love but of luck?[9] Indeed, if we treat life itself as a gift, is it a gift of God? Or is it not just the effect of a quirky molecular mutation taken in some far-off corner of the universe, just an idiosyncratic turn of events in the great cosmic stupidity as it hurtles its way into entropic dissipation? Here we touch upon the question of the gift and its enigmatic hermeneutic.

In terms of the specific problematic of the impossible, the question is this: Can one desire to think what cannot be thought, or to hope against hope, *without* implicating oneself in God or religion? With God, nothing is impossible, but might the impossible be possible without God? Is the "highest potentiation" of our powers an independent phenomenological structure that stands with or without God, with or without religion? By confining ourselves to a rigorously phenomenological ground, have we actually pulled the rug out from under religion? Even if the name of God is the name of the possibility of the impossible, might "the possibility of the impossible" go under another name than "God?" Might the name of God be an incognito under which the possibility of the impossible travels? Might the impossible still be possible, even without the God of the Jewish and Christian Scriptures, with whom nothing is impossible? Might there be an experience of the impossible that would belong to a certain religion that we can call a religion *without religion*, which gets along without what the Scriptures call a loving father? Might the work that is performed by (in) the "name of God" be carried out in other ways and under other names? Might a certain "religion" survive as a residue of biblical religion in the phenomenological structures it leaves behind (if biblical religion has been left behind, which I doubt)? Are not these structures inscribed deep within our "experience," which is the experience of us westerners who have been shaped by (among other things) these very Scriptures, like it or not?

We concede that our lives are tossed about by the winds of chance and there is no benign design behind it all. We hang on to such happiness as we have by a tenuous gossamer thread, knowing full well that it can be broken by the slightest shift in the cosmic winds. Johannes de Silentio said that without faith in God, with whom all things are possible, we can only get as far as infinite resignation; we need faith in God to believe that we will get Isaac *back*, that there will be a *repetition*, for after having given Isaac up one would actually be embarrassed to get him back. For faith is not just believing something in "childlike naïveté and innocence," which, though it is a beautiful thing that can "bring the very stones to tears...does not dare, in the pain of resignation, to look the impossibility in the eye."[10] That is true, and far be it for me to take on as redoubtable a phenomenologist as Johannes de Silentio. *But* since I take the results achieved by Johannes Climacus and Johannes de Silentio to be phenomenological, I can conclude that one might use the name of God as a kind of "placeholder" or "incognito" for our hope against hope.

After all, the name of God means the possibility of the impossible. I did not invent that, and it is not up to me to ban that linguistic usage, to try to outlaw it. The name of God is the name of one who can make the impossible possible; the impossible is where we look for God. That is a large part of what the *name* of God signifies in the biblical tradition, which I am treating here as its phenomenological content, its detachable phenomenological content. For the phenomenon stands with or without the historical religions, constituting a certain religion with or without the historical religions. (The next question is this: Is "the possibility of the impossible" a kind of freestanding phenomenological unit which sometimes goes under the name of "God" in religion? Or is it radically parasitic upon the historical Scriptural traditions, from which we learned it in the first place?) Things happen in this sphere beyond our control "gratuitously," like a grace, but the gift may well be a gift of chance, a bit of fortuitousness, not the gratuity of a divine graciousness. We believed against all the odds and kept the faith in order to keep the future open, but we were prepared for the worst, prepared to go under. Still, we caught a break and our faith and hope were "rewarded." The impersonal course of things took a fortuitous turn. If there is a "gift" here, the gift is not the doing of anyone's generosity and there is no one to thank; if we express our gratitude to the stars, we are engaged in a monologue and we are simply purging ourselves of a need to express our gratitude. We thank our lucky stars, but the stars, alas, do not know we are here.

Still the phenomenological structure of ineradicable faith, hope, and love, the phenomenological structure of this passion for the impossible, remains in place, but without the historical religions, constituting the structure of what Derrida calls a religion without religion. By this Derrida means, and I am following him here, a passion for the experience of the impossible, which is a passion that outstrips the conditions of possibility imposed upon experience by modernist criticism. Modernity is marked by a needless and distortive secularization of our experience, which is why it has come under increasing fire ever since Kierkegaard first gave it a piece of his formidable mind.

There is an ineradicable undecidability here between "God" and "the gods," the gift of God and the gift of chance, mysterious love and blind chance, between two different ways to regard the gift and to treat the course of events, whose discernment constitutes the stuff of what I like to call a "more radical hermeneutics." One might well think that a repetition, however impossible, is just the sort of thing that might be brought about by the shifting tides of time and chance, which could bring Isaac back just as easily as they snatched him away, just so long as we do not give up, which is what the Scriptural traditions call God. We got lucky, the gods smiled upon us – *or* we were blessed by God – and the impossible happened. To be sure, no such hermeneutics, radical or more radical, will be able to provide a general formula for resolving the difference, for there is no higher axiom in virtue of which one could name, identify, or resolve the irresolvable fluctuation in the experience of the impossible. Making a move in this impossible situation is what I mean by radical hermeneutics, which does not set out to resolve this conflict but to identify the precise point of fluctuation at which a resolution, if there is one, would be carried out.

I can – indeed, I would say as a phenomenological matter, I must – love the impossible and think that anything is possible, even the impossible, for only the impossible will do. And if the impossible happens I thank God, *or* my lucky stars. I love God because I love the impossible, but I love the impossible in any case. When the impossible happens, I thank what the great Patristic phenomenologist Augustine of Hippo called in the most intimate and the most powerful phenomenological terms *deus meus*, "my God." Speaking strictly as a phenomenologist, I would say that I thank God because with God nothing is impossible, but the question is, as Augustine also said, "what do I love when I love my God?"[11]

Now, by way of a parting gesture, a concluding impudent postscript, let us thicken the plot and complicate the paradox with a final twist that would call for another and extended analysis: Suppose one said that nothing turns on how one resolves this fluctuation, that as a phenomenological matter faith is faith, hope is hope, and love is love, so long as each is fired by the experience of the impossible, so that it does not matter whether one makes use of the name of God at all? Then what difference would there be between standing by the beloved until the end, even though the situation is impossible, *in the name of God*, for with God nothing is impossible, and standing by the beloved until the end, *tout court*? I have been arguing that the "experience of the impossible" is the way in which the "experience of God" is given. But might the "experience of God" be no more than a name we have for the experience of the impossible, and the "love of God" be no more than a name we have for our love of the impossible? Perhaps. But now we ask, as long as one hopes against hope and loves beyond love, does that matter? Recalling that the *peira* of experience and *praxis* share a common root, does not a certain *transformation into praxis* occur at this point in virtue of which the experience of God and the experience of the impossible are caught up in a cognitive fluctuation that is resolved in the doing, in loving God in spirit and in truth, in spending oneself on behalf of the democracy to come? *Facere veritatem.*

Could it be that the experience of God is given in an experience in which the name of God never comes up? Unlike landing on the moon, might one undergo an experience of God and never even know that that is what happened? Would that not correspond rather nicely to what Derrida calls a "gift," where no one suspects that anyone gave anyone anything? Again, would it not correspond to what theology calls God's *kenosis*, where God slips out of sight in order to let the world come into view, where God withdraws in order to make things possible, all things, including the impossible, for with God nothing is impossible?

NOTES

1. A phenomenology is always concerned with the precise sense of appearing, with the structure of phenomenality, rather than the objective reality of an appearance. Minimally, it would bracket a causal or realist account of experience and adhere closely to a descriptive account, without being in principle committed to a Husserlian theory of "consciousness" and the primacy of the cognitive, as the history of phenomenology after Husserl testifies. In the case of the Scriptures, it would concentrate on the "sense" of a faith that can move mountains rather than worrying about its objective physical or metaphysical possibility, on the sense of the angel Gabriel's Annunciation to the Virgin Mary rather than whether the evangelist records an actual historical episode.
2. Given the many meanings of the word "impossible," it would be arbitrary to restrict the notion of the impossible to the objectivistic sense of a simple logical contradiction, which is but one of its many meanings. Some things, for example, are possible for women that are impossible for men, possible for the wealthy or strong that are impossible for the poor or weak, or possible for God that are impossible for human beings; this last sense plays an important role in this chapter.
3. *Kierkegaard's Writings*, vol. VII, *Philosophical Fragments, or A Fragment of Philosophy* and *Johannes Climacus, or De Omnibus Dubitandum est,* trans. and ed. Howard Hong and Edna Hong (Princeton: Princeton University Press, 1985), p. 37. Kierkegaard's pseudonyms constitute clear antecedent figures in the history of phenomenology: what else are their descriptions of freedom, possibility, anxiety, despair, etc. than phenomenologies *avant la lettre*?
4. Joseph T. Shipley, *The Origins of English Words* (Baltimore: Johns Hopkins University Press, 1984), "per III," p. 304.

5. The name of God is not primarily a matter for philosophical or theological speculation but a historical expression in which a community articulates how "God" has entered into the structure of its everyday life – its births and deaths, joys and sorrows. Its primary sense is found in its *use*, in a greeting – "God be with you" – or a prayer – "O God," – before its occurrence in any philosophical treatise. The name of God will flourish as long as there are such communities, and the speculations of the philosophers and theologians about this name will always be parasitic upon these practices. Philosophers have neither the means nor the authority to ban its use; their main role is to respond to the learned despisers of this name. As William F. Nietmann says, in a religious language, the name of God is not something requiring justification or explanation, but something that is invoked in the face of the meaninglessness of life. See his *The Unmaking of God* (Lanham, Md.: University Press of America, 1994).

6. *De Possest*, No. 59; see the translation of *De Possest* in Jasper Hopkins, *A Concise Introduction to the Philosophy of Nicholas of Cusa*, 3rd edn (Minneapolis: Arthur J. Banning Press, 1986). In *De Possest*, Nicholas of Cusa is content to show the coincidence of possibility and actuality in God: *posse est, posse/esse, possest*, where God is the actuality of every possibility. But in *On the Vision of God* (*De Visione Dei*), he ventures further to show that God is also the coincidence of necessity and impossibility, since God by the necessity of his infinite being is capable of what is impossible for us. There he writes, "I thank You, my God, for disclosing to me that there is no other way of approaching You than this way which seems to all men, including the most learned philosophers, altogether inaccessible and impossible. For You have shown me that You cannot be seen elsewhere than where impossibility appears and stands in the way. And You, O Lord, who are the Nourishment of the full-grown, have encouraged me to do violence to myself, because impossibility coincides with necessity." See *Nicholas of Cusa's Dialectical Mysticism, Text, Translation, and Interpretive Study of De Visione Dei*, 3rd edn by Jasper Hopkins (Minneapolis: Arthur J. Banning Press, 1988), No. 39.

7. I do not think that Ricoeur's attempt to distinguish a phenomenology of essences from a hermeneutic of historical texts and cultures can stand up; see Paul Ricoeur, "Experience and Language in Religious Discourse," in *Phenomenology and the Theological Turn: The French Debate*, ed. Dominique Janicaud et al. (New York: Fordham University Press, 2000), pp. 127–46.

8. One can say this without a trace of supersessionism, for in stressing love the New Testament is just being as Jewish as possible, despite the polemics of the new "Way" against the older Jewish traditions. See E. P. Sanders, *Jesus and Judaism* (Philadelphia: Fortress, 1985).

9. The *phronimos*, for example, knows as well as any reader of the Scriptures that not everything is under his control and that he can only be praised or blamed for the things that are up to him. As for the rest, he leaves that up to *moira* or "the gods," which are an essential element (over and above his own virtue) in what he calls *eudaimonia*. *Eudaimonia*, which we usually translate as "happiness," means having a "good spirit," like a "guardian angel," accompany you through

life and protect you from fortune's more outrageous turns. You need the good fortune *not* to be born stupid, ugly, poor, or dispositionally unlovable, or all of these at once, and to enjoy good luck as life goes on. A good *daimon* bears a resemblance to the loving hand of what the Scriptures call "God" watching out for the least among us, or what Jesus called his *abba* keeping a loving care over us, but within a framework governed not by love but by luck, by the shifting tides of happenstance, catching a break in the cosmic twists and turns.

10. Søren Kierkegaard, *Fear and Trembling*, trans. Howard Hong and Edna Hong (Princeton: Princeton University Press, 1983), p. 47.
11. See Augustine, *Confessions* x.6.

CHAPTER 10

Jewish philosophy after metaphysics

Leora Batnitzky

The intellectual biographies of Emmanuel Levinas and Leo Strauss are re-markably similar. Both are post-Holocaust thinkers attempting to rethink the philosophical possibility of morality after the Nazi genocide and they use many of the same philosophical resources to do so. Both studied with Husserl and Heidegger in the 1920s, both claim a methodological return to Husserl in arguing against what each maintains is the amorality of Heidegger's philosophy, and both claim Franz Rosenzweig as a, if not the, major influence in so doing. The exegesis of classic Jewish texts matters greatly to both of them, and each claims to be returning to Plato. Both have had significant Catholic receptions and both continue to have important in-fluences on contemporary discussions of ethics and politics. Nevertheless, despite these striking historical similarities, from the perspective of their philosophies themselves, one might think that Levinas and Strauss do not have much in common *philosophically* with one another. And if one made this claim, it would be based largely on yet another remarkable similar-ity between Levinas and Strauss, which is their respective constructions of the relation between what Levinas calls "Greek" and "Hebrew" and what Strauss calls "Athens" and "Jerusalem."

As has been argued by a number of recent interpreters, the crux of Levinas's philosophy is his reorientation of "Greek" by way of "Hebrew." In this light, Levinas is thought to be a Jewish philosopher whose achievement is to have revived the Jewish tradition philosophically. In contrast, with the exception of a few recent interpretations, Strauss has been viewed largely as a political philosopher for whom revelation is, at best, of instrumental significance. While Strauss maintained that what he called "Athens" is in necessary tension with what he called "Jerusalem," many if not most of Strauss's interpreters continue to argue that Strauss comes down largely on the side of "Athens." Therefore, Levinas's decidedly "Hebrew" thought would seem to be opposed philosophically to Strauss's decidedly "Greek" thought.

In this essay, I would like to begin to dismantle these assumptions. I argue that there is a profound *philosophical* affinity between Levinas and Strauss precisely in regard to their arguments about the *philosophical possibility* of revelation (and here I emphasize both "philosophical" and "possibility"). Once we appreciate this philosophical affinity we must rethink the view of Strauss as an affiliate of "Athens" and of Levinas as an affiliate of "Jerusalem." I suggest that Levinas and Strauss can be more fully understood in relation to one another than they can be in relation to current conversations about post-modernism (in the case of Levinas) or neo-conservatism (in the case of Strauss).

Let me state clearly that my purpose is not to deny Levinas's or Strauss's philosophical relevance to contemporary post-modern or neo-conservative discussions, and certainly not to limit their philosophies to a kind of identity-politics. Far from it. (Indeed, nothing would be more repugnant to the spirit of each of their philosophies!) Nor is my point to deny the profound, if not irreconcilable, philosophical differences between Levinas and Strauss. Instead, I would like to complicate the frameworks that have been applied to them in order to question what I shall argue has been a largely Christian, if not Protestant, story about religious thought after and "during" metaphysics. I shall suggest that this more complicated story is philosophically significant in relation to questions about the *modern meanings of philosophy* and only by virtue of this about the modern meanings of "religion."

I ON THE IMPOSSIBILITY AND POSSIBILITY OF JEWISH PHILOSOPHY

Let me begin with the title of this essay. The title – "Jewish Philosophy after Metaphysics" – is potentially misleading. My claim is that there is Jewish philosophy neither after nor "during" metaphysics in the sense that Jewish philosophy has *not* been concerned primarily with foundational *proofs* for God's existence. But "Jewish philosophy" *is* concerned with a kind of metaphysics that is not utilized for the purpose of ontological grounding, but rather for its ethical or political implications. Before turning to the details of the position I am describing, let us recall Heidegger's notions of metaphysics and onto-theology, notions that are assumed by much of contemporary discussion of "religion after metaphysics," and notions to which both Levinas and Strauss respond.

As Heidegger defined it in his 1929 inaugural lecture, "What is Metaphysics?," "Metaphysics means questioning beyond beings so as to regain them, as such and in the unity of a whole, for understanding."[1] For Heidegger, metaphysics is coequal with philosophy. Heidegger ends this lecture by suggesting that "Philosophy... means simply enacting the metaphysics in which philosophy comes to itself and to its explicit tasks."[2] For Heidegger, technology is a defining moment in the history of metaphysics because the world of modern technology blocks out what he argues "most matters," which is to "open the space for beings in terms of a whole; then liberate ourselves for the nothing, i.e., free ourselves from the idols that each of us has and goes cringing to."[3] Technology is not merely hardware or software or even scientific method. Most fundamentally, it is the way in which being discloses itself to us today. Entities are too present in the age of technology because we believe that we can truly "know" and manipulate them. Ironically, perhaps, because they are too present, the entities of technology cannot disclose themselves and we cannot "liberate ourselves for the nothing." For this reason, Heidegger sought to return to the pre-Socratics, who he maintained had a pre-metaphysical notion of disclosure. His own philosophy would prepare the way for a new, post-metaphysical beginning. For Heidegger, the end of metaphysics *is* a return to ontology, by which he means a return to the concealment and revelation of being or, as Thomas Sheehan has recently translated *Dasein*, the "being-open" or "the open-that-we-are."[4]

According to Heidegger, the Western philosophical tradition's concealment of being is intimately connected to the history of Western theology. In a 1957 lecture titled "The Onto-theological Constitution of Metaphysics," Heidegger argued that the Western philosophical tradition is itself onto-theological in nature. Onto-theology is the metaphysical quest to ground the being of entities in the being of a highest entity, but onto-theology also characterizes the Western philosophical tradition's fundamental forgetfulness of being. Heidegger maintained that theology's quest to ground the being of entities in the being of a highest entity is made possible by the error of metaphysics itself, which is the inability to distinguish between the being of entities and the being of being. The overcoming of metaphysics is thus by definition also the overcoming of theology (which he understands as always being "onto-theology") as it has been historically known.

Heidegger links metaphysics with the Western philosophical tradition that begins with Plato. As Heidegger remarked in his Nietzsche lectures, "all Western philosophy is Platonism. Metaphysics, Idealism, and Platonism mean essentially the same thing... Plato has become the prototypal philosopher."[5] In an early work defining his philosophical agenda, Levinas revalues this assertion of Heidegger's, declaring that "all philosophy is

Platonic."[6] Levinas, like Strauss, seeks to resuscitate Plato after Heidegger has declared an end of metaphysics. So both Levinas and Strauss seek to resuscitate Western philosophy, though, as we shall see below, with important differences. Levinas and Strauss are further linked by their claim that Platonism itself must be understood within the context of and by way of Jewish revelation. In fact, for both it is *Jewish revelation* that holds the key to rereading Plato after Heidegger and thus, both argue, for the possibility of *the moral restoration* of Western civilization after the Nazi genocide.

More particularly, for both Levinas and Strauss, the medieval Jewish philosopher Moses Maimonides is the paradigm for the revitalization of philosophy and also Western civilization. For Levinas, Maimonides marks the peak of Jewish religion as well as the de-ontologization of ethics and religion. In Levinas's words,

Jewish monotheism does not exalt a sacred power, a *numen* triumphing over other numinous powers but still participating in their clandestine and mysterious life . . . Here, Judaism feels very close to the West, by which I mean philosophy. It is not by virtue of simple chance that the way towards the synthesis of the Jewish revelation and Greek thought was masterfully traced by Maimonides.[7]

Like Levinas, Strauss argues that Maimonides is truly a Platonist. And like Levinas, Strauss places the explication of the possibility of a philosophical return to Maimonides at the center of his thought.

Yet there is a fundamental difference between Levinas's and Strauss's reading of Maimonides, a difference that is in fact noted by Levinas in a comment whose referent seems to be Strauss.[8] Concurring with, though not acknowledging, Hermann Cohen's reading of Maimonides, Levinas states that

Maimonides is not an accident of Holy History . . . in Maimonides himself, to whom rational knowledge of God, metaphysical knowledge, is the supreme good of the human person . . . The imitation of God! The love of one's neighbor is at the summit of a life devoted to supreme knowledge. *This is a remarkable reversal, unless we are to question the sincerity of this teacher, suggesting that he may have spoken otherwise than he thought, to avoid unsettling pious minds.*[9]

In what Levinas calls Maimonides' "remarkable reversal," we find a summary of Levinas's own philosophical project: to present what he calls metaphysical knowledge that is not fundamentally ontological in nature – and thereby not onto-theological – but ethical. It is Strauss who has, in Levinas's words, questioned "the sincerity of this teacher," a position that Levinas elsewhere dismisses.[10]

Whether Strauss considers Maimonides insincere is a matter not only of interpretation but speculation. And one's interpretation of and speculation about this question will depend in large part on whether one accepts or rejects Strauss's basic premise, which is that revealed religion and philosophy are fundamentally irreconcilable. If one disagrees with Strauss's premise, it is difficult to imagine that Strauss considers Maimonides philosophically sincere. On the other hand, if one takes Strauss's premise seriously – that the relation between revealed religion and philosophy is *philosophically* irreconcilable – then one might understand Strauss's reading of Maimonides as a reflection on what Strauss argues (and argues that Maimonides argues) is a, if not the, *profound* philosophical problem.

This seemingly irreconcilable difference between Strauss and Levinas on the question of the relation between revealed religion and Judaism masks what is in fact a deep formal similarity in their arguments. Both attempt to argue that Jewish revelation *provides philosophy* with its most fundamental insight, which is philosophy's need of revelation. *Revelation*, to be sure, means something different for each of them. For Strauss, revelation attests to a divine ordering of the world, while for Levinas, revelation is and remains an interhuman experience. As we shall see in the next section, this difference is highly significant. But in order to gauge the significance of this difference we must first appreciate the formal similarity of Strauss's and Levinas's arguments. To do so, we must turn to a more detailed discussion of their arguments about the relation between Judaism and philosophy.

Neither Strauss nor Levinas attempts to harmonize Judaism and philosophy. For Strauss, such a harmonization is impossible because Judaism and philosophy represent two fundamentally opposing attitudes toward the world. Though they both seek wisdom, the wisdom of biblical religion and the wisdom of philosophical reflection are in marked contrast to one another. Philosophy for Strauss is the search for wisdom that begins with the thinker's unending quest for the nature of the good.[11] In contrast, Judaism is rooted in revelation, which begins not in thought, but in obedience to God and the revealed law.

Strauss argues that we must *choose* between Jerusalem and Athens not only because they are fundamentally different but also because they are in basic opposition to one another.[12] This doesn't mean that one can't be a Jew interested in philosophy or a philosopher interested in Judaism. Indeed, as Strauss puts it, "every one of us can be and ought to be either...the philosopher open to the challenge of theology or the theologian open to the challenge of philosophy."[13] But this formulation only underscores Strauss's well-known statement that "being a Jew and being a philosopher *are* mutually exclusive"[14] because such an identity is self-contradictory.

Like Strauss, Levinas does not believe in the harmonization of Judaism and philosophy. His reason, however, is not that they are fundamentally opposed, but that they are fundamentally similar. In Levinas's words, "I have never aimed explicitly to 'harmonize' . . . both traditions. If they happen to be in harmony it is probably because every philosophical thought rests on pre-philosophical experiences, and . . . the Bible has belonged to these founding experiences."[15] Judaism and philosophy are similarly oriented, according to Levinas. Both approach the goodness beyond being embodied in the responsibility for the other. As Levinas puts it even more explicitly, "philosophy derives [*dérive*] . . . from religion. It is called for by religion adrift [*en dérive*], and in all likelihood religion is always adrift."[16] Philosophy and religion thus exist in a relation of mutuality, for Levinas. Philosophy derives from religion, but philosophy also gives direction and purpose to religion. Judaism and philosophy do not need to be harmonized for Levinas because they are already in fundamental harmony with one another. Judaism, or what Levinas elsewhere calls "religiosity" (*le religieux*) is the pre-philosophical stuff out of which philosophy arises. Judaism and philosophy are thus organically connected. From Levinas's perspective, Jewish philosophy is impossible because it is redundant.

"Jewish philosophy" is impossible for both Levinas and Strauss, but for opposite reasons. Because he believes that Judaism and philosophy ultimately mean the same thing, the notion of Jewish philosophy is at best superfluous for Levinas. In contrast, Jewish philosophy is incoherent for Strauss because such a notion betrays the meanings of both Judaism and philosophy. While Levinas and Strauss both make a claim for the impossibility of Jewish philosophy, both also claim that "Judaism" – as the originator of monotheism – somehow makes not Jewish philosophy possible, but philosophy itself possible. To put it simply, their shared claim is that "Judaism" understands something that philosophy *anticipates but cannot quite articulate* on its own terms. Significantly, Levinas and Strauss each make this point with reference to Plato. For both, Plato anticipates but does not fully articulate revelation. In *Totality and Infinity*, Levinas maintains that the true universality of reason is predicated upon Plato's conception of discourse, which "implies transcendence . . . [and] the revelation of the other to me."[17] It is in fact this Platonic anticipation of revelation that defines ethics as first philosophy, for Levinas. Recall that *Totality and Infinity* is, as its subtitle indicates, "an essay on exteriority." Philosophy, for Levinas, anticipates the exteriority of revelation. Therefore, philosophy is bound to revelation, which reorients philosophy. *Totality and Infinity* ends with a succinct summary of this reorientation:

Freedom is not justified by freedom. To account for being or to be in truth is not to comprehend nor to take hold of... but rather to encounter the Other without allergy, that is, in justice.[18]

Freedom, for Levinas, which includes philosophical freedom, cannot justify itself on its own terms. My freedom is justified by the other, by the other's revelation to me.

Strauss, I maintain, from a formal perspective at least, puts forward this very argument about philosophy's bondage to revelation. Note Strauss's very Levinasian formulation in his early work *Philosophy and Law*, in which he argues that philosophy's *"freedom depends upon its bondage*. Philosophy is not sovereign. The beginning of philosophy is not the beginning simply."[19] While *Philosophy and Law* is admittedly a transitional work for Strauss, the theme of philosophy's dependence on and anticipation of revelation marks Strauss's mature work.[20] Recall, for instance, Strauss's argument in *Natural Right and History* that: "Philosophy has to grant that revelation is possible. But to grant that revelation is possible means to grant that philosophy is perhaps not the one thing needful... or [that] philosophy suffers from a fatal weakness."[21]

The notion that philosophy requires and anticipates revelation is a constant theme throughout Strauss's writings, a theme that, from a formal perspective at least, parallels Levinas's own arguments. One might object that Strauss rejects Jerusalem for the sake of Athens or, at the very least, that we don't know where Strauss comes down on the question of Jerusalem or Athens. In my view, this often-stated objection (whatever its form) misses the mark, and here I believe that the parallels with Levinas are not only important, but in fact decisive.

Before turning to the implications of comparing Strauss with Levinas for understanding the import of Strauss's view of revelation, let me say that even on "Straussian" terms the question about Strauss's "own" view of revelation skews what I suggest is the philosophical question that he poses in regard to revelation. As Strauss puts it in regard to Nietzsche, "Through judging others, Nietzsche had himself established the criterion by which his doctrine is to be judged."[22] Among the criteria by which Strauss is to be judged is his own claim that "the problem inherent in the surface of things, and only in the surface of things, is the heart of things."[23] As Strauss puts it in his discussion about the tensions between Jerusalem and Athens, "If we wish to understand Plato, we must take him seriously. We must take seriously in particular his defense of Socrates."²⁴ Just as Strauss urges us to take seriously Plato's defense of Socrates if we are to take Plato seriously, if we are to take Strauss seriously we must take seriously Strauss's philosophical arguments about revelation. A comparison with Levinas, I suggest, allows us to appreciate the serious philosophical nature of Strauss's arguments about revelation.

If Jewish philosophy is as impossible for Levinas as it is for Strauss, then what we are able to see is that Levinas and Strauss make very similar claims about the *philosophical status of revelation*. Indeed, both of their arguments concern not the philosophical vindication of "Judaism" and revelation – for both Levinas and Strauss, such a proof would be impossible – *but the inadequacy of philosophy conceived without "Judaism" or revelation*. Strauss, like Levinas, poses a fundamental question about philosophy's need to recognize its own possible bondage to something outside of philosophy. If his thought is understood in this way, it does not matter what Strauss's "own" views of revelation actually are, for the *philosophical* question remains the same: Does philosophy require the philosophical possibility of revelation?

In order to begin to answer this question, let us return to Strauss's treatment of Plato. For Strauss it is the Plato of the *Laws* and not of the *Republic* (or, as Levinas argues in greater detail in *Totality and Infinity*, the Plato of the *Phaedrus*) that is definitive for recognizing philosophy's anticipation of revelation. While I do not mean to discount the different conceptions of ethics and politics that emerge from Strauss's and Levinas's respective interpretations of Plato (a subject beyond the scope of this essay), note the striking formal similarity of Strauss's and Levinas's use of Plato. Each uses Plato to argue for philosophy's anticipation, but not full articulation of revelation. Strauss argues that in the *Laws*,

Plato transforms the "divine laws" of Greek antiquity into truly divine laws, or recognizes them as truly divine laws. In this approximation to the revelation without the guidance of the revelation we grasp at its origin the unbelieving, philosophic foundation of the belief in revelation . . . Platonic philosophy had suffered from an *aporia* in principle that had been remedied only by the revelation.²⁵

Strauss analyzes the life world of medieval Jewish philosophy in which "the situation of philosophy was altered *from the ground up* by the reality of revelation."²⁶ Like Levinas, Strauss follows Husserl in the attempt to describe phenomenologically the pre-philosophical life world out of which philosophy arises. What Levinas does for the Bible Strauss does for medieval Jewish philosophy. Levinas and Strauss's phenomenological analyses of these respective pre-modern "Jewish" life worlds attempt to establish the *possibility* of the truth of revelation, a possibility that for both Levinas and Strauss must alter our very conceptions of ethics and politics in the contemporary world.

Most basically, Strauss's and Levinas's interpretations of Plato are in the service of altering the contemporary view that ethics is shaped by culture and history. Each argues that philosophy's bondage to revelation makes possible a *philosophical* glimpse of a non-historicist conception of morality in the contemporary world. In the abstract of his doctoral thesis, which later became *Totality and Infinity*, Levinas writes that ethics

is not a byproduct of self-knowledge. It is completely heteronomous... To state that the Other, revealed by the visage, is the first intelligible... is to affirm also the independence of ethics with regard to history... To show that the first signification emerges in morality... is a return to Platonism.[27]

The common strategy of Strauss's "political" reading of Plato and of Levinas's "ethical" reading of Plato becomes clear. Strauss and Levinas both maintain that when philosophy understands itself primarily with regard to questions of ontology (and here the reference for both is primarily to Heidegger), philosophy loses sight of its most important pre-philosophical foundation, which for Strauss and Levinas concerns nothing less than the possibility of human goodness.

As Strauss puts it in *Philosophy and Law*,

The necessary connection between politics and theology (metaphysics)... vouches for the fact that the interpretation of medieval Jewish philosophy beginning from Platonic politics... does not have to lose sight of the metaphysical problems that stand in the foreground for the medieval philosophers themselves. And this procedure, so far from resulting in the underestimation of these problems, actually offers the only guarantee of understanding their proper, that is their human, meaning. If, on the other hand, one begins from the metaphysical problems, one misses... the political problem, in which is concealed nothing less than the foundation of philosophy, the philosophic elucidation of the presupposition of philosophizing.[28]

Metaphysics for Strauss, as for Levinas, serves political and ethical ends.[29] For both, metaphysics and ethics exist in a necessary tension. Metaphysical speculation philosophically secures the ethical possibilities of society, but politics and ethics make metaphysics possible in the first place. Because metaphysics for Levinas and Strauss is not primarily ontological in character – neither is interested in grounding the being of entities in the being of a highest entity – their shared claim for metaphysics is for a non-onto-theological metaphysics. As Strauss puts it, "the philosophic foundation of the law, in spite of outward appearances, is not *a* teaching among others but is the place in the system of the Islamic Aristotelians and their Jewish pupils where the *presupposition* of their philosophizing comes under discussion."[30] While they understand Maimonides differently, both Strauss and Levinas present a picture of Jewish philosophical thinking – both medieval and modern – that is not concerned primarily with ontological foundationalism. Rather Levinas and Strauss are both concerned with the interrelation between philosophical (what they each call metaphysical) reflection and the possibility of ethics and politics. Indeed, Strauss and Levinas both argue that this is the case for the Hebrew Bible as well. As Strauss puts it,

What kind of God is He?...This question was addressed to God Himself by Moses...God replied: "*Ehyeh-Asher-Ehyeh.*" This is mostly translated: "I am That (Who) I am." One has called that reply "the metaphysics of Exodus" in order to indicate its fundamental character...but we hesitate to call it metaphysical, since the notion of *physis* is alien to the Bible. I believe that we ought to render this statement by "I shall be What I shall be," thus preserving the connection between God's name and the fact that He makes covenants with men, i.e., that He reveals Himself to men above all by His commandments and by His promises and His fulfillment of the promises.[31]

Here Strauss uses the term "metaphysics" in an "onto-theological" sense and argues that the Bible is not concerned with the onto-theological status of God. Levinas agrees in finding the meaning of the Bible and its subsequent interpretations not in attempting to ground the being of beings in some highest entity but in what he calls the rupture of ethics.[32]

We have seen that Levinas and Strauss both utilize a conception of Jewish revelation to defend *not the philosophical truth of Judaism* but the *true possibility of philosophy*, which for both is the possibility of morality. Levinas and Strauss's respective arguments for the impossibility of Jewish philosophy are premised on a shared argument for the philosophical possibility of the truth of revelation. I would like to suggest that as such, when compared with one another, Levinas's and Strauss's philosophies do enact *philosophically* a type of twentieth-century Jewish philosophy. Jewish philosophy would here be defined *only* by the negative task of showing philosophically that Jewish revelation cannot be disproved philosophically and that this conclusion has profound implications for philosophy itself.

Indeed, both Levinas and Strauss fit Strauss's description of the medieval Jewish philosopher Judah Halevi's argument in the *Kuzari*:

In defending Judaism, which, according to him [Halevi], is the only true revealed religion, against the philosophers, he was conscious of defending morality itself and therewith the cause, not only of Judaism, but of mankind at large. His basic objection to philosophy was then not particularly Jewish, nor even particularly religious, but moral.[33]

The "Jewish philosophy" of Levinas and Strauss thus attempts to defend morality to humanity at large. Part of the goal of this essay has been to show not only that there is a profound if at first unlikely *philosophical* affinity between Levinas and Strauss but also that *Strauss's thought* fits this characterization of "Jewish philosophy."

2   ON THE DIFFERENCES BETWEEN LEVINAS AND STRAUSS OR ON THE MODERN MEANINGS OF PHILOSOPHY

If comparing Levinas and Strauss helps us to rethink Strauss's place within the context of the rubric of "Jewish philosophy," the comparison also helps us to rethink Levinas in a number of ways. Perhaps ironically, comparing Levinas and Strauss on the impossibility and possibility of Jewish philosophy shows Levinas to be more of a defender of philosophy (and not of Jewish revelation) than Strauss is. Indeed, this is the implication of their difference on the relationship between Judaism and philosophy. To return to Strauss's characterization of Halevi, Strauss writes:

by going so far with the philosophers . . . he [Halevi] discover[s] the fundamental weakness of the philosophic position and the deepest reason why philosophy is so enormously dangerous. For if the philosophers are right in their appraisal of natural morality, of morality not based on Divine revelation, natural morality is . . . *no morality at all*.[34]

Here, Strauss emerges as the defender of the moral necessity of revelation against Levinas, who maintains that philosophy is not fundamentally atheistic in regard to the proper, philosophical understanding of revelation and that therefore "at no moment [does] the Western philosophical tradition . . . lose its right to the last word."[35] Whereas Strauss argues that philosophy qua philosophy cannot give the law (or revelation) to itself, the implication of Levinas's philosophy is that philosophy qua philosophy can come to revelation on its own terms.[36] Could it be then that Levinas is a modern defender of philosophy while Strauss is a defender of revelation?

As a preliminary answer, I would venture "yes." Recall Levinas's statement, "philosophy derives [*dérive*] . . . from religion. It is called for by religion adrift [*en dérive*], and in all likelihood religion is always adrift."[37] While Levinas is critical of aspects of the Western philosophical tradition, his task is to return this tradition to what he argues is its true meaning: Plato's notion of a good beyond being. One could argue that Strauss's task also is to return the Western philosophical tradition to its former glory. While this is certainly one aspect of Strauss's project, the comparison with

Levinas allows us to see that for Strauss, philosophy is much more limited when it comes to ethical and political matters than it is for Levinas. Strauss argues strongly that philosophy *itself* cannot articulate a universal ground for morality, while Levinas contends that it is a matter of finding the right philosophy to articulate this philosophical ground.

Strauss argues that philosophy is fundamentally limited, but he nevertheless reserves a role for philosophy in social and moral thought. Strauss argues perhaps most clearly in *Natural Right and History* that if philosophers acknowledge the philosophical relevance of the non-philosophical foundation of revelation, philosophers have a clarifying role in deducing a social philosophy. Yet if philosophers do not acknowledge the possibility of revelation, philosophers can only have an adversarial role in regard to social and moral philosophy. This is because for Strauss philosophy is not fundamentally social in character.

In regarding philosophy as asocial and religion as social, Strauss is more Heideggerian than Levinas. The important philosophical and historical issue here is about the respective association between the public realm and religion on the one hand, and the private realm and philosophy on the other. Unfortunately, arguments about the relation between individual and public experience often degenerate too quickly into reductive judgments about mass–elite distinctions. Certainly a consideration of such distinctions is philosophically important, but we miss an opportunity for critical reflection by jumping too quickly into political judgment on these matters. We need to ask first about the philosophical descriptions they provide of "philosophy" and "religion" respectively, and only then, I'd like to suggest, about the political implications of these suggestions.

More recent Heidegger scholarship has complicated this issue in terms of Heidegger's thought as much of the secondary literature has moved toward recognition of the philosophical importance of sociality for Heidegger.[38] Where the early "existentialist" reading of Heidegger insisted on a dichotomy between sociality and authentic being in the world, many recent interpreters have questioned it. As Thomas Sheehan puts it, for Heidegger, "Our sociality – co-extensive with finitude, and its first gift – is what makes it possible and necessary to take-as and to understand 'is.' Our sociality is *die Sache selbst*."[39] It is beyond the scope of this essay to provide a full account of sociality in Heidegger, but from our very brief discussion a helpful point can be made, which is relevant for our consideration of Strauss.

Strauss shares with Heidegger the notion that philosophy is grounded upon a prior sociality for which philosophy cannot account. And Strauss concludes with Heidegger that philosophy itself is incapable of transcending sociality. Instead of concluding too quickly that Strauss wants to maintain an illiberal elite–mass distinction (which still may be the case), why not recognize first that Strauss, like Heidegger, insists on a fundamental limitation of philosophy as it has come to be understood in the modern period? Strauss's view of the moral and political limitation of philosophy has everything to do with his association of "religion" with the public and social sphere. Strauss's argument in this regard is intimately connected to what is, historically, an accurate depiction of Jewish religion. Jewish religion, as opposed to Protestant religion, is concerned fundamentally (though not exclusively) with outer forms of social life, forms that are enacted primarily in public.

Here the contrast with Levinas is instructive. Levinas wants to maintain that philosophy *can* ultimately account for the *truth* of religion and that this accounting has profound social implications (indeed, one could sum up Levinas's entire project with this one sentence). Contending that prophecy is the "fundamental fact of man's humanity," Levinas argues that "next to the unlimited ethical exigency, prophecy interprets itself in concrete forms… In these concrete forms, become religions, men find consolations. But this by no means puts the rigorous structure I [Levinas] have tried to define back into doubt."[40] The rigorous structure that Levinas has in mind is the result of philosophical reflection. Levinas argues that religions offer consolation while philosophy may not, and that "a humanity which can do without these consolations perhaps may not be worthy of them."[41] Nevertheless, it is philosophy that articulates the truth of religion and marks what, for Levinas, is the deep structure of human existence, one that is "outside of every sacramental signification."[42] Philosophy does not overcome the truth of religion, for Levinas, but nonetheless articulates the ground of this very truth in a kind of transcendental reflection that has universal implications for human behavior.

While Levinas and Strauss share with Heidegger the notion that philosophy's most fundamental insight begins in and does not transcend our natural attitude toward the world, Levinas maintains a role for philosophy that is closer to Husserl's than it is to Heidegger's.[43] Like Husserl, Levinas is a defender of the modern, philosophical project: to articulate a universal, philosophical account of what it means to be human. No doubt, the endpoints of Husserl and Levinas's projects are different. For Husserl, the task of phenomenology is to "know thy self."[44] For Levinas, the task of phenomenology is recognition of how the other constitutes me. Nonetheless, Levinas understands his philosophy as continuous with the Husserlian project. As Levinas puts it,

The framework of Husserlian phenomenology may have been broken open in the course of the transcendental analysis, but the "destruction" of the dominant *me* in which it was anchored is not some step along the way to the insignificance of the person... The "discovery" of others (not as *datum* exactly, but as a face!) subverts the transcendental approach of the *I*, but retains the egological primacy of this *I* that remains unique and chosen in its incontestable responsibility.[45]

Levinas assumes a social and political status for philosophy that Strauss puts into question. In Strauss's words:

In most of the current reflections on the relation between philosophy and society, it is somehow taken for granted that philosophy always possessed political or social status... Here, we are touching on what, from the point of view of the sociology of philosophy, is the most important difference between Christianity on the one hand, and Islam as well as Judaism on the other. For the Christian, the sacred doctrine is revealed theology; for the Jew and the Muslim, the sacred doctrine is, at least primarily, the legal interpretation of the Divine Law (*talmud* or *fiqh*). The sacred doctrine in the latter sense has, to say the least, much less in common with philosophy than the sacred doctrine in the former sense. It is ultimately for this reason that the status of philosophy was, as a matter of principle, much more precarious in Judaism and in Islam than in Christianity: in Christianity philosophy became an integral part of the officially recognized and even required training of the student of the sacred doctrine. This difference explains partly the eventual collapse of philosophic inquiry in the Islamic and in the Jewish world, a collapse which has no parallel in the Western Christian world.[46]

This long quotation comes from the introduction to Strauss's *Persecution and the Art of Writing*. These comments are of course related to Strauss's hermeneutical approach to philosophical and political texts, in which he maintains that awareness of the historical lack of social status of philosophy should alert us to the complex relation between esoteric and exoteric writing. It is not, however, this much-debated aspect of Strauss's contention that I would like to examine. Instead, I would like to focus on the philosophical and historical issues that Strauss raises here in regard to contemporary conceptions of what philosophy "is."

In his early *Philosophy and Law*, Strauss states that "medieval philosophy differs from ancient, as from modern, philosophy because of the situation given with the reality of the revelation."[47] We have seen throughout this essay some of the reasons why Strauss claims that medieval philosophy is dependent on revelation and why, in Strauss's words referring to Maimonides, "a philosopher as a philosopher may have an interest in the revelation."[48] For Strauss, it is not only for political reasons that "philosophy" properly understood does not have social status. Strauss also has a philosophical point.

Much like Heidegger, Strauss maintains that philosophy cannot ground or even articulate, on its own terms, social practice. Levinas, in contrast, argues that the modern philosophical project of providing a transcendental description of the self – albeit a self who is beholden to another – is one worth maintaining, preserving, and revitalizing.

CONCLUSION: IMPLICATIONS FOR "RELIGION AFTER METAPHYSICS"

I have argued in this essay for a reading of Levinas and Strauss that considers both the content and the form of their respective arguments in terms of the question of religion after metaphysics. In terms of the content of their respective arguments, I have suggested that neither presents an onto-theological picture of Jewish revelation, while both nonetheless make claims for the necessity of metaphysics after Heidegger. In different ways, Levinas and Strauss both argue that the Jewish philosophical tradition, and the medieval tradition in particular, is not oriented around ontological foundationalism, but around ethical and political presuppositions.

In terms of the form of their respective arguments, I have suggested that the real argument between Levinas and Strauss is not about "religion," *but about philosophy itself*. Although Levinas is today often considered a philosophical defender of Jewish revelation, I have suggested that Levinas's project is in fact to defend the possibilities of Western philosophy for directing social and ethical life. In contrast, I have suggested that while Strauss argues that philosophy has a clarifying role in society, he is critical of what he argues is the modern premise that philosophy itself has the ability to direct moral and social life. Hence, when compared with Levinas, Strauss in fact emerges as a defender of the philosophical *possibility* of revelation.

These conclusions raise a twofold question about "religion after metaphysics" which is both historical and philosophical. First, the paradigm of metaphysics as onto-theology assumes a fusing of philosophy and revealed religion as well as an ontological orientation for philosophy and religion that in many cases is historically inaccurate. The assumption that religious truths are fundamentally "onto-theological" in character is in tension with at least some dominant aspects of the historical Jewish tradition's primary (but not exclusive) emphasis on the social and political forms of religious life. We should appreciate that the story about "religion *after* metaphysics" may be a very particular, if not misleading, story. This story is infused with what I would suggest is a particular Protestant narrative (which may not do justice to the full array of the Protestant tradition) that disassociates "religion" from public life. While I am aware that it is all too simple to call this Protestant caricature, and what is likely a caricature of Protestantism, symptomatic of modernity, I'd like to suggest that there is some truth to this claim. Could it be that the dissociation of "religion" from public life goes hand in hand with a particularly modern claim that philosophy is capable of grounding social and political life? And could it be that a rejection of this modern role for philosophy opens up the possibilities of conceiving religion as a public, and not only a private, matter? These questions are no doubt complex. Still it is necessary to begin to acknowledge that historically speaking there are religions and not "religion" as well as traditions within a "tradition." This isn't just a question about the relationship between Judaism and Christianity, but also one about the constitution of Christianity itself.[49]

Philosophically, the debate about "religion after metaphysics" reveals more about the current status (or lack of status) of philosophy than it does about "religion." I am in agreement here with Hent de Vries, who, in his very interesting book *Philosophy and the Turn to Religion*, attempts "to demonstrate the philosophical relevance of the religious without resorting to the axioms or the types of argumentation of either *metaphysica specialis* (that is, ontotheology) or its mirror image, the empirical study of religion as an ontic or positive (cultural, anthropological, social, psychological, linguistic) phenomenon."[50] Yet I wonder if, on his own terms, de Vries, or Derrida for that matter, is justified in claiming (purportedly against Heidegger) that "one can – or, perhaps, cannot but be – on both sides of the line at once, that is to say, that this line dividing the philosophical and the theological was never given (certain or theoretically justifiable) in the first place."[51] As Derrida himself asks, in relation to Levinas, does not the claim that the "line dividing the philosophical and the theological" fall back to the philosophical?[52] When de Vries, following Derrida, states that in regard to "religions," he is interested "less in their theological message than in the structural inflection of what is commonly held to be possible and what not," is this not a philosophical question? I cannot offer any conclusive answers here, but I can suggest that Strauss's impulse to question the philosophical relation between philosophy and revealed religion may still be worth considering.

Finally, if, as I have argued, the question about "religion after metaphysics" is largely a question about the status of philosophy, what is the philosophical question that is at stake here? There are certainly strictly philosophical reasons to question the modern status of philosophy, but there are also pressing existential reasons, the most important of which are the perceived evils of the twentieth century. If philosophy in the late twentieth century turned to religion, it did so largely in response to these particular horrors. As Derrida, drawing on Kant, writes in "Faith and Knowledge," "The possibility of *radical evil* both destroys and institutes the religious."[53] It is certainly an attempt to account for evil that is at the root of both Levinas's and Strauss's philosophical projects. Their claim for metaphysics is simultaneously a claim that an account of evil requires metaphysics, no less (if not more) than an account of the good does. The question of religion after metaphysics raises the question of whether evil can be accounted for philosophically without metaphysics. It is this *philosophical* question that shapes Levinas's and Strauss's attempts to think about what it would mean to reinvigorate philosophy itself.

NOTES

1. Translated in Thomas Sheehan, "Reading Heidegger's 'What is Metaphysics?,'" *The New Yearbook for Phenomenology and Phenomenological Philosophy* 1 (2001), p. 196.
2. *Ibid.*, p. 199.
3. *Ibid.*
4. *Ibid.*, p. 182.
5. Martin Heidegger, *Nietzsche*, ed. David F. Krell (San Francisco: HarperCollins, 1991), vol. IV, p. 164.
6. Emmanuel Levinas, *Noms propres*, 2nd edn (Paris: Livre de Poche, 1987), pp. 57–8.
7. Emmanuel Levinas, "A Religion for Adults," in *Difficult Freedom*, trans. Sean Hand (Baltimore: Johns Hopkins University Press, 1990), pp. 14–15.
8. See Levinas's comments about Strauss, whom he characterizes as "the American philosopher," in "Have You Reread Baruch?," translated in *Difficult Freedom*, p. 111.
9. Emmanuel Levinas, *In the Time of the Nations*, trans. Michael B. Smith (Bloomington: University of Indiana Press, 1994), p. 172, my italics.
10. Again, see "Have You Reread Baruch?" in *Difficult Freedom*.
11. In contrast, Judaism is rooted in revelation, which begins not in thought but in obedience to God and the revealed law. In Strauss's words "the beginning of wisdom is fear of the Lord; according to the Greek philosophers, the beginning of wisdom is wonder" ("Jerusalem and Athens," in *Jewish Philosophy and the Crisis of Modernity*, ed. Kenneth Hart Green [Albany: State University of New York Press, 1997], pp. 379–80). Because these basic perspectives are so different, Strauss maintains that "We are thus compelled from the very beginning to make a choice, to take a stand" (p. 380).
12. In marked contrast to the philosophical perspective, the human being from a biblical perspective "is not master of how to begin; before he begins to write

he is already confronted with writings, with the holy writings, which impose their law on him" ("On the Interpretation of Genesis," in *Jewish Philsophy and the Crisis of Modernity*, p. 374).

13. Leo Strauss, "The Mutual Influence of Theology and Philosophy," *Independent Journal of Philosophy* 3 (1979), p. iii.

14. Leo Strauss, *Persecution and the Art of Writing* (Chicago: University of Chicago Press, 1988), p. 19, my italics.

15. Emmanuel Levinas, *Ethics and Infinity*, trans. Richard Cohen (Pittsburgh: Duquesne University Press, 1985), p. 24.

16. Emmanuel Levinas, *Du sacré au sainte* (Paris: Les Editions de Minuit, 1977), p. 156.

17. Emmanuel Levinas, *Totalité et infini*, 4th edn (The Hague: Martinus Nijhoff, 1971), trans. Alphonso Lingis as *Totality and Infinity* (Pittsburgh: Duquesne University Press, 1969), p. 73.

18. *Totality and Infinity*, p. 303.

19. Leo Strauss, *Philosophy and Law: Contributions to the Understanding of Maimonides and his Predecessors*, trans. Eve Adler (Albany: State University of New York Press, 1995), p. 88.

20. On this point, see Kenneth Hart Green, *Jew and Philosophy: The Return to Maimonides in the Jewish Thought of Leo Strauss* (Albany: State University of New York Press, 1993).

21. Leo Strauss, *Natural Right and History* (Chicago: University of Chicago Press, 1950), pp. 75–6.

22. Leo Strauss, *Spinoza's Critique of Religion* (Chicago: University of Chicago Press, 1965), p. 12.

23. Leo Strauss, *Thoughts on Machiavelli* (Glencoe, Ill.: Free Press, 1958), p. 13.

24. Strauss, "Jerusalem and Athens," in *Jewish Philosophy and the Crisis of Modernity*, p. 400.

25. Strauss, *Philosophy and Law*, p. 76.

26. *Ibid.*, p. 57.

27. Emmanuel Levinas, "Totalité et infini," *Annales de l'Université de Paris* 31 (1961), p. 386.

28. Strauss, *Philosophy and Law*, pp. 78–9.

29. Strauss and Levinas of course value "politics" differently. For the purposes of clarity, however, I use the variants of the phrase "politics and ethics" to talk about both Strauss and Levinas. Although Levinas is critical of "politics," he nonetheless has a positive evaluation of politics when it is informed by "ethics." For this reason, I don't believe that this phrasing is inaccurate with regard to Levinas.

30. Strauss, *Philosophy and Law*, p. 75, my italics.

31. Strauss, "Jerusalem and Athens," p. 393.

32. See especially Emmanuel Levinas, "From Ethics to Exegesis," in *In the Time of the Nations*, pp. 109–13.

33. "The Law of Reason in the *Kuzari*," in Strauss, *Persecution and the Art of Writing*, p. 141. Interestingly, Levinas offers a somewhat similar reading of

Halevi. He writes, "What matters to me in that work [the *Kuzari*] . . . is the possibility of an original thinking and intelligibility other than the immanence of knowledge . . . The proximity and sociality that the philosophers will seek in *knowledge* will appear in Judah Halevi as irreducible possibilities of the meaningful. Sociality together with transcendence! . . . Religion is the excellence proper to sociality with the Absolute, or, if you will, in the positive sense of the expression, Peace with the other" (Levinas, *In the Time of the Nations*, pp. 170–1). Levinas is, however, far more dismissive of Halevi than Strauss is.

34. Strauss, *Persecution and the Art of Writing*, p. 140, my italics.
35. Levinas, *Ethics and Infinity*, p. 24.
36. In Strauss's words, "the philosopher cannot give this law either to himself or to others; for while he can indeed, *qua* philosopher, *know* the principles of a law in general and the principles of the rational law in particular, he can never *divine* the concrete individual ordinances of the ideal law, whose precise stipulation is the only way the law can become effectual, or simply, can become – law" (*Philosophy and Law*, p. 71).
37. Levinas, *Du sacré au sainte*, p. 156.
38. It is worth noting that the social dimension of Heidegger's thought was pursued almost immediately by his students Hannah Arendt and Karl Löwith.
39. Thomas Sheehan, "A Paradigm Shift in Heidegger Research," *Continental Philosophy Review* 34 (2001), p. 200. Indeed, Levinas agrees with Sheehan's description and, interestingly, he does so in the context of a criticism of Martin Buber. See "Martin Buber's Theory of Knowledge," trans. Michael B. Smith, in *Proper Names* (Stanford: Stanford University Press, 1996). Prefacing his remarks with the qualification that "It is not, surely, to Heidegger that one should turn for instruction in the love of man or social justice," Levinas defends Heidegger against Buber on the issue of care and mutuality: "But *Fürsorge*, as response to essential destitution, is a mode of access to the otherness of the Other . . . But Buber allows himself to say 'All dialogue draws its authenticity from consciousness of the element of *Umfassung* [embracing].' [Yet] Consciousness reappears behind *Umfassung* . . . Relation itself, apart from its goal, differs from knowledge" (pp. 33–4, translation altered slightly).
40. Levinas, *Ethics and Infinity*, p. 114.
41. *Ibid.*, p. 118.
42. *Ibid.*, pp. 117–18
43. As Levinas puts it, "The phenomenological epoche does not destroy the truths proper to the natural attitude but wants only to clarify their sense." See Emmanuel Levinas, *The Theory of Intuition in Husserl's Phenomenology*, 2nd edn, trans. André Orianne (Evanston: Northwestern University Press, 1995), p. 147.
44. See in particular the end of Husserl's *Cartesian Meditations*, trans. Dorion Cairns (The Hague: Kluwer Academic Publishers, 1977).
45. Levinas, *In the Time of the Nations*, pp. 181–2.
46. Strauss, *Persecution and the Art of Writing*, pp. 18–19.
47. Strauss, *Philosophy and Law*, p. 58.
48. *Ibid.*, p. 64.

49. This said, Strauss's own contention mentioned above, that the Catholic tradition of natural law represents this fusing, might also be historically inaccurate, as a number of recent interpreters have argued in the context of Thomas Aquinas. See John A. Bowlin, *Contingency and Fortune in Aquinas's Ethics* (New York and Cambridge: Cambridge University Press, 1999), as well as Victor Preller, *Divine Science and the Science of God: A Reformulation of Thomas Aquinas* (Princeton: Princeton University Press, 1967).

50. Hent de Vries, *Philosophy and the Turn to Religion* (Baltimore: Johns Hopkins University Press, 1999), p. 38.

51. *Ibid.*, p. 42.

52. "Violence and Metaphysics: An Essay on the Thought of Emmanuel Levinas," in *Writing and Difference*, trans. Alan Bass (Chicago: University of Chicago Press, 1978), pp. 79–153.

53. "Faith and Knowledge," in *Religion*, ed. Jacques Derrida and Gianni Vattimo (Stanford University Press, 1998), p. 65.

The "end of metaphysics" as a possibility

Jean-Luc Marion
Translated by Daryl Lee

The reference to what is unthought in philosophy is not a criticism of philosophy.[1]

More than a thesis, the "end of metaphysics" announces itself as a theme – the theme of a question, and of a question that remains yet open. That this phrase is most often misunderstood, and only taken in a polemical sense, simply betrays a twofold ignorance: that of the disguised, complex, and paradoxical history of the concept of "metaphysics," and that of Heidegger's long and complex meditation on the phrase, "end of metaphysics." Having attempted to assess the first term elsewhere,[2] in this chapter I would like to clarify the second.[3]

The most perfect misinterpretation possible regarding what Heidegger is attempting to think under the title of "end of metaphysics"[4] would consist of ascribing to it the reductive slogans of the usual iconoclasms; the ones, moreover – regularly refuted by real thinking – according to which metaphysics has already disappeared, or will surely disappear soon, or again should have disappeared, or in any case has no right to continue, to the point, finally, where it must be gotten rid of (for example, Hume, the Enlightenment, Comte, or Carnap, etc.). For Heidegger, on the contrary, it is essentially a matter of understanding that "this 'overcoming of metaphysics' does not abolish metaphysics."[5] This is so for two principal reasons. First, because if metaphysics is coming to an end today, the time for the "ending (*Verendung*) lasts longer than the previous history of metaphysics"[6] – in other words, we will not be finished with metaphysics by thinking its overcoming, but are obligated to dwell within this overcoming as if within an epoch of thinking, an epoch that will continue. Next, because "with the end of philosophy, thinking is not also at its end, but in transition to another beginning"[7] – in other words, we will only linger within the overcoming of metaphysics in order to prepare or wait for a revival of thinking (or of philosophy) itself.

To broach this inquiry, I will follow the central theme of one of Heidegger's last lectures, given in 1964 under the title "The End of Philosophy and the Task of Thinking."[8]

I CULMINATION[9]

If metaphysics carries on at the very moment it is coming to an end, it is because, strictly speaking, that end is achieved – because it accomplishes its own end in the mode of a culmination. The most elementary misinterpretation would consist, on the contrary, in supposing that metaphysics reaches its end in just the way that one makes an end or is at the end, that one can be done with something, in short, just like a death or an end game. Yet metaphysics finds its end only in attaining its goal, thus, in accomplishing its finality. "What is meant by the talk about the end of philosophy? We understand the end of something all too easily in the negative sense as mere cessation, as the lack of continuation, perhaps even as decline and impotence. In contrast, what we say about the end of philosophy means the completion of metaphysics."[10] Indeed, given that in old German *Ende* meant the same as *Ort*, or "place," one may understand that "the end of philosophy is the place, that place in which the whole of philosophy's history is gathered together in its most extreme possibility."[11] And not only must a culmination be seen here, but a completion of possibilities. These possibilities define so many of the forms of beings, therefore so many historically imaginable and playable versions of metaphysics – already thought and therefore already played. For the succession of major metaphysical doctrines does not add up to the nonsensical sum of all the absurdities that could have been pronounced concerning beings; rather, it lays out the almost necessary and exhaustive series of all the conceptual forms made possible by the initial deal of the being of beings.[12] Instead of railing against the philosophers, it would almost be necessary to claim that not a single great metaphysician has ever gotten it wrong, since in the face of the beings to be thought and thematized, each has played the right card or cards, at the very least the best cards possible from among those that the tradition had transmitted and dealt to him. Each metaphysician, having formed an interpretation of beings that had a marked influence on his age, has thus arrived at this end-place, because he managed to make the best hand possible with the cards at his disposal. From one winning hand to the next, metaphysics has played all of its cards and has finally fulfilled its contract. From Plato to Nietzsche, all the possible forms for being have been imposed upon beings (or rather: beings have laid claim to all of the useful and necessary forms of being). Metaphysics does surely arrive at its term, because it arrives at the end of the game; but the game reaches its end only because metaphysics won it.[13]

"But then what does it mean, 'the end of metaphysics'? It means the historical moment (*Augenblick*) in which *the essential possibilities* of metaphysics are exhausted."[14] Or again: "With Nietzsche's metaphysics, philosophy is completed (*vollendet*). That means: It has gone through the sphere of prefigured possibilities."[15] Or yet again: it is "a stage in Western metaphysics that is probably its final stage; for inasmuch as through Nietzsche metaphysics has in a certain sense divested itself of its own essential possibility, other possibilities of metaphysics can no longer appear."[16] This understanding of metaphysics as organized around its endpoint, with this end taken as a culmination that exhausts all of its final possibilities, has raised many questions. More than anything it has nourished an unending polemic between Nietzsche specialists who, quite often, consider it an infamy to continue to include the thinker of Eternal Return in the continuity of metaphysics. This reaction seems nevertheless a fragile one, if only because it owes so much to the Heideggerian interpretation. It owes Heidegger first of all the possibility even of discussing the place of Nietzsche in the history of philosophy, since – it must not be forgotten – prior to Heidegger's lectures, Nietzsche did not, strictly speaking, belong to philosophy, but rather, in the best of cases was perceived as a moralist or a "poet," and in the worst was redeemed by the most nauseating of ideologies. Next, this reaction owes to the Heideggerian interpretation the very concept of metaphysics, as a historical and critical category, without which it would not even be possible to dream of excluding Nietzsche. That the question concerning the precise metaphysical status of Nietzsche's philosophy remains open is one thing (and without Heidegger his interpreters are making no headway on this mission); that metaphysics remains an insurmountable horizon for Nietzsche is another thing, one it would be difficult to broach. Nor can one honestly reproach Heidegger for a certain hermeneutic imperialism – as if, in the manner of Aristotle and Hegel, he were reinterpreting the history of philosophy to his own profit and according to his own position. This cannot be, precisely because Heidegger expounded his thinking on the end of metaphysics *after* having *renounced*, during the *Kehre* (and wherever one might wish to place it exactly), the 1927 project of a fundamental ontology as an "impasse."[17] Unlike the metaphysicians (including, on this count, Nietzsche himself), Heidegger does not describe metaphysics as the system of *aporias* that his own doctrine would resolve; rather, he confronts it without defense and without presuppositions, precisely because his first theoretical effort was unable to liberate itself from it entirely, or to overcome it.

More than anything, this effort alone to understand metaphysics as an accomplishment, which victoriously exhausts all of the possibilities, allows from the beginning the overcoming of one of the deepest difficulties which confounds other conceptions of philosophy: what to make of technology, that is, of the modernity of our world, as it extends itself further and has continued to build strength for more than a century. Mainstream philosophy has typically tended to fall into an aporetic alternative: Either one constructs philosophy in opposition to or ignorant of technology (existentialism, "spiritualism," a part of the analytic tradition, philosophy of language, etc.), or one dissolves philosophy into a simple commentary on science and technology, arriving late and often unfavorably viewed (positivism, part of analytic philosophy, the cognitive sciences, etc.). Here, on the contrary, "the end of philosophy proves to be the triumph of the manipulable arrangement of a scientific-technological world and of the social order proper to this world. The end of philosophy means the beginning of the world civilization that is based upon Western European thinking."[18] In other words: "The name 'technology' is understood here in such an essential way that its meaning coincides with the term 'completed metaphysics' (*deckt mit dem Titel: die vollendete Metaphysik*)."[19] Not only are we not able to read in this any rejection (whether romantic or ideological) of modernity, but we are obliged in the end instead to see a radical effort to attribute a conceptual significance to technology and to steal it away from the insignificance that so often makes it barbarously absurd to us. We must admit to bearing the responsibility not only for understanding rationality, but also for thinking it as a "world civilization that is just now beginning (*jetzt erst beginnende*),"[20] as "an order of the earth which will supposedly last for a long time (*lang dauernde*)."[21] Yet why would technology arise from the culmination of metaphysics? Apparently because its destiny is wrapped up in that of the flourishing of the sciences. But especially because this flourishing itself draws its own possibility from the modern figures of metaphysics: representation as the redefinition of beings, the ego as the determination of mankind implementing the *Mathesis Universalis*, the principle of sufficient reason as a unique point of access to phenomenality, etc. Technology synthesizes in fact all of the possibilities that metaphysics has realized and embodies it throughout – or rather, manifests its disembodiment. And if technology progresses without end and without any other goal than its own expansion, it is due to the fact that no other possibility presents itself to technology, or to us. Technology reproduces itself and expands because it has no other choice, no other possibility than persevering in its closed beingness. Without end – without ceasing, but also, without goal. Technology does not only accomplish all the acquired possibilities of metaphysics – it also realizes the absence of any new possibility for metaphysics. And this absence of new possibilities is precisely what provokes progress – which for Heidegger means an accumulation, distracted by nothing, of the same in its eternal return.

Thus, far from holding philosophy back, the "end of metaphysics," paradoxically perhaps, returns terrain to philosophy – the revision and the accomplishment of all of its possibilities – and opens it to the most difficult and determinant problem of our time – thinking technology in its true motivation, which may in no way be reduced to mathematical rationality, which it in fact puts into play, and which it does not have to think.

2   DESTRUCTION

To interpret the "end of metaphysics" as a completion (and even as the exhaustion of every new possibility) would have no meaning if it were impossible to specify what it accomplishes and achieves in its very exhaustion. But in order to recognize it, it is necessary to look at metaphysics not only as a totality, but also from a point of view that transcends it. Heidegger names this elect point of view *destruction*: "We understand this task as one in which by taking *the question of Being as our clue*, we are to *destroy* the traditional content of ancient ontology."[22] Still, it must be remembered that destruction, understood thus, does not seek to ruin, but on the contrary to institute, liberate and open:

> But this destruction is just as far from having the *negative* sense of shaking off the ontological tradition. We must, on the contrary, stake out the positive possibilities of that tradition, and this always means keeping it within its *limits*; these in turn are given factically in the way the question is formulated at the time, and in the way the possible field for investigation is thus bounded off. On its negative side, this destruction does not relate itself towards the past; its criticism is aimed at "today" and at the prevalent way of treating the history of ontology, whether it is headed towards doxography, towards intellectual history, or towards a history of problems. But to bury the past in nullity [*Nichtigkeit*] is not the purpose of this destruction; its aim is positive; its negative function remains unexpressed and indirect.[23]

In fact, destruction destroys nothing, so much as it makes manifest – "only the gradual removal (*Abbau*) of these obscuring covers – that is what is meant by 'destruction.'"[24] For destruction – in opposition to recent "deconstruction" – brings out (negatively) only that which in the metaphysical tradition of *ontologia* dissimulates and hides (even more negatively) the question of being under the auspices of an inquiry into beings, like stucco that covers a façade or a coating that conceals a fresco. Destruction denies negation, uncovers a covering – in a word, it attempts to make visible, to draw into the light as a rightful phenomenon, what metaphysics has made invisible, namely, being as being, hidden by the science of beings in their being and by the domination of beings. In clearing out the space of the question, destruction operates in the manner of a phenomenological reduction: just as reduction returns objective perceptions back to the primary given of the lived experiences of consciousness, in an abstraction from objects supposed to be already constituted, so too destruction channels ontic enunciations to the point where they conceal the being of beings, but as being, and the ontological difference as such. In order to draw out the mode of being through subtraction, destruction also works by bracketing off into parentheses: no longer the objects in their reality, but beings in their beingness. We thus see why the positive nature of destruction remains hidden behind a mask – as long as attention is focused on beings – and why this positivity illuminates as soon as the gaze allows beings to withdraw into the background and the being of beings as such to step into the foreground.

But destruction could not assume this strictly phenomenological function if it weren't a matter of making manifest, as is always the case in good phenomenology, a phenomenon that, above all, did not show itself. What remains hidden here, or what "remains unthought in the matter of philosophy as well as in its method"?[25] Heidegger never ceased responding to this question in the same way, though with different formulations. In 1943: "In the beingness of beings, metaphysics thinks being, yet without being able to ponder the truth of being in the manner of its own thinking."[26] In 1945, this impotence is more accurately ascribed to the metaphysical mode of thinking, representation, which inescapably privileges the permanence of presence, thus beings: "Metaphysics, insofar as it always represents only beings as beings, does not recall Being itself,"[27] or: "In fact, metaphysics never answers the question concerning the truth of Being, for it never asks this question. Metaphysics does not ask this question because it thinks Being only by representing beings as beings."[28] Only the 1957 lecture devoted to "The Onto-theo-logical Constitution of Metaphysics" definitively demarcates what remains unthought in, about and by metaphysics: "For it still remains unthought by what unity ontologic and theologic belong together, what the origin of this unity is, and what [is] the difference of the differentiated which this unity unifies."[29] Metaphysics thinks beings, because it thinks only in the mode of representation; it thus only broaches ontological

difference within the horizon of beings and their mode of being. It therefore substitutes an ontic difference in place of the ontological difference –
that of beings in general with beings par excellence; onto-theological difference (and its unity) unavoidably masks the difference between being and
beings, which from that point on remains unthought. Metaphysics does
of course think in terms of ontological difference – where else could it be
found but in this difference? – but it does not think this difference as such.
Ultimately, then, the ontological difference in metaphysics appears neither
ontological nor even theological (in the sense of Revelation), but uniquely
ontic.

Reading the history of metaphysics from this standpoint would not
simply amount to reconstituting the doctrines of philosophers in order to
measure them against the question of the principles of beings and draw out
these principles simply from the history of ideas;[30] it also means developing
a hermeneutic of "destruction." Destruction first reviews all of the forms
of metaphysics as so many onto-theologies (of formulations of the ontic
difference between the theological and the ontological), then regards these
ontic differences as so many decisions regarding the being of beings as
beings, and finally, thinks through how the fact that beings are privileged
in their beingness points each time toward being even as it masks it. For
"history is not the succession of eras, but a unique nearness of the Same
that, in incalculable modes of destining and out of changing immediacy,
approaches and concerns thinking."[31]

3 NIHILISM

To consider the history of philosophy as metaphysics dealing out possible
forms of beings (in their being, no doubt, but always only as beings) implies
the attempt to understand the deal for what it claims for itself (the forms
of onto-theology) as well as for what it does not allow to be seen – which is
to say, being as such obfuscated by beings as beings and enslaved by beings.
Metaphysics must therefore be read on two levels: for what it shows – beings
in their being; and for what it does not show – being as such. Nevertheless,
as surprising as these two orientations appear, they can scarcely be discussed.

This is true because metaphysicians – and this fact is hardly in question –
are silent on the question of being in itself and never work on anything
but beings or in view of establishing beings (by a supreme being or by the
being of beings). They ask what beings are as beings and respond to this
question as Aristotle did through the *ousia* or its later figures: the *existentia*,
the *cogitatum*, the *Setzung*, the concept, the will to power, etc., thus always

and again through the beingness of beings. In short, in metaphysics, the question, like the answer, always revolves around beings; and even when there is concern for being – *especially* when there is explicit concern – reassurance comes by defining, in response, the mode of the being of beings, in fact, a mode of beingness. But on being itself, we find nothing. As a result, in metaphysics, "*nowhere do we find such an experiencing of Being itself*. Nowhere are we confronted by a thinking that thinks the truth of Being itself and therewith thinks truth itself as Being... The history of being begins, and indeed necessarily, *with the forgetting of being*."[32] One clue that identifies and confirms this forgetting of being arises from a similar powerlessness to think nothingness as such: it always falls back into the simple negation of being, without its ever being suspected that such a negation of being in its totality draws its potential for transcendence from the beings of nothingness – that is, from its function as a prologemenon to being: "the nothing makes itself known with beings."[33] This occurs in such a way that "perhaps the essence of nihilism consists in *not* taking the question of the nothing seriously."[34] The phenomenological reading (in other words, destruction as defined above) of the history of metaphysics (of metaphysics as a history that is internally coherent, as the initial deal and all of the successive hands which do nothing but display and affirm its destinal unity) requires then a two-fold task: first, interpreting philosophical doctrines according to their onto-theological constitution; and second, reading what these versions of onto-theology leave unthought and how they leave it unthought – being as such.

The immense difficulty of such a task suggests at the very least that it is absolutely not a question of teleological reading, whether direct (truth appearing in the end: Hegel, Marx, or Nietzsche), indirect (truth being found in the past and thus temporarily neglected: neo-Thomism, neo-Kantianism, neo-Platonism, etc.), or inverted (truth being found in a forgotten origin: the Greeks, the pre-Socratics). Heidegger rejected more forcefully than anyone else this latter thesis, that of a phantasmatic return to the origin, by asking (in the conclusion of the text we are in the process of following) nothing less than that we "experience *aletheia* in a Greek manner as unconcealment," *consequently*, not as a return to the way in which the Greeks considered it, *but* thinking it "above and beyond the Greek... as the clearing of self-concealing."[35] For the privilege granted to beings follows inevitably from this mode of thinking, which privileges the representation of stable presence. Properly speaking, being, which is not reducible to beings, *is* not, because it does not establish itself in presence, precisely because it establishes presence. It does not dwell, making itself available for its representation, but takes place unexpectedly and withdraws, like lightning, an event without substance or background. Would overcoming metaphysics then mean overcoming the mode of thinking that has predominated to the point of imperialism – the imperialism of representation, armed with the power of ordering and mathematical calculation?

No doubt. What remains is to know what such an overcoming of representational thinking requires. For it is a matter of just that: "The task of thinking would then be the surrender of previous thinking to the determination of the matter for thinking"[36]; that is, abandoning the thinking still in force – representation, classification, and calculation, in short, thinking that dispenses with thinking because it has no use for it in order to master beings, science; or, to be more precise, the thinking of technology as an informational science of computers (for this is exactly what Heidegger had anticipated in speaking of "cybernetics") – in order to think the non-representable, the non-orderable, the non-calculable, being. And that requires making appear what cannot be shown as beings, what is phenomenalizable without assuming the forms of beings. It is always still a phenomenology, but this "phenomenology is a phenomenology of the inapparent."[37] Here we arrive at a troubling paradox. Many have taken this as a contradiction of terms, if not a dangerous absurdity. It is not my place here to defend this formulation (it stands up on its own as it is) or to illustrate it (that task remains far beyond us). The very least we can do is underscore its perfect coherence. Being that presents beings never presents itself as part of beings; never presenting itself, by definition it escapes representation. Only a meditation without representation, thus lacking order and calculation (without the *Mathesis Universalis*), could possibly reach this. While we wait for this we will have to learn to interpret the concealment of being without evidence of beings, as the paradoxical mode of engaging being in the world. Because even, if not especially, in nihilism, "metaphysics occurs *(sich ereignet)* in virtue of Being, and the overcoming of metaphysics occurs as the incorporation of Being (*die Überwindung der Metaphysik als Verwindung des Seins*)."[38] The term *Verwindung*, which is barely translatable, indicates that one gets over something by coming back from what one desired or refused and by overcoming it. We must accept that being will inevitably and necessarily withdraw, whenever representation rules metaphysical thinking; but accepting this loss and pursuing this mourning would allow, first of all, withdrawing from metaphysics, in order to see clearly what it says and what it will never be able to say; and then, this would allow for the reconsideration of the question of being as a question that it and it alone poses – according to its conditions and with its own demands. By means of this *Verwindung* yet to be defined, the *Überwindung* reaches a profound meaning – neither a deconstruction nor a reconstruction, but the possibility, at least in outline, of conceiving what it would mean to "think Being without beings, that is to say: to think Being without regard to metaphysics... to cease all overcoming, and leave metaphysics to itself."[39] Metaphysics must therefore first let itself be constituted onto-theologically, thus elevated to the status of a thinking of beings in their being (unthought as such), in order to provide the privileged ontic phenomenon (like *Dasein*'s position in the question of being attempted by *Being and Time*) on which the questioning of being as such could itself take place.

4 WHAT IS SAID IN THE "IT GIVES"

Destruction draws out what in nihilism continues to point toward being – toward being as it is folded back into beings, not even in the figure of the being of beings. To refer to what is unthought in this way is tantamount to shedding light onto something phenomenologically. This is what Heidegger calls, using a term that is hardly illuminating, a *clearing*.[40] How are we to understand this? In the following way, to be sure: the clearing does not bring fully to light, but at least it no longer preserves the shadow. Like twilight, the clearing already dissipates shadow, which recedes precisely as shadow, because clarity, without causing it to disappear, forces it to withdraw and encircles it as such. Now, we find ourselves today in just such a clearing at this historical moment. To this point in the history of philosophy, it has been a matter of making a simple diagnosis, in the trivial sense of the word, concerning the state of philosophy as metaphysics: the diagnosis of a transition, the destruction of which has recognized a bygone age (with the being of beings figuring as a nihilism unto itself), without the coming age having come out of its obscure clarity. But in many of Heidegger's texts, and not merely on a superficial reading, he seems to disappoint expectations by driving "thinking" toward a phantasmatic "task."[41] The very last words of the text, which serve as a guide, seem to confirm this by offering a vague tautology: "The task of thinking would then be the surrender of previous thinking to the determination of the matter for thinking." But if we attend patiently to the penultimate sentence of this text, what comes to light is the true question, the one that imposes silence on too hasty answers, because it involves a substantial and very specific difficulty.

"Does the title for the task of thinking then read, instead of *Being and Time*: *Lichtung und Answesenheit*, Clearing and Presence? But where does

the clearing come from and how is it given? What speaks in the 'There is /
It gives'?"[42]

Let us pause on these brief lines. Our first task involves proposing a
substitution – that of rejecting the problematic of being and time (and
therefore also of the book that bears these words for its title, *Sein und Zeit*),
in which being must liberate itself from its subjection to beings, to erect
itself as a question sufficient to itself based on one privileged entity (*Dasein*)
and in alignment with temporality, in order to open an investigation into
the presence of being as such (*Anwesenheit*); for this presence would no
longer approach *Dasein* from its remarkable being of beings, as the 1927
work had supposed, but from being itself, or rather from something even
prior to this being, the clearing. A decisive essay from 1962, "Zeit und
Sein," had in fact accomplished this substitution two years before the essay
guiding our inquiry:

We say of beings: they are. With regard to the matter "Being" and with regard to
the matter "time," we remain cautious. We do not say: Being is, time is, but rather:
there is Being and there is time. For the moment we have only changed the idiom
with this expression. Instead of saying "it is," we say "there is," "It gives."[43]

It is obvious that with this substitution we have already gotten much further.
What remains to be determined is what is happening here – what step have
we in fact made, groping along, without yet understanding it? But, in
fact, bringing these two texts together appears at first glance to conjoin
erroneously two very distinct theses: in 1962 it involved substituting "there
is" [*il y a*] for "it is" [*il est*], whereas in 1964 it was a matter of replacing
"Being and time" with "presence and clearing." This distinction remains
superficial, however, because the 1964 text makes it clear that the shift to
"presence and clearing" itself presupposes confronting a question far more
radical, which it alone makes thinkable – the question "how does it come
about that 'there is' [*il y a*] the clearing?" It is in exactly this way that we
recover the situation of the 1962 text, in which there is already the shift
from "it is" [*il est*] to "there is" [*il y a*]. How, indeed, does the clearing come
about if we are, as is the case with being and time, unable to reach it by
saying that it 'is'? We are unable to do this because all that is, and being
itself, even and especially "Being without regard to metaphysics," "Being
without regard to its being grounded in terms of beings,"[44] manages to
come to us only through it – the clearing. It must therefore come to us
from elsewhere, if not prior to the "it is" [*il est*], so that it comes from what
Heidegger constantly calls the "there is" [*il y a*]. Or rather, what he calls "*es
gibt*," which the French renders as *il y a*, but which literally should translate

as "it gives" [*cela donne*] – *es gibt*. In the sense, of course, of a donation that arrives; in the sense also in which the painter, sculptor, or certain artisans distance themselves from their immediate work, in order to see with some detachment what it gives – in short, in order to see the work appear in its proper unfolding, remote from its worker, as if freely and no longer an object reducible to its production. Searching out the "it gives" (rather than the "it is"), affords the possibility of accessing, on this side of (or beyond) beings, what precedes it – being, time, presence, and the clearing. For in the *it gives* – *es gibt*, and in it alone, is played and drawn out an *Anwesenheit* more originary than the being of beings of metaphysics. It is only in the "it gives" that the clearing comes to inscribe itself. The question of the clearing now becomes one and the same with that of the "it gives."

It is from this vantage point that we may more easily understand that the question of the "it gives – *es gibt*," in the last place, is the one that enables an access to the clearing and a new passage from the being of beings to being itself. From here, everything depends on what is played out in this "it" in the simple formulation, "it gives – *es gibt*," supposing that what it pronounces is given and specifically gives itself to us. In addition, from this perspective the last question of the text corresponds to the next to the last one (how does the clearing come about?), because it asks "what speaks in the 'it gives'?" In other words, in the final account, in the final question, in the final "destruction," the overcoming of metaphysics depends on the determination of what the "it gives – *es gibt*" involves. Let us fully measure the stakes of this final question. It is certainly not about hastily affixing an identity to "it – *es*," as if forcing it back to the status of beings – Heidegger's strict warning on this count must remain in force here.[45] Instead, it is a matter of drawing out the stakes of what lets itself be given, when "it gives," which requires a much more arduous effort, since it is left without any way out ontically or ontologically. How then do we attempt to respond to the question? First, by establishing what, in the eyes of Heidegger himself, lets itself be manifest in the "it gives – *es gibt*." Next, by examining whether this "it gives – *es gibt*" is tied to the question of being, or goes beyond it.

5 THE INDECISION OF WHAT GIVES

In confronting this phrase – "it gives" – there is room for hesitation. Isn't it merely an expression from everyday language, without conceptual validity? What is more, does it not singularly belong to the German language? The French "there is" [*il y a*] omits the reference to the infinitive "to give" [*donner*] and thus spatializes the phrase, and the English "there is" makes do with the verb "to be," thus negating the distancing effect that Heidegger was searching for. This widely accepted and sensible objection would be valid only if, in Heidegger's German, the phrase *es gibt* remained idiosyncratic or a play on language without conceptual reach; in this case, it would certainly be wrong to grant it philosophical authority. If, on the contrary, it so happens that *es gibt* attains a conceptual status and sustains rigorous analysis, then in clothing itself in conceptual dignity it would be imperative to grant it rights even in the vernacular languages which on their own ignored it. In short, in order to follow what is advanced in the German, we should search out equivalents elsewhere, with the hope of thinking simply what it involves; we would, therefore, validate the expression "it gives" as a legitimate conceptual formulation.

Are we obligated to grant the expression "*es gibt* – it gives" the status of concept? If we study the occurrences of this term in Heidegger's writings, it seems that this formulation, far from intervening superficially or belatedly, like some sleight of hand without conceptual consequence, arises in Heidegger's earliest observations and regularly marks his advances. It is worth revisiting those occurrences. (A) As early as 1927, *Being and Time* underscores the fact that in order to say "being," it is necessary to reject the phrase "it is" and use instead "*es gibt* – it gives": "Only so long as Dasein *is*... 'is there' [*gibt es*] being."[46] Which is exactly what another passage confirms: "Being (not entities) is something which 'there is' only in so far as truth is. And truth *is* only in so far as and as long as Dasein is."[47] In this way, *es gibt* intervenes in order to speak the clearing of being, as it differs from beings and beingness through *Dasein*. (B) When in 1929 *What is Metaphysics?* returns to and radicalizes the analysis of anxiety, once "the nothing is conceded (*zugegeben*)" even by its scientific rejection, the question of its status arises immediately in terms of the it gives: "Is the nothing given only because the 'not,' i.e., negation, is given? Or is it the other way around? Are negation and the 'not' given only because the nothing is given?" And in that case, is it not necessary to take the next step and inquire "if the nothing itself is to be questioned as we have been questioning it, then it must be given beforehand"?[48] (C) Yet, once it is determined that being as such, in opposition to beings (and to the being of beings), itself *is* not, but comes from the "it gives, *es gibt*," the question then arises as to the status of the "it – *es*." The texts that precede "On Time and Being" (1962) unfailingly show some hesitation and indecision. On the one hand, the "Letter on Humanism" relates the "it – *es*" directly to being: "For the 'it' that 'gives' is being itself. The 'gives' names the essence of being that is giving, granting its truth. The self-giving into the open, along with the open region itself, is being itself."[49] Likewise the Introduction, added to the 1929 lecture in 1949, reasserts *in fine* this same conflation, when it stands amazed "that with Being It is really nothing" for metaphysics.[50] In contrast, the 1955 text "On the Question of Being" seems to ascribe to the "it – *es*" its own proper and enigmatic singularity:

> Nor can we ponder it for so long as we fail to ask: What is "it" that does the "giving" here? In what kind of giving does it give? To what extent does there belong to this "giving of being and nothing" something that gives and entrusts itself to this gift in preserving it? We can easily say: There is a giving [*es gibt*]. Being no more "is" than nothing. But *there is a giving* of both.[51]

Univocally assigning the "it – *es*" to being itself seems to be held in suspension from this point on, precisely because being (on the same level with the nothing) depends upon the unnamed event which gives it and therefore precedes it.

Which one of these two hypotheses should we choose? What follows from each? Before deciding anything, it would no doubt be worth measuring the stakes of such a choice from the outset. If we take as a given the possibility of reaching being as such, separate from beings, through the nothing or anxiety, this access to being would not fall upon beings, but upon the fact that "it gives – *es gibt*" the nothing, being, time; this anteriority traces a gap. Two paths present themselves regarding such a gap: either repatriating the "it gives – *es gibt*" in the last event to what it makes possible – once again, and as always, assigning it to being; or confirming the primacy of the "it gives – *es gibt*" over everything it makes possible and first of all over being – thus preserving its essential anonymity. Following the first path, the overcoming of metaphysics would go well beyond nihilism, but in view of being as such – and the thinking to come will remain a thinking of being. Following the second path, the overcoming of metaphysics will most certainly reach being as such, but from the standpoint of the "it gives – *es gibt*," so in a field which is by definition more vast than being (because it makes being possible) – and the thinking to come will become a thinking of what gives.

6   THE QUESTION OF DONATION AS SUCH

Any overcoming of metaphysics is beholden to the clearing of being as such. Yet, since this clearing opens up in its turn only to the extent of what it gives, the operation of overcoming, no less than the horizon that it opens, is decided according to the "it – *es*" that gives – or, more precisely, according to the answer to the question that gives this "it – *es*," which is operating in "it gives." But in order not to proscribe any possible answer, it would first be advisable to let the question formulate itself properly. Heidegger can once again guide us in this difficult work, especially since he himself seems sometimes to hesitate. For this we will follow the indications furnished in 1962 in *On Time and Being*, a text whose Protocol (dated the same year) gathers support from the same §43 of *Sein und Zeit*, which first mentions the fact that being *is* not, but that "'it gives' being." In this "it gives" Heidegger clearly recognizes "a '*neutrale tantum*', the neutral 'and' in the title 'time and Being.'"[52] We must question this neutrality.

A first, definitive given is readily apparent from the start: because "We do not say: Being is... but rather: it gives Being and it gives time," it follows that "instead of saying 'it is,' we say... 'it gives.'"[53] The question of the "it gives" therefore precedes most clearly that of being, from the simple fact that the former question makes the latter possible. Still, this "it gives" does not show itself in person in the being that it permits and places; it is rather the reverse, since "in the beginning of Western thinking, Being is thought, but not the 'It gives' as such."[54] Strictly speaking, the question of being sheds its primacy, all the while passing over in silence that from which it originates, the "it gives." Whence this paradox that, taken literally, the overcoming of metaphysics leaps not only beyond the being of beings, but well beyond *being* itself, with a view to and in accordance with the "it gives" and its irreducible neutrality. In other words, being no longer arises from itself. "What is peculiar to Being is not anything having the character of Being (*Das Eigentümliche des Seins ist nichts Seinsartiges*)."[55] Consequently, *Dasein* can do nothing but disappear from the game, in the form of a being which transcends beingness towards being, in order to become "Man: standing within the approach of presence, but in such a way that he receives as a gift the presencing that It gives."[56] *Dasein*, too, disappears (or is accomplished), because it is no longer a case of opening beings,[57] even privileged ones, to being, but of exposing itself to the "it gives," that is, of welcoming the gift. Being (and beings) disappear in another event, which in the same movement renders it possible and precedes it.

Given the primacy of the "it gives – *es gibt*" over the question even of being and a fortiori over the question of the being of beings, there follows a second given, still more remarkable. Indeed, the well-known and most frequent conclusion – by which metaphysics is stigmatized as a thinking of the being of beings that leaves the ontological difference unthought, because it leaves being itself unthought[58] – remains unintelligible today, as long as it does not explain the cause of this inability to think being in its difference from beings; unintelligible and therefore, in appearance, arbitrary. To the contrary, the motivations behind what is obstinately unthought become visible as soon as the difference between being and beings is transposed (or translated) in the very terms of the "it gives"; for, each time that "it gives" (*es gibt*), there necessarily follows a gift or donation (*die Gabe*). Now, this gift or donation persists there, precisely because it is truly given, and as if abandoned to itself in its henceforth independent presence; in persisting there, it occupies it, as an actor occupies a scene. Thus, by occupying the scene, it hides what placed it in the scene, the giving itself (*das Geben*);[59] for the property of giving is to give a gift (something given), to deliver it, thus to deposit it in presence, from which at the same instant it abstains, since it does not give itself as something given. The director only places actors in the scene, but never the staging itself (without its becoming another actor). Henceforth, the giving (*das Geben*, or better, in verb form, the *geben*) disappears precisely and to the extent that it has made to appear the gift that it gives (*die Gabe*). Which is to say, the "it gives" itself "withdraws in favor of the gift which It gives. That gift is thought and conceptualized from then on exclusively as Being with regard to beings. A giving which gives only its gift, but in the giving holds itself back and withdraws, such a giving we call sending."[60] From which it follows that "to giving as sending there belongs keeping back... What we have mentioned just now – keeping back, denial, withholding – shows something like a self-withdrawing, something we might call for short: withdrawal."[61] Why, then, does being remain unthought? Not because of the ideological or psychological deficiencies of philosophers; or for epistemological reasons (transcendence, inconceivability, etc.); or even for strictly ontological reasons (the privilege of presence, etc.). It remains unthought because it withdraws *on its own* on this side of phenomenality; and it does so because it is obedient, in a manner more originary than for the ontological difference itself, to the "it gives," on which it thoroughly depends. Being conceals itself in non-manifestation, because it arises from donation and because "the sending in the destiny of Being has been characterized as a giving in which the sending source keeps itself back and, thus, withdraws from unconcealment."[62] In donation, in fact, the giving (*Geben*) gives to presence the gift (*Gabe*), so completely and radically that this gift alone occupies presence and, in appearing, necessarily masks its own donation; or, more properly speaking, the gift (*Gabe*, beings) has no need of illegitimately obfuscating the giving (*Geben*, being), since it is the right of the giving itself, on the contrary, not to be able to give the gift, to offer it, to deliver it, to put it to the fore, but by concealing itself behind it, because giving can never appear as something given since it exhausts and accomplishes itself in allowing to appear – it does not occupy the opening, because it opens it.[63] The unthought belongs then to being by virtue of its more essential determination – through the "it gives," through donation. Wide is the way that opens up: the "end of metaphysics" leads, in the end, all the way to the horizon of donation.

Why is it that Heidegger does not admit this? Because he doesn't in any strict manner adhere to the "it gives" through to the end; he moves away from it at the end, in order to fall back upon an entirely other instance, *Ereignis*: "Accordingly, the It that gives in 'It gives Being,' 'It gives time,' proves to be Appropriation (*Ereignis*)."[64] This transposition is evidently, and uniquely, desirable for being able to suspend the register of donation. It is all the more surprising that this transposition explicitly contradicts Heidegger's insistent call to vigilance in "bring[ing] the It and its giving into view, and capitaliz[ing] the 'It,'"[65] so as to preserve its "undetermined" and "enigmatic" character, which is, in fact, "something distinctive." This transposition even contradicts a warning made perfectly clear just prior to this: "There is a growing danger that when we speak of 'It,' we arbitrarily posit an indeterminate power which is supposed to bring about all giving of Being and of time"[66] – in short, identifying the It – *Es* would threaten to reduce it to the level of a being operating as a foundation, if not some causality. But is it not true that turning to the noun *Ereignis* leads precisely to introducing an indeterminate force, if not to sketching the shadow of a being? In the end, "Appropriation appropriates";[67] while the tautological form of this claim will not be questioned (it is perfectly acceptable in good logic), what will be criticized is that it seriously compromises the phenomenological and speculative force of the "it gives," from which it comes but which it also masks. To conclude that "Being [is] the event of Appropriation"[68] doesn't say too much – for the question of being most certainly goes beyond being – but in fact says too little – for the difference between being and beings leads back, beyond *Ereignis*, to donation.

7   THE POSSIBILITY OF A RADICAL OVERCOMING

Let us return to the penultimate line and final question of the 1964 text: "What speaks in the 'There is / It gives'?"[69] The end of philosophy, which for Heidegger equates to the overcoming of metaphysics (for "philosophy is metaphysics," says the opening of the same text[70]), accomplishes itself only by recourse to the "it gives – *es gibt*." The true implement for overcoming metaphysics is found in the donation, because the contrasting game of giving and the gift requires the surpassing of representational thinking – and it is only this game that affords it. But, then, how to avoid a paradox brimming with contradictions? The overcoming of metaphysics by means of donation does not merely lead to the thinking of being without considering beings, that is, to leaving metaphysics to itself, but leads into an entirely other dimension than being – that of the "it gives – *es gibt*," thus, a dimension of giving, of the gift, and of the contrasting game between the two. Everything takes place as though, in order to escape the being of beings – in other words to escape being held under the privilege of beings – it were necessary to overcome being itself. And, in fact, even in limiting ourselves to his withdrawal into *Ereignis*, that appears to be Heidegger's final intention – the question of non-metaphysical thinking no longer arises from, or aims any longer at, existence. It seeks a non-ontological case. Only in this context does it become possible to stigmatize how Heidegger brutally stops his own advance by thrusting donation back onto *Ereignis*. Only in this context does it also become necessary to follow Heidegger against himself and take donation seriously – to ask what speaks in the "it gives."

The question of the overcoming of metaphysics could thus require overcoming the question of being itself. At the very least, Heidegger's itinerary uncontestably shows the possibility of this overcoming. If from behind the being of beings, from behind the ontological difference that remains unthought and behind the onto-theological constitution, being does not emerge, but something other than being, the "task of thinking" will consist first of all in determining this new horizon.

Metaphysics is defined as an overcoming. The crux of the matter becomes one of defining precisely what it overcomes. It could overcome the being of beings, if not being itself, provided that it is understood on the basis of donation. This self-transcendence would not destroy it, but would render it impossible to overcome, for at each overcoming – including the overcoming of itself – it would accomplish its own essential definition. And if it were necessary definitively to abandon the name and notion of metaphysics, if only to avoid its confusions and restorations, it would not for all that require abandoning the name of philosophy (despite Heidegger's repeated conflation of the two). Indeed, *philosophy* is not defined directly by wisdom (or, for that matter, by knowledge, and even less so by science or representation), but by its strange, complex, and unquestioned relation to wisdom. A relation of affinity, of inclination, of familiarity, of desire, and of lack as well – a relation to what it lacks and loves to possess. Philosophy does not know wisdom, does not produce it, but reaches for it, anticipates it like a gift one would offer. In sum, it might be that in order to define philosophy, especially after metaphysics and perhaps even beyond the question of being, we cannot follow any other path than that indicated by the question: "What speaks in the 'It gives'?"

1. "The End of Philosophy and the Task of Thinking," in Heidegger, *Basic Writings*, ed. David Farrell Krell (New York: Harper & Row, 1993), p. 446 / "Das Ende der Philosophie und die Aufgabe des Denkens," in *Zur Sache des Denkens* (*ZSD*) (Tübingen: M. Niemeyer Verlag, 1969), p. 76.
2. "La science toujours recherchée et toujours manquante," in *La métaphysique: son histoire, sa critique, ses enjeux*, ed. Jean-Marc Narbonne and L. Langlois (Paris: Librairie Philosophique J. Vrin, 1999).
3. At issue here is the correction and completion of a previous essay's arguments, "The End of the End of Metaphysics," *Epoché* 2 (1994), pp. 1–22.
4. The phrase "end of metaphysics," furthermore, must be rigorously and doubly distinguished from the phrases "end of philosophy" and "overcoming of metaphysics."
5. Martin Heidegger, "Introduction to 'What is Metaphysics?,'" in *Pathmarks*, ed. William McNeill (Cambridge University Press, 1998), p. 279 / "Einleitung zu 'Was ist Metaphysik?,'" in *Gesamtausgabe*, vol. IX: *Wegmarken* (*GA* IX) (Frankfurt-on-Main: Klostermann, 1976), p. 367.
6. "Overcoming Metaphysics," in *The End of Philosophy*, trans. Joan Stambaugh (New York: Harper & Row, 1973), p. 85 / *Gesamtausgabe*, vol. VII: *Vorträge und Aufsätze* (*GA* VII) (Frankfurt-on-Main: Klostermann, 2000), p. 69.
7. "Overcoming Metaphysics," p. 96 / *GA* VII, p. 81.
8. This text was first delivered in French by J. Beaufret at UNESCO in April 1964.
9. [Translator's note: The French *achèvement*, translated here as "culmination," implies completion, perfection, accomplishment, the finality of death; its verbal pair, *(s')achever*, means to come to or bring to an end, to die out or kill off. *Achèvement* is the term used in the French version of "Das Ende der Philosophie und die Aufgabe des Denkens"; the semantic range of Heidegger's *Vollendung*, which is akin to the English term "full," implies wholeness or completion.]
10. "The End of Philosophy and the Task of Thinking," p. 432 / *ZSD*, p. 62.
11. "The End of Philosophy and the Task of Thinking," p. 433 / *ZSD*, p. 63, translation modified.
12. [Translator's note: In this paragraph Marion exploits a network of terms relating to card playing: *carte*s (cards), *jouer* (to play), *gagner* (to win), *la levée* (the act of gathering up cards), *fin de partie* (the final phase of a game, or, more fruitfully here, an endgame – metaphysics is the endgame), and, significantly, *la donne* (of cards, a hand or deal). While the dealing out of cards evokes Heidegger's concept of "the dispensation," since the substantive *donne* is linked to the infinitive *donner*, "to give," Marion is playing off the German term with

so much currency in Heidegger's essay and commenting on it later in the essay through the French *cela donne, es gibt*, the "it gives."]

13. John Sallis, in an otherwise illuminating study, claims on the contrary that accomplishment (*Vollendung*) must not be understood in the sense of perfection (*Vollkommenheit*). *Delimitations: Phenomenology and the End of Metaphysics* (Bloomington: Indiana University Press, 1986). This is certainly true if it involves challenging accomplishment in the Hegelian sense of the term; but this does not exclude that even the final nihilism assumes the form of an accomplishment, which sums up and puts the final touches on the possibilities of the initial hand dealt by metaphysics.

14. Martin Heidegger, "European Nihilism," in *Nietzsche*, vol. IV, trans. Joan Stambaugh, David Farrell Krell, and Frank A. Capuzzi (New York: Harper & Row, 1991), p. 148 / *Gesamtausgabe*, vol. VI.2: *Nietzsche*, vol. II (*GA* VI.2) (Frankfurt-on-Main: Klostermann, 1997), p. 179. It follows that this "moment" permits and demands a "historical decision" ("European Nihilism," p. 149 / *GA* VI.2, p. 180): we must bring ourselves (in the form of *Dasein* accomplishing the "anticipatory resoluteness"?) to positing and thinking the end of metaphysics – no longer to play the hand of metaphysics, but to prepare (or wait for the next distribution of cards, the new hand [*le new deal*]).

15. "Overcoming Metaphysics," p. 95 / *GA* VII, p. 81.

16. "The Word of Nietzsche: 'God is Dead,'" in *The Question Concerning Technology and Other Essays*, trans. William Lovitt (New York: Harper & Row, 1977), p. 53 / *Gesamtausgabe*, vol. V: *Holzwege* (*GA* V), p. 209.

17. [Translator's note: the German term is *Sackgasse*, a "blind alley" in the English translation.] "Letter on Humanism," *Pathmarks*, p. 261 / "Brief über den Humanismus," in *GA* IX, p. 343. (This term, it is true, has been taken up, here with reservation, by objectors.) At the same time, it is the abandonment of the 1929 substitutive project of a "metaphysics of *Dasein*" (*Kant and the Problem of Metaphysics*, trans. Richard Taft [Bloomington: Indiana University Press, 1997], §41, pp. 157ff., *Gesamtausgabe*, vol. III: *Kant und das Problem der Metaphysik* [Frankfurt-on-Main: Klostermann, 1991], §41, pp. 230ff., or "What is Metaphysics?" in *Pathmarks*, p. 96, "Was ist Metaphysik?," in *GA* IX, p. 122) alone that has allowed this question of the interpretation of metaphysics in its essence following the lectures on Nietzsche to be reopened.

18. "The End of Philosophy and the Task of Thinking," p. 435 / *ZSD*, p. 65.

19. "Overcoming Metaphysics," p. 93 / *GA* VII, p. 79.

20. "The End of Philosophy and the Task of Thinking," p. 437 / *ZSD*, p. 67.

21. "Overcoming Metaphysics," p. 95 / *GA* VII, p. 81.

22. *Being and Time*, trans. John Macquarrie and Edward Robinson (New York: Harper & Row, 1962), p. 44, *Gesamtausgabe*, vol. II: *Sein und Zeit* (*GA* II) (Frankfurt-on-Main: Klostermann, 1977), p. 30.

23. *Being and Time*, p. 44 / *GA* II, pp. 30–1.

24. "Time and Being," in *On Time and Being*, trans. Joan Stambaugh (New York: Harper, 1972), p. 9 (translation modified), "Zeit und Sein," in *ZSD*, p. 9. This is a late response to an earlier declaration: "a *destruction* (*Destruktion*) – a

critical process (*Abbau*) in which the traditional concepts, which at first must necessarily be employed, are deconstructed down to the sources from which they were drawn. Only by means of this destruction can ontology fully assure itself in a phenomenological way of the genuine character of its concepts." *The Basic Problems of Phenomenology*, rev. edn, trans. Albert Hofstadter (Bloomington: Indiana University Press, 1982), p. 23, *Gesamtausgabe*, vol. XXIV: *Grundprobleme der Phänomenologie* (Frankfurt-on-Main: Klostermann, 1975), p. 31.

25. "The End of Philosophy and the Task of Thinking," p. 441 / *ZSD*, p. 71.
26. "Postscript to 'What is Metaphysics?,'" in *Pathmarks*, p. 232, "Nachwort zu 'Was ist Metaphysik?,'" in *GA* IX, p. 304.
27. "Introduction to 'What is Metaphysics?,'" p. 278 / *GA* IX, p. 367.
28. "Introduction to 'What is Metaphysics?,'" p. 281 / *GA* IX, p. 370.
29. "The Onto-theo-logical Constitution of Metaphysics," in *Identity and Difference*, trans. Joan Stambaugh (University of Chicago Press, 1969), p. 60, "Die Onto-theo-logische Verfassung der Metaphysik," in *Identität und Differenz* (Pfullingen: G. Neske, 1957), p. 52.
30. On these tasks, and their specificity and legitimacy, see my study "D'une quadruple méthode pour lire les textes de la philosophie – la pertinence d'Henri Gouhier," *Le regard d'Henri Gouhier*, ed. Denise Leduc-Fayette (Paris: Vrin, 1999).
31. "The Word of Nietzsche: 'God is Dead,'" p. 57 / *GA* V, p. 212.
32. "The Word of Nietzsche: 'God is Dead,'" p. 108–9 / *GA* V, p. 263.
33. "What is Metaphysics?," p. 90 / *GA* IX, p. 113. See *GA* IX, pp. 114, 115 (Heidegger's marginal notes added later), and pp. 120, 307.
34. "European Nihilism," p. 21 / *GA* IV.2, p. 43. It will be noted that in the page preceding this citation are a response to and critique of Bergson's critique of the idea of nothingness. *L'évolution créatrice*, ch. 4, in *Œuvres* (Paris: Presses Universitaires de France, 1959), p. 728, taken from "L'idée de néant," *Revue philosophique* 62 (1906), pp. 449–66.
35. "The End of Philosophy and the Task of Thinking," p. 448 / *ZSD*, p. 79. Likewise: it is "from the beginning (*sogleich*)" that the Greeks think unconcealment as representation. For "the natural concept of truth does not mean unconcealment, not in the philosophy of the Greeks either" ("The End of Philosophy and the Task of Thinking," p. 447 / *ZSD*, p. 77). This radical and essential thesis can be traced to *Being and Time*, pp. 22, 70, 201 / *GA* II, pp. 4–5, 60, 211.
36. "The End of Philosophy and the Task of Thinking," p. 449 / *ZSD*, p. 80.
37. "Zähringen Seminar," in *Gesamtausgabe*, vol. 15: *Seminare* (Frankfurt-on-Main: Klostermann, 1986), p. 399.
38. "Overcoming Metaphysics," p. 85 / *GA* VII, p. 70. Contrary to what a note from the French translation leads one to believe, *Verwindung*, which derives from *verwinden* and as such indicates turning over or change of direction (a tailspin in aeronautics), does not relate to *verwenden*, to employ or utilize, which the translation situates in relation to "being able to accept." In

fact, Heidegger makes use of *Verwindung* in order to reverse the term that Carnap had used against *What is Metaphysics?* in his own "Überwindung der Metaphysik durch logische Analyse der Sprache," *Erkenntnis* 2 (1931), translated as "The Elimination of Metaphysics through Logical Analysis of Language," in *Logical Positivism*, ed. A. J. Ayer (Glencoe, Ill.: Free Press, 1959).

39. "Time and Being," p. 24 (translation modified) / *ZSD*, p. 25.

40. [Translator's note: the French term *éclaircie* suggests, in its climatological sense, a burst of light in a cloudy or rainy sky – connoting simultaneously clarity and opening, and therefore echoing the German *Lichtung* as it pertains to a clearing or glade in a forest. The French word for glade, the feminine noun *clairière*, derives from a related semantic field, since both *éclaircie* and *clairière* draw their meaning from a root in the Latin *clarus*, "clear" or "light."]

41. In this vein, and in tandem with many other similar readings, see A. Renault, "La fin de Heidegger et la tâche de la philosophie," *Les Etudes Philosophiques* 4 (1977), pp. 485–92.

42. "The End of Philosophy and the Task of Thinking," p. 449 / *ZSD*, p. 80. Cf. n. 36 above.

43. "Time and Being," pp. 4–5 / *ZSD*, pp. 4–5.

44. "Time and Being," pp. 24, 2 / *ZSD*, pp. 25, 2.

45. "Time and Being," pp. 5, 18–19 / *ZSD*, pp. 5, 18–19. It is so important to respect this warning that it can legitimately be turned back against Heidegger himself, who was too quick to baptize the "it – *es*" also as a noun – as it happens, *Ereignis* ("Time and Being," p. 19 / *ZSD*, p. 20). See my *Etant donné. Essai d'une phénoménologie de la donation* (Paris: Presses Universitaires de France, 1998), §3, pp. 54 ff., translated as *Being Given: Toward a Phenomenology of Givenness*, trans. Jeffrey L. Kosky (Stanford: Stanford University Press, 2002).

46. *Being and Time*, p. 255 / *GA* II, p. 281, translation modified. This text is cited explicitly in "Letter on Humanism," pp. 254, 256 / *GA* IX, pp. 334, 336–7 (see note 49).

47. *Being and Time*, p. 272 / *GA* II, p. 304. See also Heidegger's reservations in *Being and Time*, p. 26 / *GA* II, p. 8: "The Being of entities 'is' not itself an entity"; and *Being and Time*, p. 228 / *GA* II, p. 244: "Being 'is' only in the understanding of... entities."

48. "What is Metaphysics?," p. 86 / *GA* IX, p. 108. Along the same lines: "The nothing unveils itself in anxiety – but not as a being. Just as little is it given as an object." "What is Metaphysics?," p. 89 / *GA* IX, p. 113. For the totality of beings, which the nothing eliminates, is also "given in advance" ("What is Metaphysics?," p. 86 / *GA* IX, p. 109), without, properly speaking, being in the mode of these or those beings.

49. "Letter on Humanism," pp. 254–5 / *GA* IX, p. 334. Along the same lines: "Being comes to destiny in that It – *es*, being, gives itself." "Letter on Humanism," p. 255 / *GA* IX, p. 335.

50. "Introduction to 'What is Metaphysics?,'" p. 290, / *GA* IX, p. 382.

51. "On the Question of Being," in *Pathmarks*, p. 317 / "Zur Seinsfrage," in *GA* IX, p. 419.

52. *On Time and Being*, p. 43 / *ZSD*, p. 47.

53. "Time and Being," pp. 4–5 / *ZSD*, p. 5, translation modified.

54. "Time and Being," p. 8 / *ZSD*, p. 8. And this is true from the very beginning, before metaphysics even constitutes itself as such: "At the beginning of Being's unconcealment, Being, *einai, eon* is thought, but not the 'It gives.' Instead, Parmenides says *esti gar einai*, 'For Being is.'" "Time and Being," p. 8 / *ZSD*, p. 8, translation modified.

55. "Time and Being," p. 10 / *ZSD*, p. 10. Along the same lines (with one decisive nuance, which I will take up shortly): "Being would be a species of Appropriation, and not the other way around . . . Being vanishes in Appropriation." "Time and Being," pp. 21–2 / *ZSD*, p. 22.

56. "Time and Being," p. 12 / *ZSD*, p. 12. This may be connected to the "ekstatische Innestehen in der Wahrheit des Seins," *GA* IX, pp. 325, 330 (the "ecstatic inherence in the truth of being," "Letter on Humanism," pp. 248, 251).

57. "Nowhere in beings is there an example for the essence of Being (*es für das Wesen des Seins nirgends im Seienden ein Beispiel gibt*)," "The Onto-theo-logical Constitution of Metaphysics," p. 66 (translation modified) / "Die Onto-theo-logische Verfassung der Metaphysik," p. 58.

58. "The Onto-theo-logical Constitution of Metaphysics," pp. 50ff., 60–1, 62, 73 / "Die Onto-theo-logische Verfassung der Metaphysik," pp. 40ff., 52, 53, 65. The text nevertheless does make one reference to the "it gives": "We represent Being in a way in which It, Being, never gives itself" ("The Onto-theo-logical Constitution of Metaphysics," p. 66 / "Die Onto-theo-logische Verfassung der Metaphysik," p. 57); but the relation between being and this "it gives" here continues to be arbitrary and superficial.

59. [Translator's note: In the German *das Geben*, the "giving" but also the term for a card deal, one can discern the card metaphor developed by Marion in §1, including the figure of *la donne*.]

60. "Time and Being," p. 8 / *ZSD*, p. 8.

61. "Time and Being," p. 22 / *ZSD*, p. 23.

62. "Time and Being," p. 22 / *ZSD*, p. 23.

63. In "The Onto-theo-logical constitution of Metaphysics," pp. 64–5 / "Die Onto-theo-logische Verfassung der Metaphysik," p. 56, Heidegger attempts to show this same mysterious drama of presence and concealment by opposing the advent of being (*Überkommnis*) to the arrival of beings (*Ankunft*); but the two terms here remain external to each other, without the phenomenological necessity of their game being discovered; what they are lacking, in fact, is the logic of the gift to articulate the one to the other, as occurs respectively with the "giving" and the "given."

64. "Time and Being," p. 19 / *ZSD*, p. 20. This occurs in such a way that it is not merely "being [that] disappears in *Ereignis*," but more than anything the "it gives" itself, meaning, finally, the phenomenological explanation of the obligatory dissimulation of being in the evidence of beings; whence, since this retreat must be named, the introduction of *Enteignis* (expropriation, *ZSD*, p. 44) – which is hardly convincing, because it undermines what *Ereignis*

does, instead of the two movements (the advance of the given, the withdrawal of giving) coinciding perfectly in the lexicon of the "it gives". Changing the phraseology therefore provokes a phenomenological regression.

65. "Time and Being," p. 5 / *ZSD*, p. 5.

66. "Time and Being," pp. 16–17 / *ZSD*, p. 17. See also "Time and Being," pp. 4–5, 17, 18 / *ZSD*, pp. 5, 18, 19. On this – Heidegger's final breach vis-à-vis donation, at the very moment of its ultimate meditation on the "it gives" – see my analysis, *Etant donné: essai d'une phénoménologie de la donation*, §3, pp. 55–60, which I hold to here.

67. "Time and Being," p. 24 / *ZSD*, p. 24.

68. "Time and Being," p. 21 / *ZSD*, p. 22. Despite its title, D. Panis's book *Il y a le il y a: l'énigme de Heidegger* (Brussels: Ousia, 1993) does not tackle this difficult topic.

69. "The End of Philosophy and the Task of Thinking," p. 449 / *ZSD*, p. 80.

70. "The End of Philosophy and the Task of Thinking," p. 432 / *ZSD*, p. 61. (See "The thinking that is to come is no longer philosophy, because it thinks more originally than metaphysics," "Letter on Humanism," p. 276 / *GA* ix, p. 364.)

Index